It All Starts Nc
Stories

Charles H. Geletzke, Jr.

Front Cover: The author's grandson, Henry Charles Geletzke is seen riding the Strasburg Railroad and is watching engine 89 run around its train at Paradise, PA on August 10, 2023. Only time will tell if he too will become a railfan or a professional railroader; but you never know…

Title Page: GTW Road Brakeman and author, Chuck Geletzke was seen working his "regular assignment," Train 547, "The Jackson Local" at Walled Lake, Michigan with the GTW RS-1 1951, the last Alco RS-1 ever built. The date was July 6, 1970…three days before author Geletzke left for Marine Corps Boot Camp. (George A. Dondero II photo)

Rear Cover: Author, Charles Geletzke at the *Lobo Del Mar Café* on South Padre Island, Texas on March 24, 2024.

All photos are by the author unless otherwise stated.

DEDICATION

    It was with a great deal of sadness that I learned of the passing of my fellow Canadian National Railroad Locomotive Engineer and friend, Joseph Ernest Greyzck on January 30, 2024. Joe was a U. S. Navy veteran, served in Vietnam and was a tremendous woodcarver and artist. In the early 1980's, Joe' artwork became famous within the railroad industry for the posting of his character "Smokin' Joe, which he drew by hand and posted on over 20,000 railroad cars. Joe was an outstanding locomotive engineer and will certainly be missed by all of his friends! You can read Joe's story and learn how we became friends in the final chapter of this book.

It All Starts <u>Here</u> and Other Railroad Stories

CONTENTS

It All Starts <u>Here</u> and Other Railroad Stories

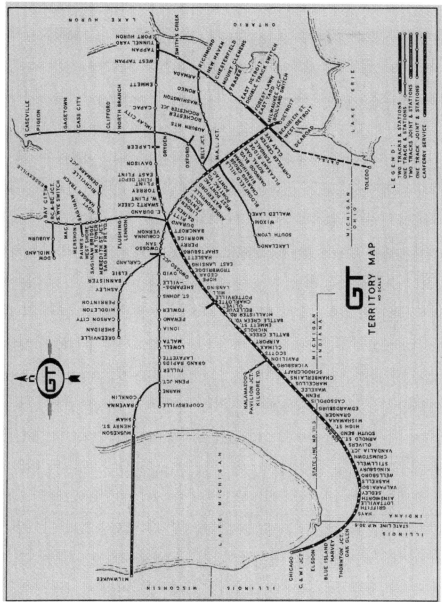

GTW Corporate Map dated October 30, 1977.

ACKNOWLEDGEMENTS

This is the ninth volume in the "and Other Railroad Stories" series. I have now published over 650 individual true railroad short stories and at this point I have still not even scratched the surface! Please permit me to thank all of the following individuals for their assistance and their photos and stories. They are…the late A. D. Anderson; Byron Babbish, Esq.; Jack Barnett; L. E. Batanian; L. R. Bolton; Richard J. Burg; Joe DeMike; the late W. D. Doncoes; Fred Furminger; the late Joseph E. Greyczk; Robert Grinn; James Harlow; M. A. Hinsdale; T. L. Hunt; J. T. Johnson; Steven A. Kaslik, Esq.; F. J. Kirkman: T. D. Klein; Kevin Korecki; the late Alfred R. Krueger; Dan Lawecki; Vyvyan Makin; Roger L. Meade; Maynard Mitchell; David J. Mrozek; the late R. K. Nairns; the late E. L. Novak; the late Richard J. O'Leary; Frederick Ottusch; Stan Sienicki; the late C. T. Stoner; D. G. Swarbrick; J. G. Tyson; Wendell "Wink" West; L. E. Williams and Robert J. Wise. And a special thanks to the members of my family…Leslie E. Geletzke; Brian A. Close; Abby K. Geletzke, M.D.; Josephine F. Close; Finn A. Close; Charles H. Geletzke III; Rachel M. Geletzke; Henry C. Geletzke; the late David B. Geletzke; Benjamin L. Geletzke; Lt./Col. Travis P. Geletzke USMC; Jennifer L. Geletzke; Julie C. Geletzke; Jonathan H. Geletzke; and Capt. Gerald W. Geletzke USN-Ret. and the late Charles H. Geletzke, Sr. All of your help was truly appreciated!

We'll show this book COMPLETE at 5:23 P.M. on July 16, 2024.
CHG

Chuck H Geletzke, Jr.

Chapter 1
The "Transition Era"

C. F. Martin

By: C. H. Geletzke, Jr.

Let me begin by stating that while I enjoy music, unlike my children, I have never been a musician!

Two Saturdays ago, we had one of our grandchildren staying with us; so for entertainment, we took him to the *Science Factory* in nearby Lancaster, Pennsylvania. This turned out to be a wonderful entertainment and educational venue for our six year old grandson.

While there, I spotted a man wearing a sweatshirt with the name, *C. F. Martin* scrolled across his chest. My immediate thought was, "It can't be!" So, without hesitation, I walked over and inquired of the gentleman the significance of the name. He explained that *C. F. Martin & Co.* is a large and famous American manufacturer of guitars, founded in 1833, and located in Nazareth, PA. The man then pointed out his wife and stated, "She works there and they have a fabulous museum!"

I then told the man that years earlier I had worked with a man on the railroad whose name just happened to be C. F. Martin and that the older guys always stated that the initials C. F. stood for "Constant Flow!" The man then just laughed and basically, that was the end of our conversation.

Since I am talking about C. F., who we normally called "Fred," I'd better tell you a little more about him. Fred served in the Marine Corps during World War II and hired out as a Grand Trunk Western Railroad (GTW) Fireman on March 23, 1951. On July 18, 1963 he was promoted to Locomotive Engineer.

Fred was known for his elaborate stories and it never mattered how well he knew the person or fellow employee that he was conversing with, if the person was willing to listen, Fred had a story for them!

When I hired out on the railroad in 1967, it was not long at all until I learned of Fred's Whopper, which he insisted right to his

Chuck H Geletzke, Jr.

last day was the truth! Have you ever heard the story of the NORTHEASTERN POWER FAILURE? It occurred on November 9, 1965 and that's when all of New York City's lights flickered and then the entire city went black! Well, I'm willing to bet that none of you heard that later that evening, or perhaps it was the next, a helicopter was flown to Detroit to pick-up Locomotive Engineer, C. F. Martin and they flew him to New York City. While there, HE RECTIFIED THE ELECTRICAL PROBLEM! And, the very next morning he was back to work on the GTW…

What else can I say!?!

Eastward GTW Train 22 is seen crossing Washington Ave. in Royal Oak, Michigan headed for Detroit early one morning in the late 1950's. In the background is the Washington Square Building, which is still standing and in use today. (Roger Meade photo)

Railroading During the "Transition Era"

By: Charles H. Geletzke, Jr.

11

It All Starts <u>Here</u> and Other Railroad Stories

As a youth, I was fortunate to have grown-up during the age of steam, with the Grand Trunk Western Railroad (GTW) down at the end of my block. The Grand Trunk used steam in everyday service through March 1960 and I was able to witness it in daily operation.

If you are like me and enjoy or are modeling the "transition era," when the railroads changed from steam to diesel, let me tell you about some of the changes that I observed, and how you might include some of these on your layout. Of course, some of these items will vary depending upon the railroad that you model and the region of the country that you are trying to duplicate.

Naturally, the first major change was the arrival of the diesel locomotives themselves. While the GTW had actually purchased its very first diesel in 1929 in the form of a J. G. Brill boxcab that was used to switch their yard and carferry in Milwaukee, Wisconsin; additional diesels did not arrive in our area until 1938 and 1941. Now for me growing up in the 1950's, I don't even recall seeing any diesels in my hometown of Royal Oak, Michigan until about 1954. Yes, the road had a fleet of 22 F3A covered wagons purchased in 1948, a fleet of Alco and EMD switchers, and the first GP9's arrived in 1954; but most of these were initially primarily used on the mainline between Chicago and Port Huron, Michigan as well as making trips south from Port Huron to Toledo, Ohio in Inter-Railroad Service over the Detroit & Toledo Shore line Railroad (D&TSL), in addition to the various yards and terminals. As for my little "neck of the woods" we were still practically all steam. I do recall the first time that I heard that different sounding horn instead of a whistle, and watched as a pair of green and yellow geeps took a westbound freight through town uphill to Pontiac...for both my Dad and me that was "kind of a big deal!" Oh yes, and before we go any further let's set the rules right now...steam locomotives were NEVER referred to as units!

Okay, so that was the major change and it was industry wide; but let's take a look at more of the subtle changes, and there were literally hundreds of them.

I know that many of you modelers love to run diesel units with the various paint schemes of your favorite roads. In our area I did not become aware of railroads "pooling" power until the mid-1960's, when Western Maryland (WM) and Chicago, Burlington & Quincy (CB&Q) units began showing-up at the Wabash Railroad's Oakwood fuel dock in southwestern Detroit. Yes, some railroads

Chuck H Geletzke, Jr.

would lease power as did the Detroit, Toledo & Ironton (DT&I) during the winter months from roads such as the Lake Superior & Ishpeming (LS&I) and the Duluth, Missabe & Iron Range (DM&IR), while the Great Lakes were closed to navigation and the power was not needed to move iron ore. On the GTW, the first use of run-through power did not occur until 1976, when Conrail power representing various former railroads began showing up on unit coal trains, which they interchanged with us. Again, study your particular road's history of operation.

The retention of steam facilities would be another huge factor for you modelers. While some railroads like the Missouri Pacific rushed in to instantaneously remove every structure pertaining to the operation and maintenance of steam, others left structures such as coal docks, water tanks, and roundhouses, many of which are still standing today. Interestingly, much of this was related to the tax laws of the various states. In some states if a structure was standing unused, it could still be taxed. In other states, all an industry had to do was to declare the building or facility abandoned "on Paper," and that was sufficient. (You will notice a great number of concrete coal docks remained years after steam's demise within the State of West Virginia.) Another factor pertaining to the removal of these structures was the expense in having them removed, whether the removal process would hinder or delay operation (i.e. block main tracks), safety, and in later year's environmental concerns such as the inclusion of asbestos. Almost any model railroad can justify having a coal dock still in place, a water tank foundation, a roundhouse floor, or a remaining turntable.

The D&TSL operating between Toledo, Ohio and Detroit was completely dieselized in 1953 and yet they retained their turntable, coal dock, and water tanks to service steam of the connections delivering and pulling from their yards. The B&O was the last railroad to deliver to the Shore Line's Lang Yard on the north side of Toledo on February 16, 1958 using their 2-10-2 Number 519. Additionally, this was the B&O's final steam run in Toledo.

My first job on the railroad was in 1967, when I hired-out as a "Fire Builder" (Laborer) in the GTW's roundhouse in Pontiac, Michigan. I always love to say that "I hired-out on a steam railroad without steam!" Yes, by this time the railroad was indeed 100% diesel; but as far as the operation went, with the exception of stopping for water and coal, the GTW was still doing practically everything exactly the same as they did during the Second World War!

Take the roundhouse for example. We still had a coal dock; but most of the "Scrapable" metal had been removed that was within reach. The ash pit and its crane were gone and the pit filled-in. We still had a water tower…in which we would occasionally swim on hot summer nights! Our roundhouse had two stationary boilers, which during the winter burned Bunker-C fuel oil unloaded from a railroad tank car. Because our diesel fuel storage tank was so small at that time, diesel fuel arrived daily by truck; although we were set-up to also unload oil from tank cars. Sand for the locomotives arrived in assigned GTW covered hoppers from the Nugent Sand Company's pit in Muskegon, Michigan. I should note that the original steam era sand house had been replaced by modern diesel era sand towers. We were still using the original 10-stall roundhouse, which still had its inspection pits, smoke jacks (which had been boarded-shut), and the tools for working on steam were still everywhere. We had a stack of firebrick for fireboxes that would never be relined. The roundhouse, which was built as a "smokeless" facility, still retained all of the asbestos covered piping to attach steam locomotives to stationary steam, so that their fires could be dropped before they ever entered the building. The piping to perform this service, was not just installed within the roundhouse, additionally on both ends of the building the pipe was covered in a steel and wooden conduit, and extended over all of the "Whisker Tracks" radiating from the turntable, which even today is still being utilized. The neatest thing about the roundhouse in Pontiac that just cried out "Transition Era," were two of the doors facing the turntable, still were stenciled "DIESEL ONLY." Inside, those two tracks had been re-equipped with special platforms designed specifically to work on diesels. Additionally, a drop-table had been added between Track #9 and #10 to remove and change out entire diesel trucks. But, if you looked around, you would also see that the drop-pit for changing locomotive drivers was still in place and even still operable!

A view of the GTW Pontiac, MI roundhouse area on August 13, 1962. The 10-stall roundhouse was out of view to the left; but you can see a portion of the turntable pit, the water tank, the covered stationary steam line, a Jordon Spreader waiting for winter, the combined Engine Crew Room & Storehouse, the coal dock, and sand tower.

As late as 1980, the roundhouse at the Detroit & Mackinaw Railroad in Tawas City, Michigan still had a 100% complete steam backshop…even though the railroad was completely dieselized in the late 1940's.

The D&TSL's Locomotive Machine Shop at Lang Yard in Toledo, Ohio as late as 1988 still had a huge metal painting hanging on an interior wall declaring "SAFETY FOR VICTORY," which had been hanging there since the start of World War II.

Up in our yard in Port Huron, Michigan, adjacent to the lead at the west end of the yard, there was still a huge coal pile, which remained there into the 1980's. This coal had been stockpiled there since who knows when...probably back in the forties…just in case the coal miners ever went out on strike!

Adjacent to the roundhouse in Pontiac, we also had a storehouse, which additionally housed the Engine Crew Dispatcher's Office. Usually, about every week or two, a wooden GTW outside braced boxcar would arrive and deliver parts, material, lube oil, etc. from the System Stores Department in Battle Creek, Michigan. Interestingly, we did not just unload this car and return it empty. No, instead the car would sit there adjacent to the storehouse dock and we would reload it with defective locomotive parts, such as air-compressor valves and used lube oil, which was returned to the "Cereal City," for rebuilding or recycling. Oh yes, we also had a

15

wooden gondola stored on one of the whisker tracks that we loaded with defective parts to be sold as scrap metal. Lastly, we even had an old Track Department bunk car, which was kept on another one of the Whisker Tracks and was intended as a place for firemen who were "force assigned" to Pontiac, and could be used as an awful, but free place to stay.

During the transition era, most roundhouses still used hostlers to move locomotives around and within the servicing area. On some roads and in some terminals, outside hostlers too were employed. These individuals were responsible for moving locomotives from the roundhouse to passenger depots and freight yards where they would be turned-over to an engine crew. Under no circumstances would a hostler be permitted to operate any locomotive with cars attached!

Now I realize that space is at a premium on all of our layouts; but how many of your roundhouses and yard offices have parking lots for all of the people that would have worked there? Stop and think, for every train and yard crew working at any given terminal, you would have to provide five parking places. Now multiply that by the number of crews on duty during each trick, and many of those jobs would probably have worked 16 hours. Remember, the Federal Hours of Service Law was not reduced to 14 hours until January 1, 1971. It later went to the current 12 hours on January 1, 1973.

Let's talk about passenger service. When steam was operated, a ready source to provide steam to heat the coaches was naturally available; but when the diesels arrived, in order to provide this same service, the locomotives had to be equipped with steam generators. With the institution of the steam generator, heavy duty water hoses had to be provided at many locations to resupply these locomotives at various points, and time had to be built into the schedules, or at least altered, to provide time for this service. During this transition or pre-Amtrak era, generally most passenger cars used on each railroad were of their own ownership. Yes, foreign cars were used, particularly baggage, mail, and express cars and reefers; but also Pullmans and even coaches when needed to meet the demands of service. Also, we cannot neglect the Railway Mail Service. U. S. Mail was transported to towns of all size in various styles of Railway Post Office cars or RPO's. Mail was picked-up from mail cranes "on the fly" and sometimes delivered and handled by the carload. A great deal of "pouched mail" was also even carried on lines without RPO contracts and handled in the baggage car.

Chuck H Geletzke, Jr.

Now as most of you know, the trainmen working in passenger service had to wear the required proper passenger uniform. But consider this, just suppose that you were working in a freight "pool" or called as a "make-up crew" off the extra board to work an extra freight in "layover" service. An example of this would be, being ordered to work west on an extra freight train from Port Huron to Battle Creek, Michigan. Now suppose after tying-up and going to the hotel, eight hours later the Chief Train Dispatcher wanted to utilize your crew on a "PX" (Passenger Extra), to perhaps handle a Football Special to Michigan State University in East Lansing. The crew would need to have their passenger uniforms. This move would have to have been anticipated the day previous, and the crew instructed to bring their uniforms. Now another question, suppose they were a "pool crew" and had their own assigned caboose…what would happen to their caboose while they were working the PX? In this case the train dispatcher would have to arrange to deadhead their cab back to the next point where they might again perform duty in freight service. During the steam and transition era it was very common to see freight trains with more than one caboose on the tailend. In this case, the "working cab," was always the one on the tailend! On holidays, sometimes a train might have five or six cabs on the tailend, trying to get crews home to be with their families, if the reduction in trains could be tolerated.

Now we'd better talk about "multiple-units" or "mu." With steam, each engine had an engine crew, which consisted of an engineer and a fireman. If a train was "double-headed" or "triple-headed," each locomotive still would have an engineman and a fireman. Now with diesels, if they were equipped for multiple-unit operation, one engine crew could operate any number of locomotives coupled together. So, take a road like the D&TSL, we would occasionally run "Pullers" to the various foreign connections around the City of Toledo with perhaps a mu equipped GP7 and a non-mu equipped SW7. In this case, each diesel locomotive would require having its own separate engine crew. In all of these instances, however, each individual train would only require a conductor and two brakemen or switchmen.

During the steam and the "transition" eras, the definitive distinction of working classes or crafts was an extremely important issue! Generally, enginemen held seniority that enabled them to work in both "yard" and "road" service. Trains working over the road generally required a conductor and two trainmen. Depending on

17

the labor agreements of each individual carrier, these men might be represented by the Order of Railway Conductors and Brakemen (ORC&B) or the Brotherhood of Railroad Trainmen (BRT), or perhaps a combination of both. In the yard, a "yard" or "ground" crew consisted of a Foreman and two Helpers. These workers were usually represented by the Switchmen's Union of North America (aka "Snakes"). Road crews generally moved trains "over the road" between terminals and additionally performed all local and industrial switching between these terminals. Most yards or terminals were normally protected by Rule 93 Yard Limits or in some cases "Switching Limits;" which according to the rules regulated how trains had to proceed through this territory and at what speed. Switchmen generally performed all of the switching and transfer work within these terminals. One of the big advantages of being a switchman was that they went home at the end of each tour of duty; while a road trainman, at a minimum, often stayed in a hotel, a bunkhouse, a railroad YMCA, a boarding house at the other end of the road or perhaps even in their own caboose. Incidentally, until the late 1970's railroad workers were allowed to stay in boarding facilities located on the property of each individual railroad. Following the huge explosion that leveled the Southern Pacific's yard in Roseville, California on April 28, 1973, Federal Law began mandating that railroad workers be housed "off the property."

Let's talk a little about how these workers were housed. Depending on the era and the contractual working agreements, if train crews were required to layover in a large terminal, they might stay in a hotel, a Railroad Y, a bunk room, or trainmen might stay in their own caboose. Interestingly, and I have never gotten over this one, when I worked for the Missouri Pacific in 1972 and 1973, train and engine crews laying-over in Vanderbilt, Texas still stayed in a "segregated" hotel! Yes, you heard me correctly…the white train and enginemen stayed in individual rooms, and the African-American trainmen stayed in one big dormitory room! On the GTW during the change from steam to diesel, at some of the terminals, such as Battle Creek and Caseville, Michigan, the train crew would stay in their caboose, while the engine crew was put-up in a bunkroom within the enginehouse.

Going along with the distinction between crafts, the handling of cabooses during the steam and the transition era was a big item! Naturally, road and yard crews had their own assigned cabooses. Additionally, there were extra cabs also, restricted for yard or road

Chuck H Geletzke, Jr.

use. Now if there were yard crews on duty within a terminal, a road crew could not "dig-out" their own caboose if it was "buried" on the caboose track! Instead, a yard crew would have to be instructed to make sure that when the road crew went on duty, that the road cab was sitting "first-out" in the caboose track, where the road crew could just "grab-it" and go. Likewise, a road crew could "tie" their own caboose on their own train within a terminal; but they could not perform any other switching aside from "throwing-out" a car that was "Bad-Ordered" by the Car Department, as long as the car was "found to be defective AFTER they tied on their own train. If a car was designated to be a "Bad-Order" or "Rip" before the road crew tied on, the car had to be set-out by a yard crew. Most of this changed during the mid-1970's after the "transition era."

In steam days, turning facilities, be it a turntable, a wye, or a loop, were much more important than when the general purpose diesels came on the scene around 1950. Naturally, most locomotive engineers and fireman preferred to operate their locomotives in a forward facing direction. Most working agreements provided that if turning facilities were available at each end of a train's run; the engineer would be permitted to turn the locomotive. When turning facilities were not available, most steam and even jobs (particularly yard assignments and locals) using a diesel, would arrange for the locomotive initially to be headed in such a manner, that the engineer would have the best visibility to perform the local work for the preponderance of the trip.

The rules governing the use of white flags and classification lights to designate extras, and green flags and class lights for sections too, were an important item in the transition from steam to diesel. Here again I would encourage you to look at a copy of an Operating Rule Book for the railroad and era that you are modeling to ensure correctness of operation. On most roads the use of flags and classification light disappeared along with train orders generally in the late 1980's.

The use of train orders and the wording of most operating rules were fairly similar from the steam into the diesel era. The big changes began to occur during the 1980's and 1990's when railroads began to hire "kids" out of colleges to head the Rules Departments that actually had little or no hands-on experience. During the transition era, I personally was qualified on the operating rules of the GTW, D&TSL, NYC, PRR (PC), Ann Arbor, Delray Connecting, Missouri Pacific, Santa Fe, and the SP. I always had a feeling of confidence when operating over a foreign railroad, that if I had a question on the interpretation of an operating rule (let's take the flagging rule...Rule 99, for example)...on every one of these roads, the Flagging Rule was Rule Number 99! Beginning after the transition era on many roads this was no longer the case and in my personal opinion created a very hazardous situation! But hey, no one asked me for my opinion!

Signal systems were another big topic of the steam and the transition era. While the vast majority of railroad operating personnel never left the tracks of their own road, the differences in signal systems, signal rules, and indications could be vastly different! Going along with this, signals built during the steam era were of much heavier construction than those that we see today. Additionally, almost all signals were located to the right of the track they governed. As time has gone on, this too is no longer the case.

During the steam and the transition era, railroads had their own personalities. Each railroad had a different type and color of ballast generally obtained from an on-line quarry. As long as the railroads still had steam locomotives, most yards and side tracks were held in place with cinders rather than ballast. Most yard leads too were built-up from layers of cinders. Additionally, as long as steam was still operating weeds were much less apparent along the right of way until after the arrival of the diesel. On most railroads during the steam era and into at least the late 1950's, a great deal of pride was exuded in their right of ways. Ballast at the edge of the ties was well manicured and tall weeds were not at all tolerated along the right of way. I will never forget as a kid seeing our local GTW Royal Oak section gang going along the right of way with their sickles. You could look down that mainline and from fence to fence the weeds were cut to a uniform appearance!

Naturally, at this time each railroad had their own paint scheme not only for their equipment; but also for their structures. You could look at two parallel railroads and instantaneously be able to distinguish which carrier was which.

Pole lines also were a good indicator of what railroad you were driving along. A branchline might only have poles holding a single insulator and one solitary copper wire, indicating that this line was still dispatched by Morse telegraph. On the GTW, most of our branchlines were dispatched with telegraph until 1971. Looking at pole lines with multiple wires and insulators of a uniform color was also a good indicator of the steam and the transition era. When a

Chuck H Geletzke, Jr.

trainman, section man, or signal maintainer needed to communicate with the train dispatcher, he would have to locate the nearest lineside phone, if the subdivision was so equipped.

As the number of diesels increased on the railroads, another item that declined was the railroad depot and eventually the interlocking towers. At one time, almost every town had its own depot painted in the owning railroad's colors with a train order signal proudly displayed on the building's trackside. As time went on, as passenger trains disappeared, and radio replaced telegraph and telephone transmission of messages, the depots and towers too disappeared.

Most of these towns also each had a freight house, where LCL (Less Than Carload) freight was picked-up and delivered. Very similar to today's *United Parcel Service (UPS)* or *Fed Ex*, these facilities loaded primarily boxcars with freight of all kinds (FAK). Trucks or even individuals would deliver items to the freight house, which had to be weighed, billed, loaded, shipped, and delivered in a fast, safe, and efficient manner without damage. Most freight houses also contracted with a local cartage company to pick-up and deliver shipments. Once again, while I was working for the Missouri Pacific in 1972 and 1973, they still handled LCL and LTL (Less Than Truck Load) freight. Most other carriers got out of the LCL business by the early 1960's.

In concert with the use of the depot was the amount of paperwork generated. Every shipment required a Bill of Lading, a Waybill, and later a Freight Bill, to collect payment for the shipment. Train and yard crews needed switch lists and other required information to perform their duties. Depending upon the size of the operation and the number of cars handled, many of these installations had huge clerical forces. On the GTW the computer began to diminish the need for these jobs in about 1967 or 1968.

On railroads like the PRR, the use of the "trainphone" began during the steam era, I believe during the 1940's. Most railroads began to equip locomotives, cabooses, towers, and depots with radios during the 1950's. Surprisingly, on my road, the GTW, we did not see the first radios until 1968! When my brother hired-out as a switchman in Pontiac in 1978, they were still switching on the lead with hand signals! Incidentally, today the use of hand signals has truly become a lost art!

What else changed during this time of transition? Let's see, first of all the iced refrigerator car began to disappear, being replaced by the mechanical reefer. Along with the old wooden reefers, the ice houses and ice platforms too went the way of steam. Throughout this era the transportation of cattle and livestock on the rails faded away, and with it, the stinky old wooden stock cars, drovers, and the rail-served stockyards themselves...all now handled by truck. I can even recall seeing our local deliver a train of races horses to my community in Santa Fe Horse Express Cars in the early 1960's...this was the one and only time! Aggregates such as sand and gravel also began to depart from the rails. Particularly in states such as Michigan, which allowed the heaviest trucks in the world, saw the disappearance of these commodities, which did not return "enough" revenue to the carrier by the late 1960's.

At one time, every town had at least one team track where any customer could order a car and load it himself for shipment anywhere in North America or similarly receive a load, even though they personally did not have their own siding. Team tracks handled every type of load imaginable and were always an excellent industry for inclusion by modelers. Today, there are still a few team tracks around; but they are few and far between.

Think about the track during the transition era. Most of it was "jointed" or what we today refer to as "stick" rail. This track was maintained by section gangs who worked out of a small shanty placed every seven to ten miles apart. All of these section men and signal maintainers too traveled over their territory on motor cars and most were only protected using a Track or Train Line-Up issued by the train dispatcher. When there was a big track or signal project to be undertaken, a traveling gang would arrive in camp cars where they would live in an adjacent siding until the work was completed. The Track, Signal, and Bridge & Building Department all had their own camp and tool cars.

Many terminals and towns had crossing towers and crossing watchmen to protect motor vehicles from opposing train movements. These were always interesting little structures, one different from the next, and all begging to be modeled.

Like the railroads serving New York Harbor, the GTW also had car ferries across Lake Michigan and across the International Border between Detroit and Windsor, Ontario and later between Port Huron and Sarnia, Ontario. These were all interesting operations any of which could be turned into an operating switching layout in and of themselves.

Chuck H Geletzke, Jr.

Lastly, let's address the attire of the railroaders themselves. With steam virtually every operating railroader wore bib-overalls and usually a Kromer cap. As the diesels appeared, the men who manned them began to dress as if they were going to the golf course. Interestingly, as time went on, bib-overalls made a reappearance on the job. Over time the baseball cap replaced many of the Kromers, steel-toed work boots became mandatory attire, and around the year 2000 those awful reflectorized vests were mandated to assure that any working railroader would forever resemble a clown! You could always spot a switchman or brakeman, because his shirt or jacket was peppered with small holes from passing signals with fusees. Every operating railroader was required to have an approved watch, which had to be inspected every month and compared for the correct time at the beginning of each tour of duty.

Yes, in the transition era we still had scales to weigh cars to charge shippers the correct amount of money for the amount of freight handled, to account for shortages, and to ensure that cars were not overloaded. Additionally, we were allowed to get on and off of moving equipment, we could "kick" and "drop" (please don't refer to it as a "Flying-switch") cars.

During the late 1960's, our locomotives and cabooses were all still equipped with kerosene lamps, each caboose and locomotive carried a red kerosene lantern for any emergency that might occur. Railroad "company mail" was transported in the baggage car on passenger trains and in the caboose on the various locals and way freights. Into the 1970's, our wooden cabooses still never had toilets. If a worker needed to go to the bathroom, generally a privy could be found adjacent to most railroad structures; if not an alternative spot had to be located.

Just like railroads today, the carriers of the transition era also had distinctive personalities of their own. In general, the GTW was a very easy and fun outfit to work for. Roads like the Missouri Pacific, the Santa Fe, the Southern, and the SP were extremely rules conscious and not necessarily known for giving a man a second chance. Here again, you will have to talk with some of the local or resident experts on the road you model as well as the railroads you interchange with to get a feeling of how they treated their employees and foreign workers on their property.

As you can tell I feel blessed to have had the opportunity to begin my railroad career during the transition era working on a steam railroad without steam; but let me conclude with one detail that was

23

not so great about those times. Just imagine hitting an automobile at a grade crossing in the middle of the night at some dirt crossing in the middle of some nondescript intermediate location. As previously stated, we had no radios, and cell phones were still in the distant future. Do you have any idea what it was like to go and bang on some farmer's front door in the middle of the night and ask him or her to call the local volunteer fire department and police station to come and assist with a fatality. That was the part of that time period that was not so much fun.

But I'll tell you what, if you ask any of the people at our Retiree's Breakfast every month, if they would go back and do it all over again…everyone of them would go in a minute if they could railroad like they did during the transition era!

CN GT Pocket Calendar 1976

Chapter 2
Practically Pure Steam

Westbound GTW Mikado 4078 (originally the 3742) with Fireman, Carl Niemi was seen at Royal Oak, Michigan during the summer of 1959. (Roger L. Meade photo)

View from the GTW sand tower in Pontiac, Michigan, looking south (railroad east) toward the coal dock on September 2, 1967. The piggy-back tracks on the left were originally constructed in the late 1920's to store and maintain excavating equipment being used to grade the new route from Yellow Cab on Pontiac's south side to Royal Oak.

Carl's Playground

By: Charles H. Geletzke, Jr.

I want you to look at this photo, which I took in August 1967 from the Grand Trunk Western Railroad sand tower in Pontiac, Michigan looking south toward downtown Pontiac. Pay particular attention to the piggyback tracks on the left. What you see here was not always an intermodal facility; what this was originally was "Carl Neimi's playground!"

The way I understand it, Carl Neimi's Dad was a machinist in the Pontiac roundhouse and he and his family lived right near there…I believe on Ojista Street at least during the 1920's. Now it was at this time that the plan was developed to move the Grand Trunk Western's right of way off of Woodward Avenue between Royal Oak and Bloomfield Hills and relocate it to its present location. The original plan was to build this new railroad line with four main tracks all the way from Pontiac to Detroit and as if that was not enough, it was intended to have a four-lane highway run overhead! As most of you know, the four tracks were built and did run from a point just west of D&M (Detroit & Milwaukee) Yard in Detroit all the way to Lincoln Street in Royal Oak. Only two of the main tracks were ever constructed between Royal Oak and Pontiac. For those of you who have ever ridden a train over this territory or back in the day maybe even walked it, you know that the right of way was graded and built to handle all four tracks. All of the viaducts were designed to accommodate four tracks as was the beautiful depot in Birmingham with its high-level platforms on each side of the mainline. Additionally, the overhead bridges and structure clearances were all constructed with the eventual plan of utilizing four tracks.

When this right of way was surveyed and graded you could see that from a point just south (compass direction) of South

26

Chuck H Geletzke, Jr.

Boulevard in Pontiac through the "S" curves to a point just north of
Maple Road (aka 15 Mile Road) and the Birmingham depot it was
necessary to excavate a tremendous "cut." The "spoils" from this cut
were then transported and built-up as an elevated "fill" between the
Birmingham depot and Washington Avenue in Royal Oak. Now I
cannot say whether all of the material from the cut was sufficient to
build this fill or whether perhaps some of this material was acquired
elsewhere…I just don't know. I do know that at about this same time
a huge cut was also excavated on the Dequindre Line on the Holly
Subdivision between Hale Street (Milepost 2.1) and Jefferson
Avenue (Milepost 0.6) within the City of Detroit; but it was also at
this time that the "High Line" was elevated over all of the street
crossings on the GTW, NYC, and the Wabash Railroads between
Milwaukee Jct. on the Mt. Clemens Subdivision and Delray. I have
no idea where all of the fill came from for that project.

Okay, okay, so what about Carl's playground? While all of
this excavating and construction was going on, the contractors
needed a place to store their equipment (i.e. steam powered railroad
steam shovels, side-dump gondolas, and flat cars). It was at this time
that the two tracks were constructed just south of the Pontiac
roundhouse, which over thirty years later would become Pontiac's
piggy-back tracks. Every evening and on weekends this equipment
would make the trek back to Pontiac and all of this machinery would
be serviced and maintained on these two tracks during the night
while the excavators and graders slept. Over a period of time, this
became Carl Neimi's playground! Carl got to know all of the
mechanics and even though this area was considered to be "out in the
country" at this time, Carl learned the inner-workings of steam
playing on this machinery and visiting his father in the 10-stall
roundhouse.

Now let's take another detour. On the GTW Railroad, all
enginemen (engineers and firemen) had "System" seniority. That is,
they could "bid-in" or be assigned to any engineman's position,
which their seniority and qualifications would allow them to hold.
GTW engineers worked out of Milwaukee Jct. (in Detroit), Pontiac,
Durand, Saginaw, Grand Rapids, Muskegon, Port Huron, Belsay (in
Flint), Lansing, Battle Creek, South Bend, Blue Island, and Elsdon
(in Chicago). At one time, there were also positions at Bay City and
Kalamazoo.

As you can imagine and this is still the case, that hiring
usually goes in cycles. There were 13 enginemen hired between

27

September 1, 1928 and March 23, 1929 with Steve Vencil being the last. It was at this time that the Great Depression struck and all hiring was stopped and many employees were furloughed…often for years! In 1937 there was a brief surge in business and Carl Joseph Ure was hired on January 1, 1937. The effects of the depression struck again in 1938 and once again, all hiring ceased.

In November of 1940 business was beginning to increase and one day the railroad wanted to run all of the scheduled jobs; but did not have enough firemen. Apparently there was a big discussion between the Engine Crew Dispatcher located in the Stores Building just south of the Pontiac roundhouse and the trainmaster located in his office at Johnson Avenue. There was a lot of work; but not enough men. Finally the crew dispatcher said. "Young Carl Neimi can fire an engine! He used to play all the time on that construction equipment over there and on these yard engines too."

The trainmaster finally relented and in desperation said, "Well, go ahead and call Carl's Mom or Dad and see if he can come and work for us."

That was on November 20, 1940. Carl borrowed a pair of his Dad's overalls and came out and fired an afternoon yard job…he was so desperately needed that he did not even have to make his three student trips! Imagine, with the exception of one man, he was the first one hired in eleven years! Carl later received his promotion to locomotive engineer on December 2, 1947.

I first met Carl in 1967 when I too worked in the Pontiac roundhouse. He now had 27-years seniority; but in reality it was more like 38! When I met him he was the regular engineer on the Caseville Local and at that time the job was working as a "turn" between Pontiac and Caseville six days a week and those were 16-hour days!

Over the years I worked with Carl many times as a brakeman and as a fireman. Carl was always a true gentlemen and one of the system's best engineers. He was truly a pleasure to work with. I believe that he retired in 1986 when the "big buyout" was offered.

It wasn't until the early 1960's that those two tracks were converted to handle piggy-back trailers. Most of the business was bottled beer that came across Lake Michigan on the Car Ferries from Milwaukee and then arrived in Pontiac and was shipped over the road by trucks to local beer distributors.

When the GTW opened the Moterm Inter-modal facility in Ferndale, Michigan in the mid-1970's the Pontiac ramps were

Chuck H Geletzke, Jr.

deactivated. Following the formation of Amtrak in 1971 and several years later the takeover of GTW's commuter business by the Southeastern Michigan Transportation Authority (SEMTA) those tracks were converted to a fully equipped passenger car maintenance facility designed to handle all passenger car repairs and maintenance. Several years later SEMTA's operation was terminated and the facility was temporarily taken over by the Blue Water Chapter of the National Railroad Historical Society and used to maintain their fleet of passenger cars. After several more years the GTW reacquired this property and turned it into a center for the repair and servicing of the railroad's Maintenance of Way equipment, which it still handles today.

I would like to thank members of the *Grand Trunk Western Railroad Historical* Society and retired locomotive engineers Roger Meade and J. T. Johnson for their assistance in providing information for this story and GTWHS member and CN signal maintainer, Jason Nates who inquired about the past use of those tracks.

Photo from the U.S. Navy Shipyard (Electric Boat Co.) in Groton, CT during WW II illustrating the building of the Submarine U.S.S. Dentuda. The "boat" was originally named *Capidoli*; but was renamed *Dentuda* on

24 September 1942. It was launched 10 October 1944.   (LIFE
magazine photo)

High School Hazing

By: C. H. Geletzke, Jr.

I don't know about all of you; but when I was in high school
we were required to sign papers that we would not join nor
participate in fraternities or sororities. College was an entirely
different proposition; but being a railroader while attending classes,
the thought never entered my mind…later for me; the United States
Marine Corps became the best fraternity of all!

Anyway, my mother graduated from high school in 1941 and
went right into defense work. Her oldest brother graduated in 1943
and two weeks after graduation was on his way to becoming a U. S.
Navy Submariner. His name was Alfred R. Krueger and he was a
tremendous basketball and baseball player. Now for the story…while
in high school he went through "Rush" and became a fraternity
member. I recall him telling me the number of silly/stupid hazing
rituals that members of his class had to endure. One fellow had to
scrub the Royal Oak, Michigan City Hall steps with a toothbrush!
But in my uncle's case, he was ordered to count all of the railroad
ties on the Grand Trunk Western Railroad between the depot in
Ferndale, MI (Milepost 11.0) and the Royal Oak depot (then at
Milepost 13). At that time there were four tracks between the two
points not to mention a tremendous number of spur and industrial
tracks. He never told me the details of his count; but regardless, I
thought it was a great story, and probably a breeze compared to his
cruises as Quartermaster aboard the Submarine U.S.S. Dentuda!

D&TSL coal dock at Dearoad Yard in River Rouge, Michigan as seen in the early 1920's. This is the only known photo showing the 5-stall enginehouse standing behind the 70 ton Ogle coaling station, which burned in 1927. (C. H. Geletzke, Jr. collection)

Dearoad Hostler

As told by: the late Dave Doncoes, FRA Inspector and retired
D&TSL Locomotive Engineer

One of my favorite stories was always the one about when the late Fred Rancich hired out in engine service on the Detroit & Toledo Shore Line Railroad (D&TSL).

After completing his fireman student trips, Fred was assigned as the afternoon hostler at Dearoad (the northernmost yard on the Shore Line). The job involved taking care of and watching the four locomotives assigned to the yard, roustabout, and puller jobs, which went on and off duty at Dearoad in River Rouge, Michigan. As part of his duties, Fred was required to coal, water, and add sand to the locomotives, move them in and out of the four-stall roundhouse, supply their cabs, and have them lined up on the Ready Track at the appropriate hour. In addition, Fred had a hostler helper who helped perform these same duties, throw switches, shake grates, dump ashes, put up coal and sand, and fill the locomotive lubricators, One last duty involved turning road and puller locomotives, which arrived from not only the Shore Line; but also the Grand Trunk Western (GTW).

On one of Fred's first days on the job, the local from Lang arrived at about 4 p.m., requiring not only water, but coal as well. Fred turned the engine, which was one of the road's Consolidations, on the turntable, and then backed down to the coal dock and water plug while the crew went to dinner.

When the engineer and fireman returned, the fireman, who was quite a lot older than Fred, jumped all over him, because he had not put enough coal in the tender. He said, "Do you realize how much work it is to carry coal from the back of the tender to the firebox?"

Poor Fred just apologized and stated that he would do better next time.

The very next day the *Mary Ann Local** crew again arrived on Fred's shift. The crew backed to the roundhouse, which was located at the south end of the yard, and informed Fred that their engine once again required servicing. As the fireman walked away, he hollered at Fred: "This time, don't skimp on the coal!"

Well, Fred, wanting to make a good impression, spotted the locomotive under the coal chute and filled the tender up. He even grabbed a scoop shovel and guided coal into every corner of empty space in the coal bunker. Then he topped off the coal pile, making as large a heap as he possibly could without allowing coal to fall off the sides.

Later, the engine crew returned, and once again Fred's work did not meet their expectations! This time it was the engineer who jumped on Fred, stating: "If you can't get more coal than this on this engine, maybe we better ask the Superintendent to find another man!"

Fred, who had given his best, was crushed. He wanted to do a good job, and he wanted to be accepted by his new fellow workers. Anyone else probably would have walked away from the job; but Fred was not a quitter. Instead, he worked out a plan for the next day.

On the third day, Fred was servicing the roustabout engine when the local arrived about suppertime. After putting the 0-8-0 switcher in the roundhouse, he climbed aboard the Consolidation, which still had plenty of coal in its tender for the return trip to Lang. Fred turned the engine, took water at the plug and then spotted it at the coal dock. However, today he did one thing differently. He not only topped off the tender with a huge mound of coal; this time he angled the coal chute right into the tender gangway and filled the cab with coal right up to the bottom of the firebox door. After that, he just walked back to the roundhouse.

On Fred's fourth day, the local crew searched him out. "Today," said the fireman, when he found Fred, "all we'll need is water."

And Fred? Oh yes, he stayed on to retire as a locomotive engineer, and D&TSL's General Chairman of the *Brotherhood of Locomotive Engineers*, in the early 1980's.

* The name *Mary Ann Local* was derived from the fact that the D&TSL local freight working between Lang Yard in Toledo, Ohio and Dearoad Yard in River Rouge, Michigan and return, operated six days a week, sixteen hours a day, and received its nickname from the Xavier Cugat song, *Mary Ann*, which was recorded in 1945...you know the words... "All Day, All Night, Mary Ann...!"

(This story originally appeared in the author's first book, *The Detroit & Toledo Shore Line Railroad-Expressway For Industry*, published in 2011.)

D&TSL Locomotive Engineer, W. D. "Dave" Doncoes, was seen at Lang Yard in Toledo, Ohio in March 1955. (C. H. Geletzke, Jr. collection)

Chuck H Geletzke, Jr.
Something truly unique…Universal Seniority!

By: the late D&TSL Locomotive Engineer and *FRA (Federal Railroad Administration)* Inspector, W. D. Doncoes and C. H. Geletzke, Jr.

Note: This story originally appeared as "Universal Seniority" in my book *Inside Railroading and Other Railroad Stories*; however, I have deemed it necessary to explain the details and "set the stage" for the following several stories.

Here is a rare working agreement that I would be willing to bet was never implemented on most other railroads.

When the late Wilbur E. Hague and I co-authored our book *The Detroit & Toledo Shore Line Railroad-Expressway For Industry* (published in 2011) neither of us were familiar with the term "Universal Seniority," and sadly we did not include an explanation or thorough history of it in our text. Unfortunately, I have not been able to pinpoint the date on which it actually took effect. As best I can tell, it had to have been in the very early 1940's, possibly around 1945 when the D&TSL discontinued running trains through from Toledo, Ohio over the tracks of the Grand Trunk Western Railroad (GTW) to terminals in Pontiac, Durand, and Flint, Michigan.

What was "Universal Seniority" you ask? That agreement enabled a "junior" man who had less seniority and was a "promoted" conductor to hold the conductor's position on a job and permitted the "senior" promoted conductor on the assignment to "bid-in" one of the brakemen positions (cutting his own pay). Similarly, a "senior" locomotive engineer might 'bid-in" the fireman's position on a train or regular yard assignment (taking a cut in pay) and fire for a man with much less seniority.

Let me state also, that **ALL regular assignments and Extra Board Positions went up for bid every 30-days on the D&TSL!!!**

The late Dave Doncoes hired-out as a locomotive fireman on the Shore Line in 1945 at the age of 17, where his father was a D&TSL engineman. He only worked for a short time and then went into the Navy. He returned shortly after the Second World War and was promoted to Locomotive Engineer in 1947. Interestingly, because Federal Laws were different at that time, he had to wait until his 21st Birthday, December 5, 1949 to actually be able to work as a Locomotive Engineer! Dave explained that only a short time after

35

turning 21 he held "the Flint Run" (Trains 521/522) as the regularly assigned engineer...**WITH STEAM...and had a man older than his father firing for him!!!** Apparently, that man just did not want the added responsibility!?!

Similarly too, as late as the early 1980's the Shore Line had a conductor, who to put it mildly was grossly over weight and senior employees would allow him to work the Conductor's position on various jobs and they would brake for him at a lower rate of pay...That will be the following story.

I would guess that most of you who are professional railroaders or even those of you who work in other occupations based on seniority would never experience nor promote anything like this???

GTW streamlined Northern 6408 is seen backing down to its train at Dearborn Station in Chicago, Illinois from the roundhouse at Elsdon on the trackage of the C&WI Railroad. (Richard K. Smith photo; C. H. Geletzke, Jr. collection)

Chuck H Geletzke, Jr.

Dual Train Numbers

By: Charles H. Geletzke, Jr.

I learned something new yesterday. Did you know that when the Grand Trunk Western Railroad's (GTW) scheduled passenger trains (this applied to the other using railroads also) operated over the tracks of the Chicago & Western Indiana Railroad (C&WI) between 49th Street and Dearborn Station in Chicago, they assumed new Train numbers and changed timetable direction?

Yesterday, while I was at a friend's home, I was looking at a copy of *C&WI Employees Time Table No. 101*, effective September 30, 1951. In it I noticed that the GTW's traditionally "odd numbered" westbound trains received new "even" numbers and changed to "Northbound," while similarly, the departing "Eastward" trains instead of using the even numbers that all of us were familiar with, used "odd" numbers and until reaching 49th Street were considered to be "Southbound's!"

GTW Eastbound

GTW No.	C&WI No.	Dep. Dearborn Station	Arr. 49th Street
20 A.M.	221	9:40 A.M.	9:51
14 P.M.	215	8:00 P.M.	8:11
6 P.M.	207	11:00 P.M.	11:11

GTW Westbound

GTW No.	C&WI No.	Dep. 49th Street	Arr. Dearborn Station
5 A.M.	206	6:45 A.M.	7:00
15 A.M.	216	7:46 A.M.	8:00
17 P.M.	218	8:07 P.M.	8:20

37

It goes to show that you learn something new every day, and hopefully for those of you with interesting bits of information, you can see how easy it is to turn it into a story and share this material with all of your railroad friends.

Vern Heyman, or what a bicycle can do…

As told by: Richard Burg

First of all, I "didn't meet" Vern Heyman in 1963. I say that because I was well aware of who he was; but not by name…I had never actually spoke to him beyond an occasional wave of my hand as I rode my bike.

Vern had spent a long career working on the Pennsylvania Railroad (PRR), eventually rising to become a Locomotive Engineer. He'd had many jobs during that career. He'd largely worked in Columbus, Ohio, Toledo, Ohio, and the Detroit area, and by 1963 was working a Detroit West Side Belt Line local out of Lincoln Yard in Lincoln Park, Michigan.

For my part, I was a kid just starting high school, who gotten his first decent bicycle for the previous Christmas, and suddenly found my world had expanded many fold!

Vern's Detroit West Side Belt local took him north out of Lincoln Yard, over the Rouge River Bridge, through Delray interlocking, past Ford's massive Rouge Assembly plant, and to the trackage rights on the old Pere Marquette mainline for a short distance until the PRR's Belt Branch veered off to the right on a dead north-south tangent. Once on the Belt Line he'd take his consist north to Fullerton Yard.

Calling Fullerton a yard was a stretch, the PRR had its main track and three stub switches on which the kick switching of cars was very problematic, because his switching lead was located around the west leg of the yard's wye. As such, he'd have a crew that was heavy in brakemen. One of them would do the uncoupling of the cars. Another would often ride the cars down into the flat storage tracks applying the handbrakes. Those two guys rotated their jobs. As the car rider would come back up to take the uncoupling job, and the "uncoupler" would ride the next car, or cut of cars. Vern couldn't see any of this around the curve of the wye, and relied on another brakeman's flare (fusee) signals from halfway around the curve. The motive power was usually an EMD SW1, or perhaps a similar horse powered Alco unit. Detroit is as flat as a pancake, so there wasn't any need for anything larger. At the cut point for the cars there was a large stack of various colored box car doors. A testament to all the errors engineers, or brakemen had made over the years of kicking cars too soon, and clipping off the doors of cars that hadn't yet cleared a turnout.

One summer day I saw a very funny example of inexperience in the ground crew. They clearly included some summer "temp" employees, or new hires. One of them pulled a car's cut-lever, and then scampered up its ladder to the brake wheel. Well, he thought that was what he was doing; but alas, he was on the "A" end of the car as it rumbled off south on the Mainline. Being new he feared climbing up onto the car's roof, and traversing to its "B" end while it was in motion, and then applying the brakes. So off he rolled to the south. I hopped on my bike and gave chase. It rolled across Plymouth Rd…then kept going across Joy Rd. (one mile!). I was working up a good sweat. Would it reach the junction with the C&O, and derail? It did slow down before that happened. The guy riding the car didn't appreciate the kid on a bike laughing along the right-of-way!

I sat in a small playground on the big metal swing-set watching almost every day in the summer, and often during the school year. This is what I blame for this lifelong addiction to the Pennsy, and most every other road too! The cars rolling past me were from every other major railroad in the U. S., in all of those amazing paint schemes of the 1950's and 1960's. "The Mainline of Mid-America," "Route of the Empire Builder," "El Capitan," the early Erie-Lackawanna two tone paint scheme, and so many more dazzled my young eyes. Made me want to see more!

The car mix could have just as easily been from the 1930's, nothing big at all, all forty foot boxcars with a handful of short gondolas, and plenty of ice hatch wooden reefers. Once Vern had his cuts of cars sorted to his liking he'd begin delivering them to the local customers. Right across Fullerton Avenue there was *Hercules Drawn Steel*, a fabricator of heavy wire cables. They only took a single gondola car for scrap on occasions into a facing point switch. The track went inside the factory, and required Vern to completely wye (turn) the car first, and have an idler car so that his engine did not enter the building. The north leg of the wye was also the Mainline of the C&O (former Pere Marquette or PM) West Detroit Branch that ran from Oak Yard to the west to an interchange with the New York Central (NYC) (former Michigan Central or MC) Junction Yard much farther east. The C&O didn't seem to do much local switching in the area, and only showed up daily with a cut of interchange cars for Vern to handle. Interestingly, they did keep a few switchers at the Fullerton facility to service customers that were farther into the city. Every evening as I lay in bed I could hear the C&O local on this line bringing out all the empty and interchange cars from deep in Detroit. It ran by slowly just up the block, clicking the rail joints at a leisurely pace. On warm summer nights I would occasionally walk up to the corner to watch it pass, with maybe as many as 40 cars at times. Behind *Hercules* stood *Rose Truck & Caster*'s small plant. It was always a storm of welding all night long, with constant flashes of white hot light illuminating its windows, as if there was a massive lightning storm going on for hours.

The C&O, PRR, and Wabash (through their subsidiary the Union Belt of Detroit or UBD) all had trackage rights on all the tracks in the area, although I never saw a Wabash engine not even once. Occasionally, Vern would have to deliver a boxcar or two to *Lochinvar Water Heater's* warehouse just up the C&O to the west. One of my first jobs was as a fork truck driver at that facility. Somehow that morphed into being the company owner's Chauffer, when he had to go to the airport. To this day I have never figured out why he would ask for me, an 18 year-old kid, to drive on every trip, using MY 1961 Ford Galaxy!?!

I asked Vern an embarrassing question once about servicing *Lochinvar*. While I worked there he'd had a mishap. He would do a "flying switch" (professional railroaders call those "drops") into the facing point switch to reach its rail dock, and a car rider would brake the cars to a stop at approximately the right spot, and we'd use one of those wedge poles to move it exactly where we wanted to unload it. Apparently one day he'd sent a Northern Pacific boxcar down the fairly long lead into the plant, and the brakeman discovered it didn't have functional brakes. He coasted past the rail dock, off the end of the track, and plowed through a chain link fence onto Coyle Ave. From there, he just kept going up the middle of the residential street, amazingly tracking straight, and not hitting any parked cars until it finally came to rest about a half a block down. The loaded car had pressed deep ruts into the blacktop...so much so, that they were later able to return the car to the end of the rails by towing it up those same ruts! I didn't get to see how they got it back on the rails; but the next day, I unloaded it. On another occasion I saw Vern's crew fail on a flying switch maneuver. The car stalled-out barely into the turnout. For the first and only time I saw a car being "poled." The crew apparently had prepared for this possibility and dug a sturdy length of pole out of the bushes to perform the task of pushing it back onto the Mainline, and off the siding.

So getting back to the real customer base on this area of the line, the big one was *A&P* (*Atlantic & Pacific*) warehouse, with two internal rail docks. I'd spend most summer mornings watching Vern pull over 15 cars up the line, and then drilling them into the two doors, after pulling out all the previous day's empties, and storing them on the Mainline in Fullerton Yard. The two doors were very different in what cars they took, and I'd dubbed them the "Warm Track" and the "Cold Track," because one of them took only wood reefers. It held about six to eight cars, I think. The other track (Warm) was slightly longer and took only boxcars, probably full of canned goods. One of my thrills, several years earlier, when I would walk to this place from home, was to see a nearly solid train of PRR X54 insulated boxcars that were brand new, come into the warehouse. They were still in numerical order, probably on their first trip from *Campbell Soup* in Camden, New Jersey. They remained a common sight all through my childhood.

Just up the tracks to the north was a small steel operation called *Copco Steel* that took all the gondolas that came up the branch other than the occasional one for *Hercules Drawn Steel*. I had a similar experience here when I saw a string of PRR G41 traverse loaded coil steel cars arrive, again still in numerical order, and clearly brand new.

There were a couple lumber yards in the area that took boxcars of wood, and one of them had a contract to replace the interior linings of the cars. They'd receive about a half-dozen cars at a time, all identical. They were from foreign roads such as the Reading.

Once I had my bike I could follow Vern for miles north into areas of the city I'd never seen. (BTW, the bike was a 1963 *Evans*, the last year they were made I was told. I still have it hanging in my garage. I just can't part with my best toy!?!) By this time Vern was very aware of "that kid" who would appear on the swings of "Shirley Green Belt Park" to watch them kick switch Fullerton Yard and then follow them up the line all the way to Ford's old *Model T* plant in Highland Park. He'd always wave to me.

Flash forward 20 years. The PRRT&HS (Pennsylvania Railroad Technical & Historical Society) sent me a letter (I was the President of the local chapter) asking if I would make contact with a retired PRR engineer who wanted to meet PRR fans in the Toledo/Detroit area. I exchanged letters with him, and he joined our society, and even began writing an occasional story for our magazine. I also went to meet him several times and talk trains! He'd tell me stories of his PRR jobs, going all the way back to firing steam. One day he asked how I got interested in the PRR and I told him much of the above information. He fell silent, "YOU were the kid on the bike!?!" We became good friends until his passing.

The *Detroit Union Produce Terminal* has always been a point of interest to me. It was featured in an article in *Railway Age* in 1929. It was the prototype for another such facility in Baltimore that opened exactly two years later.

Vern was, for a time, the engineer of the PRR local serving the *Detroit Union Produce Terminal* circa 1950. He told me stories of how competitive the vendors could become. As his engine approached the terminal with its consist they'd be met by vendors down the tracks of the Union Belt Railroad. They would throw cases of various products up onto the engine's deck as offerings, and yell out car numbers the wanted spotted first, so they could unload them, and be the first on the floor of the Sale Room with their goods. Vern said, "we'd get so much produce that everybody in our neighborhoods got fresh produce for free, and even then, they'd have to go offer it to others."

Vern seemed to have started his railroad career at Grogan Yard in Columbus, Ohio firing on shifters (PRR term for switchers or yard engines). He said he didn't mind firing in one half of the yard that serviced general freight; but the other half was a "Hell of a job!" They'd call the two halves of Grogan the Light and Heavy Sides (Just like the D&TSL's Lang Yard in Toledo, Ohio). There was the general freight Light Side and the coal drag "Heavy Side." All firing jobs were not equal!

He graduated to working a through freight headed north to Detroit. It was a Hot Shot perishable freight headed to the produce terminal mostly, with a bit of other freight along to fill out the tonnage. Vern said that this was a good train at the start; but as time went by, the PRR kept adding in switching along the route until the

Chuck H Geletzke, Jr.

Hot Shot was little more than glorified peddler freight. The perishable traffic slowly dried-up and went to other lines.

Running trains into Detroit was a different world. There was no heavy steam power. The PRR crossed the Maumee River Bridge, and then made a sharp right turn to Toledo's Cherry Street passenger station. In the early days (1920's) the Pennsy had attempted to run I1s Decapods up the line; but an alarming percentage of them were derailing at that sharp right curve, and the idea was scrapped. As such, many trains headed into town with a pair of H10s Consolidations, or possibly L1s 2-8-2's. But there was one vestige of "heavy" power. There were the PRR N1s 2-10-2 engines running out their last miles. The engines proved to be pretty agile around that sharp curve, although new crew members were alerted to not hold the tender or engine handrail while traversing the curve, as they would firmly plant themselves into the engine's cab or tender's corner.

Here is the PRR 7312 stored in Chicago on April 14, 1946. This photo would have been taken just before the engine was moved to Detroit for service on the viaduct. You can see the headlight is wrapped up and the stack covered. An additional air tank has been added to the pilot deck, the pop valves appear to have some sort of mufflers applied, which makes

43

sense for a locomotive that is going to be used in a passenger station. The engine has the "claw" classification and marker lights on both the pilot and tender deck. The tender has had its arch bar trucks replaced with PRR dolphin trucks. A second sander pipe has also been added to the back of the drivers. (John Harris, Sr. photo; Richard Burg collection)

Vern eventually moved up to Detroit as an engineer. By the late 1940's, he had landed the Detroit Fort Street Union Depot Pool of jobs and often got to switch the Depot itself, via the 1890's viaduct running over Fort Street. The viaduct was hopelessly outdated and the weight of the power allowed on it very restricted. The PRR's crack train, the Detroit Arrow to and from Chicago, and the Red Arrow to and from the East were both powered by K4s Pacific's; but the class was too heavy to go on the viaduct. Thus, lighter engines ran up to the depot to bring down the departing trains and to pull the arriving trains into the station. In about 1948 the task was assigned to a rare old H6sb 2-8-0 numbered 7312. Vern had made that engine his own, nobody else would use it. It was old and lightweight; but Vern said he'd never used an engine that steamed as well as good old #7312! When running on the viaduct, there were restrictions. The viaduct was open below the rails and ties. Porters on passenger trains guarded the rest rooms lest a patron go in and flush the toilet onto the tracks and street below! Another problem was the loss of hot embers from the firebox of the locomotive. On one day, Vern's fireman forgot, and began shaking his fire grate, while tending the fire, sending a cascade of hot coals down onto the street below. On the street, sitting in traffic, was a fancy convertible Cadillac. The coals burned holes through its roof and trashed its interior!

Chuck H Geletzke, Jr.

PRR K4s 5253 was seen at 23rd Street waiting for the *Red Arrow* to be pulled down off the viaduct from Fort St. Depot in Detroit, MI, to take it to Columbus, Ohio on October 16, 1940. (E. L. Novak photo)

About the summer of 1948 Vern took a vacation and while he was gone an extra board engineer ran "his baby." When he came back, it was nowhere in sight. Inquiring at the yard office, he was told the sad news. His replacement had derailed her and broken her frame. She'd gone to scrap. Vern bemoaned to me that he never thought to take a photo of her. Learning this, I approached my good friend, John F. Harris, Sr. asking if he might have a photo of the engine. Sure enough, he loaned me a negative of it in Chicago and I presented Vern with an 8 X 10 print. The look on his face was priceless!

Early in Vern's Detroit career he didn't rent an apartment or house. There were a couple unused class N6B wood cabin cars (cabooses) parked at Lincoln Yard, and he was given permission to use one of them as his home. Vern was still fairly young and would date local women at times. A few he'd invite home for dinner (he liked to cook). He told me at times he'd get some pretty worried looks from them when he took them "home" and turned into a dark railroad yard at night! They relaxed when they arrived at his "caboose," complete with curtains, and flower boxes on the windows!

Lincoln Yard was planned to eventually become a 10,000 car yard; but never became much more than a few hundred car minor yard. It was a dangerous yard to work at night, because there was very little lighting of the tracks; but it did have one new innovation. The PRR had developed an "adjustable hump" and Detroit was one of the first installations. It is still buried in the dirt near the Outer Drive bridge at the middle of the yard.

Sam Rea, then President of the Pennsylvania Railroad, had big plans to enter the New York Central's fortress of Detroit, and tap into the rich automobile traffic. Sam had the encouragement of Henry Ford who felt that the NYC was raping him with their rates, because they had no effective competition other than the nearly bankrupt, at times, Pere Marquette Railroad.

The Pennsy quietly bought up land to establish a tangent mainline from the Pere Marquette at Carlton, Michigan to Lincoln Park, and then more land. At what was then, in the middle of the teens, the outskirts of Detroit to build a belt line, and a second yard, on the city's east side (Today's Detroit City Airport). Ford wanted them to reach his Highland Park plant, and the Pennsy wanted to go all the way around town, at a distance outside the NYC's and GTW's Detroit Terminal Railroad line to harvest the next level of industrial development of the city.

All was going according to plan; the PRR built the tangent line and the start of Lincoln Yard; but without an engine facility! They didn't need one to begin business as they had the friendly PM and Wabash also in town (who they partially owned). Passenger locomotives would be serviced at the PM facility at 16th Street on the Detroit River under the Ambassador Bridge. The freight engines could be serviced at the Wabash roundhouse at Delray. The West Detroit Belt was built also. But WWI intervened and the element of surprise was lost because the United States Railway Administration (USRA) took control of all the rail traffic for a couple years, stopping all construction. The Pennsy did run trains into Detroit during this time; but not on their unfinished line. Instead it moved over the PM and Wabash via Romulus, Michigan. Anyone who has ever seen the connection at that junction knows that the trains had to traverse a very tight curve and go very slowly, even then. After the War, the PRR's own line was quickly finished and service started. A

large freight station was built in Detroit, and soon the produce
terminal; but Henry Ford had his own ideas. He'd purchased the
Detroit, Toledo & Ironton Railroad (DT&I) and started his own line
to siphon off the planned traffic. It was a primitive line, using
trackage rights over the rival NYC, and at some points, running
down the middle of a street in Tecumseh, Michigan. These problems
were slowly corrected with a new line and Ford's dream of
electrifying the line; but eventually he grew tired of the I.C.C.
(Interstate Commerce Commission) regulations and labor rules, and
sold the line to the PRR. So, the Pennsy now had two routes into
Detroit…and the Depression hit!

The PRR H10s 9453 was photographed at the Wabash Railroad's Delray
enginehouse, which was used by the PRR to service freight locomotives on
Detroit's southwest side. (Charles H. Geletzke, Sr. photo)

Vern had retired by the time I was an adult; but we kept in
touch. He lived on a farm in Northwest Ohio. He called the place the
Hibernian Manor, if I recall correctly? It was a well maintained,
beautiful place. On an occasion I took my young son, about 11, to
visit Vern with me. My son, Ray, was not interested in trains; but did
have an interest in the Civil War from my influence. He'd never seen
a farm and found the place interesting and especially loved the fresh
spring water. (Vern gave him a big glass bottle of it to take home.)
Vern seemed to love kids and talked a lot to Ray, between our
discussions about the PRR. This brought up the Civil War, at which
time Vern lead him to a back bedroom turned into a library. Inside, I

too was amazed to find shelves to the ceiling of old books. They didn't just cover the walls, it was like a real library, with rows of shelves filling the room. It had that smell you only get in a room full of old books. Every book was a Civil War history from the past. To this day I wonder what became of that room?

Vern and I somewhat lost connection as my family life and heavy work schedule filled my time. I'd met Reverend Jon Barker, also via the PRRT&HS, and to my surprise learned he too was Vern's friend; but never acted on that fact…until one day Jon called me and told me, "Vern's dying of Cancer in Toledo!"

"Let's go visit him, Jon."

Plans were made very soon and Jon drove up from Cincinnati and I drove down from Ypsilanti. We met at the hospital. There we were met by his daughter and (I think, perhaps a niece). I'd never known that Vern even had kids; nor did Jon. She told us the sad news. "Vern's been in a coma for two days now, and we are just waiting for the end; but you can go in and see him if you wish."

We went in quietly and sat by his bed, first chatting quietly about our memories of Vern with each other, and then Pastor Jon addressed Vern directly. "Vern, if you can hear us, it's Rich Burg and I, Jon Barker, here to visit you." Jon had a strong "Minister's voice."

Vern's eyes fluttered a bit, and then opened…looking at us. A faint smile came to his face. "Hello friends" came in a weak voice. His family was in shock and watched! We quietly told him how much we loved him and how important he'd been to each of us. His relatives came in and joined the discussion. He soon murmured, "I'm tired," and closed his eyes. We left. A lot of tears were shed in the hallway with the family.

Vern passed a couple hours later.

Chuck H Geletzke, Jr.

Author Geletzke's friend's father's PRR Employee Pass from 1903.
Written on back of pass, "Good on Engines."

Chapter 3
Becoming a Model Railroader and a Railfan

Just completed the 8th grade and had to ride the train to Durand, MI to do a little railfanning on June 21, 1963. At that time the GTW Mikado 4070 was still sitting in one of the Grocery House Tracks.

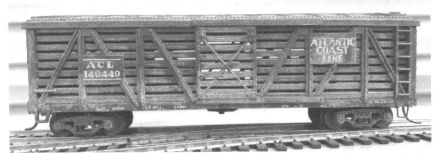

The author's HO scale *Varney* stock car, which he received new in 1955.

Fifty Years and 75 Miles!

By: C. H. Geletzke, Jr.

Chuck H Geletzke, Jr.

Let me begin by stating that from the time I was little more than an infant I was terrified of going to the doctor's office...not because of the exam; no, I was scared to death of getting shots! Normally, my parents' would hold me while the nurse would inject the serum. I am proud to state that all of that changed when I joined the Marine Corps!

For all of you who were living in the mid-1950's and dealt with the affects of Polio and probably many people in the last few years that had to receive injections for Covid witnessed people with the same phobias.

I distinctly recall seeing a huge number of people...particularly children wearing braces on their legs because they had contracted Polio! I also remember the discussions between adults of the day cheering the coming arrival of polio shots and the end of that dreaded illness! [Incidentally, my wife still has a copy of the second page of the *Philadelphia Inquirer* dated April 19, 1955 (the same day that Albert Einstein died) with her photo as the first child in Philadelphia to receive a Polio shot!] I believe that I was a student in the first or second grade when the vaccine finally arrived in my hometown of Royal Oak, Michigan in about 1955 or 1956. I recall my parents' discussing how ALL of us would go to the local health department and receive our injections. I also remember begging and pleading with them..."Please don't make me get that shot!" I truly believed that the illness would not be anywhere near as bad or painful as the shot!

Naturally, my parents were not about to give in to the demands of a seven or eight year old child; but believe it or not, I was able to coax one concession from them. I begged and pleaded, "If I get the shot, may I get ONE HO SCALE FREIGHT CAR KIT!?!" At that time I had a fairly elaborate *Lionel* O27 layout (compared to my friends); but I knew in my heart that I was ready to make the move into HO.

Being an otherwise pretty well behaved kid and both my Mom and my Dad were certainly aware of my love for trains, they folded and agreed to my DEMANDS!

A short time later (possibly as much as several weeks) I recall standing in a block-long line in front of the *Royal Oak Health Department* and waiting our turns for the impending and dreaded injection. I know that you will find it amazing; but we all survived the visit and praise the Lord, so far I have never contracted the much dreaded and debilitating illness!

51

It All Starts Here and Other Railroad Stories

Now I do not recall if it was that same evening or perhaps the next; but my Dad (whom I have written about before who allegedly was never a railfan…but sometimes I still wonder???) fulfilled his part of the contract and drove me down to *Models Hobby Supply* in Ferndale, Michigan to purchase one HO scale freight car kit. Thinking back, I believe my Dad made the actual choice and we returned home with a *Varney* Atlantic Coast Line plastic stock car kit in the bright yellow and black box. Additionally, my Dad purchased one nine inch section of *Atlas Snap Track*. I can no longer recall if Dad assembled the kit that evening or the next; but because I was so young, and HO scale was so small, we all agreed that Dad would complete assembly. The following morning I arose to the assembled boxcar red ACL stock car sitting on our living room coffee table on the short section of track. Yes, I was enamored! In my heart I knew that in no time at all we would be expanding the empire!

And expand we did and over the next six or seven years I would have three more layouts in that home on East Bloomfield, and yes, that ACL stock car always continued to play a prominent roll in the operation.

During my freshman year of high school my parents had a new home built, and over the Christmas holiday we made the move…the new home was only six blocks away. Because I had to dismantle the existing layout prior to the move, it turned out to be several months before I would commence building another layout.

Now I have no idea how or exactly when it happened; but apparently during the move, one of the sliding doors of the stock car fell off and disappeared…never to be found. Naturally, I continued to run and use the car and since my next layout was "Point to point," I just kept the side with missing door facing the wall.

As you might imagine there is more to this story. That freight car and many others languished in my parent's basement until after several other moves and a conversion to O scale. With the blessings of the railroad, my wife and I moved to Toledo, Ohio in 1979, where we purchased our first home and I began another layout, only in O scale this time. Then, in 1992 we moved only 3-1/2 miles north, back across the State Line, to the little town of Temperance, Michigan. After finally deciding that to build my dream PRR Shamokin Branch in O scale, would require a supermarket! Thus, I made a final conversion back to HO.

Okay, here is the unbelievable part of the story. One morning in about 2005 I was walking our two Jack Russell Terriers, Gracie

Chuck H Geletzke, Jr.

and Dolly, on our almost daily three mile walk in a subdivision just north of us. The dogs and I crossed Camden Lane and headed east on Woodland Drive. I must admit that I had noticed a day or two previously that the occupants of one of the homes right there were in the process of moving…in or out, I'm not sure? But as the dogs and I stepped into the street, I looked down and lying right by the curb was what I thought was a plastic door for a *Varney* stock car! I picked the small item up, inserted it in my pocket, completed the walk, and headed for home. Back in the basement I dug out the stock car and would you believe that the door was a perfect match!?!

But here is the major question…if you are a mathematician, what are the odds of finding the exact correctly needed door lying on the pavement fifty years later and seventy-five miles south of where the original piece disappeared??? Unbelievable!!

Discovering Model Railroading Magazines

By: Dan Lawecki

In his previous book, *"Soak It!!!"…and Other Railroad Stories*, Chuck Geletzke shared the story of his purchase of the then-new 1958 issue of *Model Railroader* Magazine, which was the first model railroading magazine that he ever owned. That nice story triggered a memory for me that, unlike Chuck's experience with a single, fresh and new magazine, involved a stack of moldy and musty smelling model railroading magazines!

In the early 1960's my interest in prototype railroading was beginning to take hold. Growing up in South Bend, Indiana I had the luxury of three railroads located just a couple of blocks away from our family residence on the West Side of town, and I spent many an hour taking in all the prototype railroad activity in that area.

Soon, I began to think about getting into model railroading as a hobby; but I was stymied by a serious lack of information about the hobby. Each year during the Christmas season the *Sears, Roebuck & Co.* store located in downtown South Bend had a large display of *Lionel* trains for sale, as did *Robertson's Department Store*. But as much as I enjoyed seeing those trains, they just didn't look as real to me as I thought they should.

One summer day in about 1963 or 1964, a number of kids from the neighborhood, including me, were hanging around doing nothing in particular when a boy named Randy told us of a misdeed that he had committed. On the street around the corner from our home was a house that had become rental property. The most recent tenants had just moved out of the house and in doing so, they neglected to lock the back door. Randy had taken note of that fact and one day he entered the house to look around. When he walked down the basement he discovered that the tenants had left behind a stack of model railroading magazines. That caught my attention, as I didn't even know at the time that there was such a thing. Randy offered to show me the stash he had found; but I was leery about entering that property and facing the consequences if we were to get caught. I declined his offer.

The group disbanded as several of us were summoned to return home for dinner; but Randy went back to that house. He went down into the basement and gathered up the magazines. Soon after we had eaten our evening meal that day, there was a knock at the back door. There stood Randy, grinning from ear to ear, clutching the magazines that he handed to me.

I carried the magazines into a spare bedroom on the main level of our Cape Cod home and lying on the floor, I began to investigate the material. There were forty-eight issues of *Railroad Model Craftsman* from the years 1950 through 1953, fully intact; but, oh did they smell awful! They had obviously gotten damp, because the odor was intense. My Mom took notice of that fact quickly, and she soon made her way down the hallway and instructed me to either place the magazines in our trash barrel near the alley, or keep them stored out in the garage. The indignities we model railroad enthusiasts have had to put up with at times!

I took the magazines out on the front porch and began studying each and every issue from cover to cover, soon learning about such modelers as John Allen and his famous Gorre & Daphetid RR, and Frank Ellison and his O scale Delta Lines. Each of those magazines included a list of hobby shops located around the country, and it didn't take long for me to notice an establishment named *Bob's Hobby Shop* in the neighboring town of Mishawaka.

I wanted badly to pay a visit to that store; but I had few options at my disposal. We were a one-car family at the time. My Mom had not as yet secured a driver's license, and my Dad needed to take the car to get to his job at the Post office. Trying to visit *Bob's Hobby Shop* during the week just wasn't going to work out. On Saturdays Dad usually had a number of tasks to tackle, including taking Mom to the grocery store. The hobby store was closed on Sundays.

There was only one other option to consider and that was me riding my bike from our home to 713 North Main Street in Mishawaka. *MapQuest* tells me today that the distance from 814 S. Kaley Street in South Bend to that building in Mishawaka is 6.4 miles; but at the time it seemed much further away. Would my folks give me the green light to make the trip? There was only one way to know and that was to ask them.

So, one evening after dinner I approached them about my idea, and to my great relief and surprise, they bought into the plan. There were of course, the expected warnings about being careful and avoiding trouble; but I think that I had demonstrated up to that point a sense of maturity and commonsense that my folks appreciated. The weather for the following day looked promising; so I made my plans to take a road trip to Mishawaka.

The following morning I tucked a couple of dollars into my pocket, grabbed my bike and headed east toward Mishawaka. I found *Bob's Hobby Shop* without any difficulty and when I entered the premises, I was blown away by all of the model railroading equipment and supplies! I was greeted warmly by the owners, Mr. and Mrs. Moorhead, whom asked me if they could be of any help. I told them that it was my first time in their store, and I wanted to look around for a time. There were shelves full of *Athearn* rolling stock kits and ready-to-run motive power, and all of that equipment looked so much more realistic to me than the *Lionel* tinplate equipment that I had seen previously. I knew in an instant that if I was going to get into the hobby, it would be as an HO scale enthusiast.

It suddenly dawned on me that the two or three dollars that I had in my pocket wasn't going to go very far that morning. *Athearn* "Blue Box" kits were available back then for about $1.49; but I didn't have enough cash on hand for track or anything else to accompany a kit. I ended up purchasing a packet of *Walthers* "brick paper" that I later used to cover the wood base on a structure that I had scratch-built.

The bike ride home seemed to go quickly. That visit would be followed by many others, especially after I acquired my driver's license in the next five or six years. The die had been cast. I was going to be a model railroading enthusiast. Who would have guessed that a pile of moldy old magazines were responsible for that!!!

NYC & C&O (former Pere Marquette) interlocking at Wayne Jct.,
Michigan in the early 1960's. (Jim Harlow photo)

A Day of Train Watching at Wayne Junction
62 Years Ago

By: David J. Mrozek

According to weather records available at *Weather Underground*, Thursday, August 9, 1962 appears to have been a pleasant, 75-degree, summer day in the Detroit area...a near perfect setting for a day of train watching at the former Michigan Central interlocking tower at Wayne Junction. Located 16.75 miles west of Detroit, the tower protected the crossing of the New York Central's double-track Detroit-Chicago mainline and the Chesapeake & Ohio's single track Toledo-Saginaw line. The operators at Wayne recorded the day's train movements for each company separately on their specific Station Record of Train Movements forms. In the NYC's case, that form was the T134-A sheet, which was required by the Interstate Commerce Commission (ICC) to be retained on-location for a 3-year period. This account only speaks to what would have been seen on the NYC that August day, since the C&O train movements document was not available, if indeed it has survived at

56

all. However, from an historical perspective, the NYC activity recorded is interesting both in terms of the shear number of trains operated, the motive power assigned, as well as the unexpected events that transpired that day.

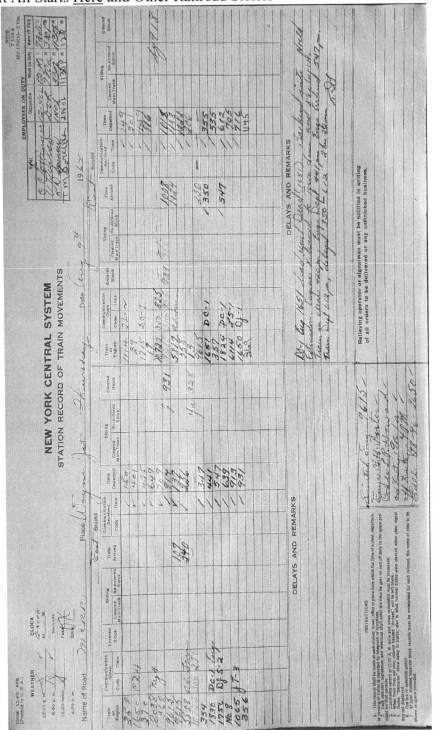

NYC Record of Train Movements at Wayne Jct., MI on August 9, 1962.

Chuck H Geletzke, Jr.

The NYC's Detroit and Michigan Division Employee Timetable #11 dated April 29, 1962 carded twelve first class trains passing through Wayne Jct. daily. There were two mail and express train exceptions-Train 13 did not run on Mondays and Train 370 did not operate on Sundays. In addition to the passenger and mail trains, the August 9th train sheet also reveals that there were six westbound freight movements (TL-2. DC-7, DC-1, LS-1, DJ-1, and an Ann Arbor Turn). Eastbound, there were five freights recorded (CD-4, NY-4, the Ann Arbor Turn, DJS-2, and JT-3).

On the motive power front, the NYC was for the most part operating with a fleet of first generation diesel locomotives in August 1962. Many of the road units were in the process of transitioning in appearance from the Central's famous lightning stripe paint scheme into a simplified black and white cigar scheme for freight units and a similar dark gray and white scheme for passenger units. In 1959, the familiar NYC oval logo had been reconfigured into its final form with bold, more modern looking script, which was applied to locomotives as they were repainted.

As can be seen on the August 9th train sheet, many of the freights were powered by streamlined EMD F-units (number series 1600-1877) or ALCO FA-units (1000-1123), with EMD GP7's (5600-5827) assigned to the Ann Arbor Turn. Passenger trains were identified only by train number and it is likely that most were hauled by EMD E7's or E8's (4000-4095), although four ALCO PA2's (4208-4211) remained on the roster until 1965 and sometimes they made rare appearances on trains in and out of Detroit. There were still a handful of Baldwin and Fairbanks Morse cab units running around as well and while none were registered on August 9th, two days later, an FM CFA16-4 (6602) lead CD-4 eastbound. Earlier that same morning a Baldwin RF-16 (3811) took TL-2 west and later that evening JT-3 was sent east with that same unit leading. No doubt the Michigan Division motive power chiefs wanted to quickly send these less-than-reliable Baldwin "sharks" back to Toledo where they came from before there were any issues with them.

A small number of second generation diesels began to appear on the property in 1961 and 1962 in the form of 15 EMD GP20's (6100-6114) and 25 ALCO RS32's (8020-8044)-both producing 2,000 horsepower. These units were generally assigned in groups to the hottest trains on the system. On August 9th, NY-4 was headed up by RS32 (8038) that morning and later that afternoon LS-1 was lead by GP20 (6114). There weren't enough of these units to power NY-4 and LS-1 everyday; so EMD F's and ALCO FA's could also be found heading up these trains. More help would be coming with ten 2,250 horsepower EMD GP30's (6115-6124) slated for delivery later that August. Subsequent train sheets showed that GP30 (6116) was assigned to LS-1 on September 16th.

NYC also had a small 80 horsepower switcher, an EMD SW8 ((9615), assigned to Wayne to service the local industries and Ford Motor Company's Wayne Assembly Plant. Ford began building Lincoln and Mercury vehicles at the newly opened facility on October 1, 1952. A station wagon plant addition to the structure was completed in 1957 to produce bodies for the then popular Mercury Colony Park wagon. Over the years the products built at Wayne changed and included long wheelbase versions of the Edsel (the Corsair and Citation models), the F100 pickup truck, and still later, Ford's first Bronco in 1966.

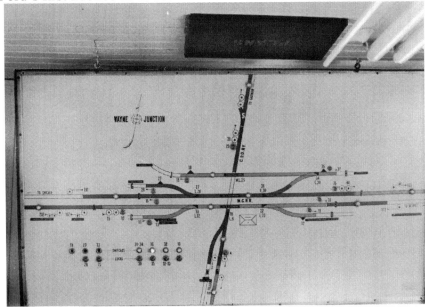

They NYC-C&O (PM) model board in the NYC interlocking tower at Wayne Jct., Michigan as seen in the early 1960's. (Jim Harlow photo)

Third trick operator, R. D. Spencer came on duty at 3:30 P.M. on August 9th with Train 354, "The New York Special," due to pass Wayne Jct. at 3:43 P.M. It was running four minutes late; but with an 80 mph speed limit for passenger trains on the mainline, it might still pull into Detroit on time at 4:10 P.M., despite the 50 mph speed restriction over the grade crossings in Dearborn. Westbound DC-1 was having locomotive problems and would need assistance before continuing its journey west. The Delays and Remarks section of the train sheet explained what transpired and read as follows…

"DC-1 Eng 1651 lead unit dead. Backed into North Extension. Engines returned to Town Line and replaced. Train in clear 4:20 P.M. Engs departed 4:41 P.M. Engs arrived 5:47 P.M. Train departed 6:12 P.M., delayed 2 hrs 22 min. RDS."

Two additional entries were recorded on the train sheet. DC-1's disabled locomotive lash-up lead by trailing F7 (1830) headed eastbound back to Town Line and ultimately Detroit departing Wayne at 4:41 P.M. The replacement set of locomotives lead by F7 (1824) ran light from Town Line to Wayne arriving at 5:47 P.M.

The balance of the shift for R. D. Spence was relatively quiet, at least on the NYC side of things, LS-1 headed west at 7:05 P.M. and was followed by DJ-1 at 7:16 P.M. Eastbound, Train 8 "The Wolverine," passed the tower at 6:39 P.M., JT-3 at 9:13 P.M., and finally Train 356, "the Twilight Limited" at 9:31 P.M.

It would have been nice to have been at Wayne Junction that day; but as an 8-year old kid, my train watching days were still four years in the future. However, in 1966, I did discover the NYC train register and block station at Town Line in Dearborn, Michigan; but that is another story…

Chapter 4
Getting Started

My High School Prom and All-Night Party

By: Charles H. Geletzke, Jr.

How many of you railroaders and shift workers have ever thought about this?

Shortly before I graduated from high school in 1967 I asked a really cute girl in my class out and we attended our Senior Prom and All-Night Party. Now I have never been a real late-night person; but I did have a good time and she was a great deal of fun.

Now please allow me to say that looking back over a 45 year railroad career, riding in locomotives and cabooses or sitting at a desk as a Trainmaster during the middle of the night, why would anyone stay up all night if they didn't have to???

If I had it to do all over again, I would probably do the prom and then take her out for brunch the next day...just saying!

A view of the GTW 10-stall Pontiac, MI roundhouse and turntable as seen near the end of steam in 1959. Notice the coaches stored on the Coach

Chuck H Geletzke, Jr.

I was just getting started and already things were beginning to change!

By: C. H. Geletzke, Jr.

I had only just begun my railroad career with the Grand Trunk Western Railroad on July 6. 1967 and by Monday afternoon, July 10th, I could already observe that things were changing! Apparently there had been a problem with the turntable shanty on the turntable at the Pontiac, Michigan roundhouse. What I did not realize was the fact that railroad management had only recently abolished the B&B (Bridge & Building) Department staff on the Detroit Division, which included the terminals of Detroit, Pontiac, and Durand. The B&B Department was the ones who maintained, repaired, and painted all of the structures and bridges belonging to the railroad. Prior to this reduction in force, a B&B gang located right there in Pontiac, would have driven less than two miles over from their shop, located within the confines of the PO&N Wye, just west of the depot and repaired the damage within several days…but not now! No, I was about to learn just how the railroad was planning to save money!

My job was that of a Laborer in the roundhouse and I worked from 3:00 P.M. until 11:00 P.M., with Thursdays and Fridays off. When I reported for duty on Monday the 10th, I immediately observed that the turntable no longer had an operator's shanty and where it had stood, now was just an exposed open platform…with several levers sticking up above it and an electric streetcar type controller or rheostat. What I did not know; but soon learned was that the B&B gang performing the work, had to drive over each morning all the way from Battle Creek, a distance of 120 miles and a two hour drive…each way! Thus the gang would spend half their working day, just driving back and forth! So, if they arrived by 9 A.M., they could work for about four hours minus thirty minutes for lunch, and then drive two hours back home.

It was quite sad to me, but by my second week on the railroad I quickly learned why a three day project could easily take over two weeks to complete…and apparently they were saving money!

63

Perhaps if I had gone on after receiving my Bachelor's degree and obtained an MBA, I would one day understand!?!

The GTW Alco S2 8198 and caboose GTW 77140 were seen working the City Job at Battle Creek, MI in the late 1960's. (Stan Sienicki collection)

Carbody Mounting Bolts

By: C. H. Geletzke, Jr.

I have told you before that my first job on the railroad was working as a Laborer for the Grand Trunk Western (GTW) in their Pontiac, Michigan roundhouse. That was in 1967. Occasionally I would be instructed to fill-in as a Machinist Helper (even though I was never paid the increased rate of pay) and assist in actually repairing one of the diesel locomotives.

One day in late August I was told to help Harold King, who was working on one of the Alco S-2 or S-4 switchers. Harold was probably twenty years my senior and had begun his career working for the Santa Fe in their Barstow, California Locomotive Shops. Harold was a very knowledgeable man and I always enjoyed working with him...and oh yes, Harold did not only work as an afternoon Machinist on the railroad…during the day, he operated a dragline in one of the Oxford, Michigan gravel pits!

On this particular day Assistant Roundhouse Foreman, Al Freeman had instructed Harold to make sure that all of the carbody mounting bolts and nuts, which were used to secure the Alco's hood to the frame of the locomotive were tight and secure. A hole in the flange along the bottom edge of the hood was placed over the bolt and then secured with a lock washer and two approximately 4-inch jam nuts from underneath the frame of the locomotive. If I recall correctly, there were four anchor bolts on each side of the engine's hood?

Now Harold cut his eye teeth working on Santa Fe steam and in his "expert opinion" (and I agree) any machinist worth his salt could easily detect if a bolt and its attached jam nuts were secure, merely by tapping them with a hammer! If one of the nuts were not tight, it would emit an entirely different sound than if they were secured properly. But in this case, apparently an ICC (Interstate Commerce Commission) Locomotive Inspector (this was prior to the formation of the FRA or Federal Railroad Administration) had found a loose nut while performing his inspection and he told Mr. Freeman that he wanted ALL of the nuts removed from all eight studs and all 16 of the jam nuts manually tightened properly! Harold King was furious about this! I still recall him stating, "I can tell you within two minutes if all of these nuts are tight by just tapping them with my hammer…this is the dumbest thing I've ever seen!"

Anyway, I was told to help Harold…for me, this was a true bonus, because I got to hear a huge number of Harold's railroad stories!

We started with the bolt and its two jam nuts on the right front corner of the locomotive. For tools we used a 4-inch box wrench, the handle on which was probably three feet long. In addition we had a 6-foot steel pipe or "cheater bar" or pipe, which we could slide over the wrench's handle to increase the amount of torque that we could apply. On each stud, we used the two tools, removed the two nuts, applied a "shot of oil" and then reapplied the lock washer and first nut. Once we had it secured as tightly as we could, we then applied the second jam nut…again as tightly as possible! When Harold was satisfied with our results, being the professional that he was, he gave each one a little tap with his hammer! When the sound was right he would say, "What a waste of time!"

Removing and retightening most of the nuts and bolts was not a big problem...except one on each side. You see this bolt was accessed in the center top of the battery box on each side of the unit. On both of these we draped old dirty burlap bags over the tops of the batteries so that we would not contact the terminals and receive a heck of a shock! On these, I would crawl inside the battery box, lying on my back on top of the burlap, and hold the box end of the wrench on the nut, while Harold turned it using the cheater bar. Would you believe that not counting our 30 minutes for lunch, we spent the remainder of our eight hour shift loosening and tightening eight bolts and 16 nuts!?! Thankfully, that was the only time that I was ever required to perform this task on the railroad!

After writing this story, I sent it to my friend, Robert "Bob: Grinn a retired GTW Machinist and asked for his comments. Here is his response...

Thankfully, I never saw an Alco locomotive! They were gone when I hired out in Detroit in 1978. Even though I believe the car body mounting bolts used lock washers and regular nuts when I started, later they used nylon nuts. The bolts holding the motor in place had the double nuts style that we hit with a hammer. We used a cheater bar, as all mechanics call it to tighten the nuts. A pipe that slid over a wrench or over a breaker bar. CN later banned them because of an injury somewhere on the system. Every shop still had a cheater bar hidden until we needed it!

The GTW 7019 was photographed at Pontiac, MI on April 2, 1992. (Jack G. Tyson photo)

"Shave and a Haircut..."

By: C. H. Geletzke, Jr.

On April 15, 1968 I made my first "paid" trip and established my seniority as a Road Brakeman for the Grand Trunk Western Railroad (GTW) working out of Milwaukee Jct. in Detroit, Michigan. The job that I was called to work was the "Mount Clemens Switch Run," Trains 586/585 and we went on duty at 8:00 A.M.

The job actually performed all of the local switching between Milepost 17.3 just east of Fraser all the way out to the east end of New Haven at approximately Milepost 33. On occasion the job would be instructed to run all the way to Richmond (Milepost 39); but this was not a normal occurrence.

On this day I was working with Engineer, Dud Field; Conductor, Neil Greiner; and Flagman Bob Craig. I was the Head Brakeman and we had the engine GTW 7019 an SW1200 built in 1955. Because there were no facilities to turn the locomotive, we backed the engine all the way to New Haven

One of the interesting parts of the job was the fact that at Mt. Clemens we had to take loaded N&W coal hopper out the 10 mph spur, a distance of about eight or nine miles to the U. S. Air Force's Selfridge Field Air Force Base, which at the time was an active Strategic Air Command facility.

To get there required us to run a distance of between two and three miles out to the gate on the southwest corner of this huge fenced facility. Once through the gate we circumnavigated three sides of the interior perimeter of the base and even rolled across the extreme north end of the main runway. Believe me, it was quite an experience to be traversing the north end of that flight path when an Air Force fighter was taking off! Once at our final destination, we set off the loaded hoppers on a clear track and then gathered the empties. I noticed that the Air Force had a switcher of their own in addition to a locomotive crane to handle all of their own switching. All of this coal was destined to the base's power and electric plant. While we did not handle any of them, a number of tracks on the base also contained a rather large number of DODX and USAX tank cars.

Now here was the interesting part of this trip. Shortly before we completed all of the switching, I noticed that Neil Greiner disappeared. Brakeman Craig did not seem concerned; so we just kept switching. Shortly we put our locomotive and our outbound cars in a clear track and walked to the nearby PX or Post Exchange where each of us ate a wonderful lunch for about two dollars. As we were all just sitting down, like magic Conductor Greiner reappeared and I noticed that he obviously had just had his hair cut! I soon found out that while we were finishing up the work, Neil paid a visit to the barbershop, also located in the PX, and had his haircut for about 50 or 75 cents...if I recall correctly at that time I believe a haircut at a commercial barbershop was about $1.75...quite a saving! With the work, tonsorial services, and our meals completed we returned to the Mt. Clemens Freight Office. The round trip out and back took us about three hours.

We then completed our work in the local *Ford Motor Company Vinyl Plant* and at the *Ford Paint Plant*...a very complicated switch. With those chores finished we departed for the town of Chesterfield and then on to switch the *New Haven Foundry* in New Haven, Michigan.

When all of the work was completed, we turned and headed back to Detroit where we yarded our train at East Yard, put the caboose away, and took the engine to the roundhouse. We then walked back to the Milwaukee Jct. yard office where we "tied-up" at

Chuck H Geletzke, Jr.

12 o'clock Midnight…only a 16 hour day…my first of many more to come!

Driving Your Own Vehicle

By: C. H. Geletzke, Jr.

When I went braking for the Grand Trunk Western Railroad (GTW) in 1968, by the time that I was called to work only my fourth trip, I quickly learned that it was common practice for the Crew Dispatcher, when he called us for duty at another terminal, to instruct us to drive our own personal vehicle…or sometimes, even ride the bus! When we were required to do this, we would be compensated for the "railroad mileage" from our home terminal to the on duty point of the assignment. Thus, if the crew caller told me (for example) to deadhead from my home terminal, Milwaukee Jct. in Detroit to Pontiac, to work an assignment there, I would be paid an additional 26 miles in addition to the mileage of the job that I was working (With a basic day of, or minimum of 100 miles). As you can see counting the trip of 26 miles up, and 26 miles back home at the end of the day, plus 100 miles for the job, I would have earned 152 miles pay…or about a day and a half pay.

The company had the option to tell us to "deadhead by train." If we did that (using passenger or freight trains), we would only be compensated the recognized deadhead mileage in addition to the mileage on the job we were working.

Now if the crew dispatcher said "use your own personal vehicle," we would receive an additional payment of the recognized allowable mileage rate as stated by the U. S. Federal Government for the deadhead portion of the day.

For me, this usually worked out very well, as I lived with my parents in Royal Oak, Michigan, which was midway between Detroit and Pontiac. Thus, even though I only drove a portion of the entire allowable and negotiated distance, I would be compensated for the entire amount!

Crew members were normally given a "two hour call" or advance notice to report for duty at our home terminal…we were not compensated for any portion of this time. However, if we were called to deadhead as in the example from Detroit to Pontiac, one hour was added to the advanced call time…thus we would be given a

69

"three hour call." Call times varied for all away from home terminals based on distance. The same amount of deadhead time would be added to the return trip before our names could be placed back on the extra board. Thus if I was returning to Detroit after working in Pontiac, instead of going "back on the board," immediately following my off duty time, I would have to absorb the one hour deadhead. I know it sounds complicated!

Interestingly, the vast majority of employees who were called to deadhead from their home terminal to another point "using their own personal vehicle" would just drive directly from their home to the out of town terminal…this was an accepted practice throughout my entire railroad career.

After filling your head with all of these details let me now get to the first part of the actual story. Please let me state that from hereon, all of the details of this story are secondhand hearsay, and let me add that this event occurred years before I went to work on the railroad and I never knew any of the individuals involved!

One day I overheard several old head enginemen talking and this was the story they were discussing. I believe that it occurred back in the early 1950's when the GTW was still running mostly steam.

Apparently one day a GTW Fireman who lived and normally worked out of Battle Creek, Michigan was called to deadhead to Lansing to fire a yard job. Living somewhere on the east side of town, he allegedly just jumped into his personal auto and headed for our State's Capitol, which was about one hour away. In route he apparently was involved in a serious accident and was killed! As you can imagine, after the dust or snow or rain settled, his wife took the case to court. It seems the railroad refused to compensate her in any manner, because her husband had never reported to the Battle Creek roundhouse or yard office and had NEVER signed the On-Duty Crew Register Sheet stating that he was reporting for duty and "fit for duty!" As far as the corporate attorneys were concerned, the victim was just out for an early morning drive…on his own time!

70

D&TSL GP7 42 and SW7 117 were seen at 4-track Edison Yard in Trenton, Michigan on January 31, 1980. The yard office was located behind the photographer's right shoulder.

Part Two

This one will shock a number of my railroad friends! Sometime in the early 1980's two former Detroit & Toledo Shore Line [D&TSL] (It was now the Grand Trunk Western [GTW] under former Detroit, Toledo & Ironton [DT&I] leadership.) trainmen were called to drive from Lang Yard in Toledo, Ohio to Edison Yard in Trenton, Michigan...a railroad distance of 35 miles each way, to work Train 808/807 an afternoon local. Now each of these two enterprising individuals decided that they would do their part to "help save the environment" and rode together, up and back, in one of the men's personal autos. The next day each man submitted an individual "time claim" for the car mileage, just as if they had elected to drive separately. When the timekeeper received the two claims, some way, some how, she became aware of the fact that the two men had decided to ride together...and would only pay one of the claims! This one minor issue created hard feelings and dissention for years within the ranks!

At Leslie and my wedding in Philadelphia, PA in 1976 we see railfan Ken Borg on the left and the late GTW Crew Dispatcher, Joe Dooley, who introduced Leslie and I to one another.

Part Three

When I became a railroad manager in 1976 I was made aware of the various fringe benefits that the railroad provided for its managers. One of these was an agreement, which stated that if the railroad officer experienced an accidental death his beneficiaries would receive a certain sum of money. If the individual was accidentally killed "on the job," the carrier had a double-indemnity policy, meaning that the beneficiaries would receive twice the amount.

In 1975 one of my best friends at work was a clerical employee who often worked as one of the Crew Dispatchers at Milwaukee Jct., named Joe Dooley. One day he told me that his wife had a childhood friend in Philadelphia who was coming out to visit for the weekend and asked if I would like to meet her and go out to dinner with them…you know, a "Blind Date!" Because of the geographical distance between our homes, I figured that I would probably never see her again; but what the heck! We met on Saturday night, October 18, 1975. Two days short of a year later, we were married!!!

In the spring of 1979 Leslie and I were transferred to Toledo, Ohio where I became the Trainmaster on the D&TSL. At about this same time, Joe Dooley followed his father's footsteps and went into GTW management and was sent to Flint, Michigan as an Assistant Trainmaster, where he normally worked one of the night jobs. By this time, Joe and his wife had two children.

One evening, Joe was driving on his way to work, and only about a mile or so from the yard office in Flint stopped for a red traffic light. When the light turned green he started to drive ahead…before he had gone even fifty feet, his car was "tee-boned" by a car carrying two escaped convicts and their mother, being pursued by the police at an estimated speed of 115 mph!!! The escapees hit the driver's side door of Joe's car and killed my good friend instantly!

A day or two later, Leslie and I drove up for the funeral. I will never forget, it was only the first week of October and yet it was already snowing during a good portion of our drive north.

At the time, Joe had two younger brothers who also worked for the railroad. One day a year or so later, I was talking with Tom, one of Joe's younger brothers, who also was a railroad manager. During our discussion I asked Tom if Joe's wife, Cindy, ever received the double-indemnity portion of the employee insurance benefit. Tom said, "No! The corporate attorney said, "How did we know that he was not on his way to the store!?!" (The fact was that Joe was due to report for work less than ten minutes from the actual time of the accident.)

Several years later I had quite a discussion with Joe's Dad, who was a high-level manager. It was quite apparent that his love and respect for the railroad had dissipated…

I still miss Joe! He was a good friend and an outstanding railroader!

Eastbound GTW Train 168 headed by GTW passenger GP9 4950 is seen handling passengers on the "engineer's side at Royal Oak, MI in October 1969.

My First Trip as a Passenger Brakeman

By: C. H. Geletzke, Jr.

I could not believe that at 2:40 A.M. on Thursday, June 13, 1968 my telephone rang and it was the Grand Trunk Western Railroad (GTW) Crew Dispatcher at Milwaukee Jct. in Detroit, Michigan calling me to work my very first trip as a "uniformed" Passenger Brakeman...of course, there was only one problem...I did not own a passenger brakeman uniform! I immediately explained that to the caller and he stated, "Just wear a dark suit and a tie!" He also informed me that since this was a pair of commuter trains (Trains 994 and 995) I would be required to deadhead to Pontiac to begin work. Thus, I was being given a three hour call instead of the normally required two hours. He stated that I would go on duty for pay purposes at Milwaukee Jct. at 4:40 A.M. and after driving my personal automobile, I would report for duty at the roundhouse

74

Chuck H Geletzke, Jr.

Book-In Room in Pontiac at 5:40 A.M. (Remember, as I stated in the first volume of this series, prior to January 1, 1971 **"Deadhead Counted as Rest!!!**

I immediately showered and put on my black suit and tie and headed for the Pontiac roundhouse where I had begun my railroad career just about a year earlier. When I walked into the Locker Room, I found that Engineer, Andy Lord and Fireman, J. T. Johnson were already out on the locomotive, which was the GTW 4918, a passenger GP9. The Conductor was old Tom Church, who began his railroad career back in the late 1930's. The Flagman was Adam Aamon (Years later I learned that he had two nicknames one was "UpandAdam," and also "Canvasback," because just as soon as he got to Brush Street Depot he would go right upstairs and spend the entire day in his bunk! We had about eight or nine coaches and because we were a lowly commuter train, we did not handle any baggage, mail, or express cars.

Conductor Church informed me that my first chore was to go out to the engine and tie it onto the east end of the string of coaches sitting in the Coach Track. This turned out to be an interesting move as each of the three switches that needed to be thrown to get the engine to the train, was a spring-switch, which did not actually require me to physically throw it! Once I had the engine tied onto the train, a car inspector coupled the air, signal, and even the steam line, which surprised me since it was almost the middle of June! That said, the engine was not producing steam and the heavy metal steam lines were actually coupled to prevent them from sustaining any damage enroute.

With this first task completed, I climbed aboard the head coach and began walking back through the train with the Car Inspector, who was making certain that the air brake trainline was properly charged and that the Conductor's signal line was working properly in each coach. During my stroll, I ran into Conductor Church in the fourth coach, where he began to explain my duties for the morning trip. Meanwhile, the Car Inspector proceeded to the rear of the train, where he observed the air pressure on the rear car and once it reached the required 110 psi, he began performing the federally mandated Initial Terminal Brake Test.

By now the entire train crew was aboard and at 6:25 P.M. Conductor Church blew two short toots on the signal whistle in the cars end platform, which in turn blew a small little whistle in the rear of the locomotive cab…a signal to "Go Ahead," and we began pulling about .6 of a mile east to the Pontiac depot located at Milepost 26.3.

Now at that time Pontiac still had a Switchtender who was assigned at the east end of the yard at Johnson Avenue, on all three shifts, and he had us lined up, all the way down the East Lead and onto the Eastward Main Track. Oh yes, I should also mention that during only the past several years, the operator, telegraph and train order office was moved from the Pontiac depot to the yard office at Johnson Avenue. As we rolled past the yard office, our train orders were hooped up to us. Shortly we arrived at the depot and the train stopped with the locomotive just west of Huron Street. At that time also, both Johnson Avenue and Huron Street still had crossing towers manned by Crossing Watchmen, who saw that the crossing gates were safely down in position to protect the movement of the train and vehicular traffic.

As we were pulling down to the depot, both Conductor Church and Flagman Aamon explained to me my duties while we were enroute. First they assured that I had my GTW Employees Time Table in my possession and explained which side of the Mainline each depot and its platform were on (Here was an instance where having been a GTW railfan really helped me!). Going east, this would be easy, as once we departed Pontiac, all of the platforms would be located on what we would refer to as the "Engineer's side of the train." Our westward trip, later that afternoon, would be much different. Conductor Church informed me that the head three coaches would be my responsibility, and that not only would I have to see that the proper doors were opened, and that the "traps" were in the correct position; but that I must call out each station name, prior to arrival, in each coach. Upon arrival at each station I was also to dismount from one of the coaches and place a step box on the station platform and assist passengers boarding the train if needed. Lastly, if any switches needed to be thrown during our trip, to properly line our route, also was to be my obligation.

After loading only a handful of people, we departed Pontiac, on-time, at 6:35 A.M. Interestingly, the next two stations were listed as "flag stops" in the timetable, meaning that a stop was only required if there were passengers present, waiting there to board the train. Both of these stations actually had flag signals, which the flagman or conductor had to make certain were extinguished upon our departure. On this day we had office workers waiting to board for Detroit at both locations; so stops became necessary. We departed Bloomfield Hills (M.P. 21.2) at 6:41 A.M. and Charing Cross (M.P. 19.9) at 6:43 A.M.

Looking east at the GTW's Birmingham, Michigan depot with its high-level platforms on October 13, 1978.

Because our next stop, Birmingham (M.P. 17.8), was a manned station with a train order office and "high-level" platforms, I had to drop or lower each doorway "trap" in each doorway in my three coaches on the engineer's side of the train. This was the only depot with a high level platform on the entire GTW Railroad! The depot was actually constructed in the 1930's with a Center Track located between the two mainlines, so that trains handling dimensional or wide loads would not strike or damage the platforms. This stop was always well patronized, and we departed on-time at 6:49 A.M. Oh yes, I did observe that we had a Clear train order signal and did not have to pick-up orders. As we pulled away from the station I walked back through my three cars of responsibility and raised the passenger traps making certain that all of the Dutch-Doors were open on the engineer's or right side of the train.

Next was the commuter location of Oakwood Blvd. (M.P. 14.3). This little unmanned station at the intersection of 12 Mile Road and Vinsetta Blvd. was elevated above ground level and actually was located within the City Limits of Royal Oak (my hometown). Here again, a huge number of local suburbanites boarded the train! I began to notice that a large proportion of them seemed to want to ride in the head coaches, which Conductor Church pointed out to me, was so they would have a shorter walk upon arrival in the Motor City. Again we were once again underway, on-time at 6:54 A.M.

Our train barely got up to speed when we had to slow down and stop at the manned depot and train order office on 11 Mile Road in Royal Oak (M.P. 13.2). Both Royal Oak and Birmingham were the two stations, which originated the greatest amount of commuter traffic. Because the vast majority of these riders rode this train daily, Monday through Friday, they did not hesitate climbing aboard and finding their seats. I don't know for sure; but I would be willing to bet that a large number of them sat in the same seats on every trip!?! Here again, we were out "on the advertised" at "straight-up" 7 o'clock.

Our seventh stop was only a little over a mile away at Pleasant Ridge (M.P. 12.0) another unmanned station with the same type of three-sided shelter as were located at Bloomfield Hills, Charing Cross, and Oakwood Blvd. It was fun observing this little station from the train because this was the same spot where my grandfather had begun kindling my interest in trains three blocks from their home, when I was only two! Oh yes, we were "on the move" at 7:03 A.M.

The next stop, Ferndale (M.P. 10.9) would be the last station where we would expect to find passengers boarding our train. This too was a "manned" station; but it did not house a ticket agent. Instead, it was the headquarters for the Grand Trunk Western Railroad's Police Department and was located just two blocks north of 9 Mile Road. As we departed, I again noted the time…on-time at 7:06 A.M. I was impressed…these guys really knew how to run a railroad!

From here on we would begin to see passengers disembark. Our next stop would be Highland Park (M.P. 6.6); but please pay attention here! Because the depot here had closed a number of years earlier, and was now boarded up; instead of stopping right at the depot, we pulled east a little further and stopped at the Chrysler Corporation's commuter stop (approximately M.P. 6.6), which at that time was located at the northeast corner of their Highland Park complex and would eventually become their corporate headquarters. Here a huge number of Chrysler employees left the train and walked

Chuck H Geletzke, Jr.

to their offices on the west side (compass direction) of the tracks. When all were off, we pulled away at 7:13 A.M.

Our second to last stop was at my home terminal on the railroad, Milwaukee Jct. (M.P. 4.1) located within the City of Detroit, just north of East Grand Blvd. The manned depot and train order office here was not a large or fancy structure, nor able to house a huge number of waiting passengers; but instead, the trains were met by D.S.R. (Detroit Street Railway) busses, which transported a huge number of riders to the Fisher Building, the General Motors Building, and Wayne State University, all located about a mile or so to the west. While the passengers were detraining the telegraph operator here handed me a message issued by the Station Master at our final stop, Detroit's Brush St. Depot and approved by the General Yardmaster at Milwaukee Jct. This handwritten message instructed us as to which Main Track (Eastbound or Westbound) we were to use from Boulevard Switch (M.P. 4.0), a spring-switch located just east of the Milwaukee Jct. station into Brush Street Depot. Additionally, it informed us as to which of five depot tracks we were to head into at Brush Street.

At this point Old Tom Church, the Conductor, made his way up to the head end and observed the handwritten message in my possession, which clearly stated: TRAIN 994 USE THE EASTWARD MAIN TRACK FROM BOULEVARD SWITCH TO BRUSH STREET DEPOT. YARD YOUR TRAIN IN DEPOT TRACK NUMBER THREE. He then carefully observed that for today's trip I had us properly lined onto the Eastward Main Track at Boulevard Switch, and to discuss the proper track to use at Brush Street Station. Tom gave the engineer a "Go Ahead" signal and we pulled away from the station at 7:20 A.M. He said, "Now understand, after we get past the Lead to City Yard, there are five useable tracks at the depot for passenger trains. They are numbered consecutively from right (the side nearest the downtown business district) going toward the Detroit River on the left. Now write this down and memorize this…Track No. 1 is the track furthest to the right, it is where they "usually" store the Business Cars; but if you ever have to use that track, you will have to have the doors open and the steps down on the right or 'City Side.' The next track to the left is No. 2 and it unloads on the 'River Side.' Next to that will be Track No. 3 with its platform on the right and there you have to unload on the 'City Side.' Track No. 4 will be the next one and it unloads on the left or 'River Side.'" Lastly, by itself is Track No. 5 and on it, you can unload on either side…generally, you will try to use the right or 'City Side' again. You will NEVER head into any of the other tracks with a passenger train! Don't even think about it!" (See my previous story, "When we had Switchtenders" in my book *Unit Trains and Other Railroad Stories*.)

Since we would be heading into Depot Track No. 3 at Brush Street, the three of us trainmen would actually be catching a little break here. The reason that I am saying this was because we already had all of the coach doors open on the right (engineer's side) and that would be the side from which the passengers would detrain…"The City Side. We raced down the hill on the "Dinky Line (Dequindre Line), rounded the 90-degree curve to the right at Jefferson Avenue not exceeding the allowed 12 mph, rolled past the Lead to City Yard and the GTW-CN carferry to Windsor, Ontario, and the engineer pulled to a stop at the Depot 3-4 Switch, which was lined for Depot 4. I dropped off the leading coach steps on the head end of the car and walked forward and lined the switch into Depot 3. I gave the engineer a "Come Ahead" signal and we pulled into the depot, stopping only several feet from the bumping post exactly as scheduled at 7:30 A.M. No sooner had we come to a stop and within seconds our train began to disgorge our passenger's from the City Side…mission accomplished!

Once all of the commuters had climbed down off the coaches, Flagman Aamon walked up through the entire train looking for items and perhaps sleeping passengers still aboard the train. When he reached the head car, all three of us plus the engine crew walked ahead into the depot and entered the Stationmaster's office where I was introduced to Bob Thiel, the Stationmaster.

By this time I had been working in freight service since April 12th; but I must admit that walking into the Crew Room of Brush Street Depot with guys I hardly knew was a little intimidating. As previously stated, Adam Aamon immediately wandered off to the crew bunkroom upstairs; however at that time, I had no idea that there was even a bunkroom in the building. The Conductor sat at one of the tables completing his paperwork and the two enginemen just sat there talking with one another. At 8 o'clock Train 996 rolled into the depot right on time and I watched the passengers unload and the crew repeat our steps into the Crew Room. Similarly, at 8:30 A.M. Train 998 pulled into the depot and once again I observed a nearly repeat performance.

Chuck H Geletzke, Jr.

Since the action seemed to be subsiding Stationmaster Thiel came over and talked with me. He explained to me that on this assignment I was basically finished until 4:30 P.M., the on-duty time for Train 995 that would return us to Pontiac. He stated, "During this time you are still under pay, and you are free to do whatever you want...just make sure that you are back here and ready to perform at 4: 30 P.M.! I do not want to hear any excuses...ever!!!" He went on to tell me that I could even catch a bus and ride back to my home in Royal Oak, if I wanted; but just be back here on time! Eventually I learned that several of the regular trainmen, with lots of seniority, even had side jobs down here working for stockbrokers and at sporting goods shops, etc. Basically, my time was my own until thirty minutes before departure time...I could not believe it! No wonder the commuter trains lost money!?!

After this little discussion, Mr. Thiel gave me a slip of paper on which was written the name of a local tailor. He said, "You have lots of time; so first go have breakfast, then walk over to this tailor shop and hand them this slip. There you will be measured and fitted for your passenger uniform, PASSENGER UNIFORM...I couldn't believe it! I never dreamed that I would have a passenger brakeman's uniform!

So, I fiddled around for a little while, then walked into downtown Detroit still wearing my black suit and tie and found a diner for breakfast. Afterward I located the tailor shop and was measured for my uniform. By that time, it was only about 10:30 A.M. and I realized that I still had about six hours until I had to report for duty...so what to do next? I decided to walk over to the local *J. L. Hudson Co.* Department Store, which I had visited many times as a child with my parents...that was THE PLACE TO SEE SANTA CLAUS every year as a child! All alone I browsed the huge number of floors in the store and I don't recall that I purchased anything. I am guessing that I stayed there until about Noon and then walked back to the depot. Not having any other place that I really wanted to go, I just decided to hang out at the depot. I noticed that several of the trainmen and enginemen seemed to be sitting at a table playing cards, while others just sat around or napped. (let me state that by the time I had worked these jobs several times and learned the ins and outs of the various jobs, I began catching the bus back to Royal Oak and going home to do things that were not nearly as boring. Believe me, I ALWAYS caught an early enough bus during the afternoon to be back in plenty of time to catch my train! Fast forward to 1970…on the day that I last worked one of the commuter trains following my enlistment in the Marines, Engineer, "Skippy" Tingue and I even rode the Bob-Lo Boat together down to Bob-Lo Island and back before train time!)

Stationmaster Bob Thiel made quite an impression on me and I was back, neatly dressed, and ready to go long before 4:30 P.M. By that time the afternoon Stationmaster, Gordon Baylis was on duty and running the show.

Our return Train was Number 995 and had freight service GP9 4137 for power and was scheduled to depart at 5:00 P.M. Prior to our departure Conductor Church took a few minutes and explained what I would be expected to do. The return trip would be a little more complex. The reason for this was the fact that on the return leg of the journey not all of the station platforms would be located on the same side of the train like they were coming down that morning. Going home Milwaukee Jct., Highland Park (Chrysler), Ferndale, Pleasant Ridge, and Royal Oak would all unload on the left or fireman's side of the train…and not only would we unload on the left; but we would discharge our passengers right on the Eastward Main Track! Thus, it was imperative that we have an eye for any and all approaching trains (which as long as everyone followed the rules, should not be a problem!). (Rule 107 stated: "Trains or engines must move with extreme care when meeting or passing a train carrying passengers which is receiving or discharging traffic at a station. They must not pass between such train and the platform at which traffic is being received or discharged unless the movement is properly protected.") At Oakwood Blvd., Birmingham, Charing Cross, Bloomfield Hills, and Pontiac we would discharge our riders on the Engineer's or right side. Thus it was imperative that we had all of the proper doors and traps set in the correct position at each station including the high-level platform at Birmingham. The last thing that Mr. Church said to me on this trip going home, "DO NOT neglect to call out the name of each of the next stations prior to our arrival! We DO NOT need a rider falling asleep and missing their stop!" Once again, I was to be responsible for the head three coaches.

At precisely 5 o'clock Conductor Church signaled the engineer to proceed and we departed Detroit. I had all of my doors open and the traps up on the left side approaching Milwaukee Jct. where the operator issued us our Clearance and train orders. Behind the depot I spotted the DSR buses, which had only minutes earlier picked-up their riders at Wayne State, the Fisher Building, and

Chuck H Geletzke, Jr.

General Motors Headquarters. The Penn Central tower operator here had us all lined-up across his railroad and again we were out on time at 5:10 P.M. As instructed, I called out all of my stops and we departed each station on-time…Highland Park at 5:17 P.M., Ferndale at 5:24 P.M., Pleasant Ridge at 5:26 P.M., and Royal Oak, where we had a clear train order signal, at 5:30 P.M. As we pulled away from Royal Oak, I began dropping the traps and closing the doors on the left side and properly positioning the doors on the right. As I walked through each car, I called out our next stop, "Oakwood Boulevard," several times. Shortly, we pulled to a stop, unloaded our riders and got underway at 5:33 P.M. Just as soon as we were moving, I began dropping the traps or platforms preparing for our arrival at Birmingham's elevated station platform at our next stop. Here again as I walked back toward the headend I called out the Name "BIRMINGHAM NEXT…BIRMINGHAM NEXT!" As we pulled to a stop at the depot, I noted that we had a Clear train order signal.

Now at our next stop, Charing Cross, I learned a valuable lesson, which Conductor Church never informed me about! As I stated earlier, the station platform was located on the right side of the train; so I raised all of the traps on the right. What I did not realize was, THE STATION'S PARKING LOT WAS LOCATED ON THE LEFT SIDE! Thus, many of the "REGULAR" riders did not want to detrain on the right and have to wait for the train to depart before being permitted to cross-over to the left side! What I observed was the "regulars" opening several of the doors and traps on the left side, getting off there, and running to their personal vehicles. I shuddered to think what might have occurred if an eastbound freight train happened to be silently drifting down Pontiac Hill! Fortunately, I never heard of any injuries ever occurring there. We pulled out of Charing Cross at 5:47 P.M.

A few minutes later we pulled into Bloomfield Hills and unloaded more patrons on the engineer's side departing at 5:50 P.M.

With only a relatively few passengers still remaining aboard the train we screamed up the steepest portion of Pontiac Hill and rolled to a stop at Pontiac at 6:00 P.M. With only two or three riders remaining we pulled west where the afternoon Switchtender had us lined up the East Lead at Johnson Avenue at the east end of Pontiac Yard. Taking advantage of the spring switches, we headed right into the Coach Track where we were met by a Car Inspector who cut the engine away from the train at 6:05 P.M. I then herded the engine and engine crew back to the roundhouse. Once in the Book-In Room Conductor Church informed me that we were tying-up at 6:10 P.M., officially a twelve hour and thirty minute day. Lastly, I climbed into my 1955 CJ-3b Willys Jeep and headed for home. Once home I called the Milwaukee Jct. Crew Dispatcher and informed him of my off-duty time at Pontiac and then added one hour for my deadhead back to "the Junction," that meant that I would be added back to the Extra Board at 7:10 P.M.; but technically would be rested at 2:10 A.M. From this you can see that my total time on duty was 14 hours and 30 minutes...definitely a long day for a college kid on summer break!

Reader request: Following this assignment, when was Brakeman Geletzke called again off the Milwaukee Jct. Brakemen's Spare Board?

The telephone rang the next morning, June 14, 1968 at 7:20 A.M. instructing him to report at 9:15 A.M. for Trains 586/585 the Mt. Clemens Switch Run...but that is another story.

View looking east of the GTW Mt. Clemens Subdivision at Mt. Clemens, MI on April 5, 1975. On the far left we can see the Team Track and loading dock. On the right is the Freight House. Once loaded the cars containing the new fire trucks would have to be switched from the far left track to the House Track on the right.

Mt. Clemens Fire Engines

By: Charles H. Geletzke, Jr.

This story is for you modelers. On the Grand Trunk Western Railroad (GTW) in the town of Mt. Clemens, Michigan we had an interesting little firm that we served…just not directly. The firm as originally established in 1957, was the *Fire Master Corporation* and it manufactured custom and commercial chassis for fire engines. In 1960 the name was changed to *Fire Trucks, Inc.* The majority of the vehicles that this company built went to the *Department of Defense*; but some went to communities too…such as the *Philadelphia Fire Department.*

Now as I stated, this company did not have their own siding. Instead when they had a vehicle that was ready to be shipped, they would contact the GTW's Freight Agent in Mt. Clemens and he would order a car for them. From my experience, all of these seemed to have been 50-foot end-door boxcars (and believe me, the GTW once had a huge number of them!). It is possible that they may have used flat cars; but, personally, I never saw any.

Before the empty car departed Detroit for loading, it was mandatory that the yardmaster make certain that the car was properly turned and the car's end door be on the east end of the car when it was positioned for loading! Once the car arrived on Local Freight 586, "The Mount Clemens Switch Run," the car would be immediately spotted at the dock at the team track located directly across the Mainline from the Freight House. There it would be loaded within only a day or two; but the car was not yet ready to go.

At this point, the Freight Agent would arrange to have the Switch Run grab the car and shove it across the Mainline and spot it at the Freight House. Once spotted, the Agent and his clerk would begin the task of blocking and bracing the fire truck for safe transport. Let me add, that they always did this on their "own time!" One question that I never asked was whether the fire truck company was ever charged for the second switch to the freight house??? This was none of my business anyway…and probably if they would have been charged, we would NOT have received the business! Thus, it was a win for all personnel involved!

Once the vehicle was properly secured it was moved to Detroit on Train 585 the Switch Run, where it would be lined-up for the trip to its final destination.

So, for you modelers, no matter which railroad or geographical region you model, you could easily add a boxcar carrying a brand new fire engine headed toward its final destination.

Oh yes, sadly *Fire Trucks, Inc.* went out of business in 1988.

Those Canadian National Covered Wagons On the GTW

By: Charles H. Geletzke, Jr.

Some time ago I was asked a question regarding the Grand Trunk Western's use of the Canadian National Railroad's covered wagons; so I did a little research. Looking back through my old timebooks this is what I was able to piece together and recall...

Wednesday January 1, 1969 I was called to work an Extra Train 580/579 "The East Detroit-Fraser Local" on duty at 1:30 P.M. Notice that I stated that it was an "Extra," because it was a holiday, the regular assignment and crew had been cancelled. We had engine GTW 4919 a passenger GP9 with engineer, Andy Lord; head brakeman, Tommy Beal; conductor, Joe Maltese; and I was the flagman. To illustrate just how different things were then, my brother, Gerry, age 12, rode along too. We ran from Milwaukee Jct. to Fraser and as I recall switched *National Lumber*, *Prince Macaroni*, the *Chatham Foodstore Warehouse*, and probably several other firms. Interestingly, we helped to solve what we were told was an ongoing theft of material at *National Lumber*, as we witnessed two of their employees using a hi-lo to load lumber on a *National Lumber* truck and drive it off the property for their own use. Needless to say, they did not work there much longer! We tied-up at 6:15 P.M.

Upon going off duty, brakeman Beal and I were asked if we would be willing to work "in the aggregate" and deadhead (in this case, drive our own personal autos) to Pontiac and bring the "Auxiliary" from Pontiac to Birmingham, as there had been a derailment on the top of the 14 Mile Road viaduct (M.P. 16.55). We

Chuck H Geletzke, Jr.

both accepted and each drove to Pontiac. On the way, I dropped my brother off at our home in Royal Oak.

At Pontiac, we quickly grabbed a quick meal and met the rest of our crew. The crew consisted of engineer, Jim McDaniel; fireman ____; head brakeman, Beal; conductor, Charlie Nelson; and again, I was the flagman. We had locomotive GTW 4441 a GP9. Because we were working in the aggregate, Tom Beal and I each showed our time on duty for this assignment as 6:15 P.M.; however, our sixteen hours would run from the previous 1:30 P.M.

My records show that we handled Crane 50007 and its idler, two flats (one with ties and the other with wheels and trucks), a generator equipped boxcar, a bunk car diner and wooden caboose GTW 77902.

As it turned out, Train 428's three GP9's were derailed. Unfortunately, I did not record their numbers, nor do I recall the cause of the derailment. Because it was dark, I never took any photos. I recall eating a wonderful pork chop dinner with plenty of good hot coffee in the diner served on actual china. We were able to rerail one of the geeps before our relief crew arrived. While rerailing I also remember clearing Train 422, which was headed by two DM&IR SD's for power and were leased to the GTW for the winter while the Great Lakes were closed to navigation.

Now for the point of the story...we deadheaded back to Pontiac aboard Train 421 to retrieve our autos and I rode in engine CN 9003 an F-3. Tom and I tied-up at 5:15 A.M. and I deadheaded back to Milwaukee Jct. in my personal vehicle.

According to my records I had four other encounters with the CN covered wagons, although I do recall seeing them on the Mainline many times and I am sure that my late friend, Jack Ozanich, could have documented his trips on them also. On Monday, January 25, 1969 I was ordered to work Train 427 on duty at Milwaukee Jct. at 8:00 A.M. with engineer, Carl Neimi; fireman, Gene Clark; student fireman, Bruce Shear; flagman, Larry Crawley; conductor, John Wilder; and I was the head brakeman. We had the CV 4552 (GP9)-GTW 9024 (F3)-GTW 9014 (F3) for power. We got our train of 133-cars at Ferndale Yard and ran to Battle Creek arriving at 8:00 P.M. After yarding our train and taking our units to the house we changed to the GTW 9022 (F3)-CV 4553 (GP9)-CN 9000 (F3) for our return trip on Train 428. Because we were so late, we ran "cab-lite" to Lansing, where we picked-up 24 cars out of the River Track. We departed Lansing and arrived at Durand and were relieved at 11:30 P.M. We then deadheaded back to Milwaukee Jct. on the train. I vividly recall riding in the CN 9000!

In the Autumn of 1969 I went to Durand to work. Incidentally, during all of this time I was attending Central Michigan University as a "full-time" student. Durand was the closest point to Mt. Pleasant where I could work and it was an 80-mile drive each way as opposed to the 165 mile drive that I had to Milwaukee Jct.!

On Friday, May 1, 1970 I was called to work Trains 422/421 out of Flint on duty at Torrey Yard at 11:30 P.M. Our crew consisted of engineer, Byron Hall; fireman, John Leatherman; head brakeman, Roger Bamber; conductor, Bill Kerr; and I was the flagman. On this trip our power was the CN 9003-CN 9001-CN 9002 all F3's. We ran from Torrey Yard to Grand River Avenue on the High Line in Detroit, swapped trains with the Detroit & Toledo Shore Line Railroad, keeping our same power and caboose and returned to Flint, going off-duty at 11:20 A.M.

Again on Saturday, May 2, 1970 I was called for Train 422/421 on-duty at Flint at 11:30 P.M. with the same crew and motive power...CN 9003-CN 9001-CN 9002. The trip was essentially the same, except that we tied-up at 11:05 A.M. in Flint. My notes say that the train "broke-in-two" twice during the trip!

Interestingly, my final trip with one of the CN 9000's, was also my final trip on the GTW with a covered wagon. On Friday, April 30, 1971 I was ordered for Trains 434/433 at Durand at 11:00 A.M. The crew was made-up of engineer, Al Kemph; head brakeman, Darryl Van Dusan; conductor, Bobby Anderson; and I was the flagman. On the headend we had the GTW 4433 (GP9) and CN 9000 (F3). On this day we ran from Durand to Ferndale Yard and return. We went off duty at Durand at 11:15 P.M. Here is the worst part of this story...many of you will note the date...this was the final day for GTW passenger service (not counting the commuter trains). During this day I saw Train 169 at Durand, 168 at Pontiac, 165 and 164 "The Mohawk" at Pontiac (at separate times) and I did NOT take a single photo, as I forgot to take my camera with me!!! In my own mind I guess that I had been taking all of this for granted and I never dreamed that this would really be the end of national passenger service as we knew it. Boy was I wrong!!!

Anyway, for those of you who are interested, I hope this answers your questions and thanks for giving me another chance to take a trip down Memory Lane.

Chuck H Geletzke, Jr.

A Believer in Seatbelts!

By: C. H. Geletzke, Jr.

The date was June 3, 1969 and for me it was the last day of final exams and the end of my Sophomore Year of college at Central Michigan University in Mt. Pleasant, Michigan (located in the geographical center of Michigan's Lower Peninsula). Believe me, I was more than ready to be finished and could not wait to head for home and best of all begin an entire summer of RAILROADING! I had everything packed and ready to go...all I had to do was carry all of my belongings (everything that I owned that I had at college) down six flights of stairs in Emmons Hall, load it into my 1955 CJ-3b Willys Jeep, have my room inspected, sign out, and head for home. The time was about 1 P.M. Once everything was loaded, I immediately got underway.

Before I go any further, allow me to also mention that in many ways, 1969 was still considered an early era in the construction of America's Interstate Highway System. That is to say, today, if you were to drive north from Detroit to Mackinaw City, Michigan up Interstate-75, when you reach Bay City, you would just continue to drive north on the highway. At the time of our story though, at Bay City one would have to veer off I-75 and head west to Midland, Michigan and then head north again and connect with the completed portion of the Interstate further north, just south of Grayling...even though it was actually a temporary detour, it was still designated as I-75.

Let me tell you a little about my jeep, which I purchased only a little over a year earlier when I hired-out as a brakeman. It was a traditional styled four-wheel drive vehicle of the era and was painted fire engine red with a white roof. The steel roof and doors could be removed in warm weather and that was my intention once I arrived home. The vehicle had a four cylinder engine with a three-speed manual "stick-shift" transmission and all of this allowed it to have a maximum top-end speed of a tad over **55 mph.** The jeep was designed to seat four people, with two seats in the front, and if additional passengers elected to ride, they could sit on the wheel-wells in the rear. I must also say that when the Willy's Engineering Department designed this all terrain vehicle they created one feature that totally disturbed me and ALWAYS made me nervous...**THE**

89

GAS TANK WAS MOUNTED ON THE VEHICLE FLOOR RIGHT BENEATH THE DRIVER'S SEAT!!! Lastly, and thank God, the previous owners elected to install one option, which was never included in the original design…they added lap-type seat belts to the two front seats!

Okay, as previously stated I loaded all of my belongings into the vehicle, and since I was traveling alone, the space was more than adequate. I even stretched a rope across the rear area of the cab from which I was able to hang all of my clothing on coat hangers. I am guessing that I departed at about 1:30 P.M. After navigating several of the Mt. Pleasant city streets I headed east on M-20, which would take me all the way to Midland and the home of the Dow Chemical Co. On the east side of Midland I entered the eastbound (perhaps under those circumstance at that time it may have been considered southbound?) lane of I-75, merged into the right lane (there was not much traffic at that time in that area), and began cruising at a steady 55 mph. Let me also state that it was a bright cool sun-shiny day and at this time the sun was shining on the rear of my vehicle. The temperature was 51-degrees.

So there I was cruising along in the right lane at a steady 55 mph approaching the town of Auburn…all at once I felt my jeep lunge ahead and I recall trying to get my hands on the steering wheel, which seemed to be beneath me, and if that was not enough, for a second, I was looking straight down at the pavement! Shortly, my Jeep came to a halt, sitting right side up, still facing east; but I was looking up at the sky…it no longer had a top! I noted that the engine was still running and I reached up and turned the key to shut it off. It was at this precise time that I noticed cars stopping on the westward side of the highway and people were exiting their vehicles to come to my aid…at that point, I was not even aware that I needed aid yet! Just then a man crossing the road pointed to a spot, perhaps fifty yards ahead of me, where a man was climbing out of his car that was further out in the field than mine. It was at that moment that I realized that I had been struck by another vehicle!

I then began looking myself over…I was still safely buckled into my seat, I had a cut on my right arm and I believe another cut on one of my legs…that was all that was apparent…oh, and I no longer had any shoes on my feet! I unbuckled and climbed out of the jeep and looked back to the west…I couldn't believe it… ALL of my personal possessions were scattered down the road for perhaps 50

Chuck H Geletzke, Jr.

yards or more! I began walking around the debris and soon found two different shoes, which I put on my feet.

Shortly the police and local volunteer fire department arrived and several of the people who actually witnessed "what was now officially an accident" began telling me exactly what they had seen.

Apparently the driver of the other vehicle (the Police later determined that the driver was under the influence) was racing along at a calculated speed of 115 mph (maximum allowed speed was 70 mph) and crashed into the rear of my Jeep! Because of the speed and the angle of impact...my Jeep flipped **END OVER END THREE TIMES!** On the first flip, it hit the AUBURN Exit Sign...Upside Down...and sheared the steel top off, right over my head! My Jeep continued to flip end over end...two more times! Fortunately, when it came to rest, it landed right side up...considering the age of the Jeep, it was a true miracle, as the vehicle was not equipped with a roll bar! Had it landed upside down, no doubt I would have been crushed!

By now the other driver was walking around the crash site and the police were interviewing him. I looked at all of my belongings strewn everywhere and surprisingly found one of my cameras in the weeds...I then took photos (2-1/4" slides) of the accident site. For you modelers would you believe that during the past semester, I built a *Walther's* O Scale combine...it was now scattered as several hundred individual pieces throughout the crash site.

Shortly a wrecker arrived and the firemen helped me load my possessions on the back of the wrecker. Both the Police and Firemen asked if I wanted to be taken to a hospital. At that point I felt so blessed to still be alive and not mixed in with that Exit Sign and my Jeep's top that I declined the offer. I really thought that I was fine.

Now remember this was probably close to 25 years before most people would have cell phones. I climbed in the cab of the tow truck with the driver and was driven to a service station and restaurant right across the highway. I immediately called my parents and arranged for them to drive up and take me and the remains of my stuff home.

I then went inside of the restaurant and ate. Afterward I made periodic trips outside to make sure that no one was bothering my belongings. About three hours later my Mom and Dad arrived and we loaded everything in their car...the remains of the Jeep were left at the service station and became a ward of my insurance carrier.

It All Starts <u>Here</u> and Other Railroad Stories

After arriving home I think I immediately went to bed…by then my muscles were getting sore. By the next morning I could hardly walk! As the day progressed I began to feel better and by suppertime was feeling pretty good. It truly was a miracle that I did not end up in a hospital or even worse. At 11:00 P.M. I called the GTW's crew dispatcher and booked-up to work. Surprisingly, I was not called to work and "laid-in" during the next two days…at that time that was a truly rare occurrence! While I was home on one of those days an insurance agent paid me a visit and since I was not injured, we settled the claim several days later. Besides not being severely injured this was the one good part of the incident. Because I needed a vehicle to drive to and from work, I was able to take the proceeds from the accident and some of my personal savings and purchased a brand-new 1969 Plymouth Roadrunner.

I was finally called to work on June 7th as the head brakeman on Train 586/585, the Mt. Clemens Switch Run, on-duty at 6:45 A.M.

One final comment: Since the date of the accident I have not even so much as backed my car out of the garage without buckling my seatbelt!

NJI&I NW2 #2 was photographed at Osborne Road in South Bend, Indiana on May 10, 1975. (Dan Lawecki photo)

Chuck H Geletzke, Jr.

Cab Rides

By: Dan Lawecki

As a lifelong resident of South Bend, Indiana, I was fortunate to grow up here during the 1960's. When there was plenty of railroad activity to observe and enjoy. Our family home on the West Side of town was but two blocks away from the parallel mainlines of the Wabash subsidiary New Jersey, Indiana, & Illinois Railroad (NJI&I), the double-tracked Grand Trunk Western's Chicago Division (GTW) mainline, and the New York Central's (NYC) Kankakee Belt. I spent many an hour trackside taking it all in.

The NJI&I was something of a mystery to me. It served some customers along Sample Street near our home; but the bulk of its activity took place at the *Studebaker Corporation* until that auto maker closed its doors in December 1963 and moved its operation to Canada. On family car rides to visit my maternal grandparents who lived on the South Side of town, our route down Olive Street took us past the NJI&I Olive Yard and roundhouse. The NJI&I's sole motive power, a 1948-built EMD NW2, was usually spotted on the Roundhouse Lead; but I was only able to catch quick glimpses of it as we drove by.

In September 1969 I began my senior year in high school and shortly thereafter I purchased my first car, a 1960 *Volkswagen Beetle*. The car served lots of practical purposes, such as getting me to and from school and to and from my part time job; but it also afforded me the luxury of being able to visit rail spots around town a bit easier than I could by riding a bike.

It dawned on me that a trip to the NJI&I Olive yard sounded like it might be interesting; but by that time the NJI&I had become a subsidiary of the Norfolk & Western Rwy., and the N&W had a reputation of being hostile to railroad enthusiasts. The last thing that I wanted to do was to run afoul of the N&W Police, or some other law enforcement entity. Not willing to take that chance, I pulled out the family portable typewriter from its berth in the dining room closet and I wrote a letter to the NJI&I requesting permission to visit Olive Yard.

My recollection is that I mailed that letter early one week, and I was more than surprised when a letter addressed to me arrived from the NJI&I before the end of the week. The letter was from Dick

Callen the NJI&I Superintendent. He thanked me for my letter, and
thanked me for my interest in the NJI&I. He went on to state that not
only did I have permission to visit the Olive yard facilities; but I
could show the letter to any law enforcement officer as proof that I
had permission to be on the property!

But the best part was yet to be found in that letter. Mr. Callen
told me that the Chief NJI&I Mechanic, Mr. Dreibelbis, would be at
the roundhouse on that Sunday, where he would be completing some
mechanical repairs on NJI&I #2, the NW2 that was mentioned
previously. He encouraged me to make the visit at that time. He
needn't have worried about asking me a second time!

I hope the Good Lord forgave me; but I had a tough time
concentrating on the words of the Gospel at our Sunday morning
Mass that day. My head was further up the road at the roundhouse!

When I arrived at the roundhouse, Mr. Dreibelbis gave me
the run of the place while he completed his repair tasks on #2. When
he finished his work, he told me that he was going to take the
switcher out into the yard trackage to make sure that everything was
operating properly. He asked me if I wanted to tag along and I
wasted no time replying in the affirmative! I scampered up into the
NW2, made my way to the fireman's seat, and got ready for my first
ever locomotive cab ride.

What I remember the most, aside from that test run not
lasting long enough, was how rough riding the locomotive felt. The
lead set of trucks seemed to lurch to the left, then back to the right
(we call that "hunting"), seemingly looking for a flaw in the
Trackwork where the switcher might derail. But stay on the tracks it
did, and before I could blink my eyes, the test run was finished. I
thanked Mr. Dreibelbis profusely for his kindness and we parted
company.

That experience has remained a pleasant memory for well
over fifty years now; but back about 1978 or 1979 I had an
opportunity for another cab ride. I had taken my twin children,
Jennifer and Dan, for a car ride that ended up at the east end of the
GTW Olivers Yard. The twins were about three or four years old at
the time, and they enjoyed watching trains with me. I parked my car
near the Olivers Yard Office on Ford Street and as if it had been
carefully scripted, a westbound GTW train soon arrived on the scene.
It was Train 511/510, the "South Bend Turn" out of Battle Creek and
the motive power was one of the GP38's that the GTW rostered. The

Chuck H Geletzke, Jr.

"Turn" set out cars at the Conrail interchange, then the diesel moved east toward the Ford Street grade crossing where it paused.

As the three of us waited to see what would happen next, the friendly engineer extended his arm out the cab window and waved us over to where the diesel was idling. As we moved closer, he asked me if the three of us would like to come up into the cab for a short ride. Three excited individuals wasted no time at all getting into the cab and we took a seat on the fireman's side. As was the case with my NJI&I cab ride, this one was entirely too short. The engineer moved the GP38west into Olivers yard trackage where cars from Conrail and the NJI&I were pulled. Once back on the Eastbound Main, the consist moved west to couple the caboose onto the end of the train. Then we headed east to a spot adjacent to the yard office, where the three of us dropped off. The twins and I thanked the engineer for his kindness and we bid him farewell. I regret that I never learned the name of the engineer; but he made the day for the twins and their Dad!

He took one heck of a chance!

C. H. Geletzke, Jr.

On May 29, 1970 I was still working the Grand Trunk Western Railroad's (GTW) Brakemen's Extra Board out of Durand, Michigan. On that day I was ordered for Trains 541 and 542, the "Greenville Local" or, "The Turkey Trail." We were to be on-duty at 2:35 P.M., which was exceptionally late for this job! The crew was made up of Engineer, Marv Lab...a real character and fun guy to work with...incidentally, I believe that Marv was probably the second to the last guy, still working, who hired-out firing steam! The remainder of the crew consisted of Fireman, Harold Reed; Conductor, Art Devoe (aka "The Parakeet"); Flagman H. R. "Home Run" "Rod" Baker; and I was the Head Brakeman. On this day we had a GP9 for power, the GTW 4540.

Now just to give you a synopsis of what this job normally did, it ran from the yard in Durand (Milepost 67) and then on to Owosso (M.P. 78.52), where sometimes it worked for one to two hours. Once the work was completed, the job got on the Ann Arbor Railroad at Owosso Jct. (M.P. 79.17) and ran on trackage rights, a distance of 20.58 miles to the little town of Ashley, switched several firms there, and then entered the Greenville Subdivision (M.P. 0.00) and worked its way over to Greenville (M.P. 40.38), where it would switch the *Gibson Refrigerator Co.* twice, switch the other firms, and then return to Durand via the reverse route.

On our westward trip we spent well over an hour switching the *Harris Milling Co.*, which was a good sized grain elevator known for feed and grain and grinding a specialized type of flour used for making biscuits, the bulk of which was shipped to bakeries in the south. Interestingly, this good-sized operation was normally switched by the GTW on days, the Ann Arbor on afternoons, and the Penn Central (former NYC) on nights.

After completing this work and serving several other small firms, we headed out to the west side of town (actually in Owosso Twp.) on the Grand Rapids Subdivision. There we switched a firm named *Moore Iron Works*, that equipped flat cars for transporting automobile frames with the proper tie-down components. Most of you probably never realized this; but when an auto manufacturer changed the design of their products, often the various tie-down and DF (damage-free) securement components had to be removed, changed, or at a minimum repositioned! Thus, each frame flat, and many bi and tri-levels were assigned in a pool to serve only one auto manufacturer and transporting parts for only one auto! Anyway, this small firm had only two stub-ended tracks, which ran inside of their building, each of which would accommodate only two 89-foot flat cars. The building was reached by a single spur off the south side of the mainline and a single track ran perhaps fifty yard to a switch, which divided into the two tracks that entered the building. Just before we encountered the switch was a derail. It was of the type that just flipped on and off the rail and to the best of my knowledge, was never locked.

So, on May 29th, Rod Baker who had wrestled in high school and was in fantastic physical shape, and I were out pulling and spotting cars at this industry. I believe that "the Parakeet" stayed back at the depot drinking coffee and talking with the agent. Oh yes, before I go any further, let me also state that we did not yet have radios on this job! When Rod and I made our last move, we shoved two empty flat cars into the western most track, secured the handbrake, gave the Fireman a signal to have the Engineer pull ahead, and then cut away. Our engine was still holding onto two boxcars. As we exited the building, both Flagman Baker and I each climbed aboard the trailing end of the rear boxcar. I grabbed a hold of the end ladder, resting my feet on the truck's sideframe and Rod swung aboard the rear side ladder on the fireman's side and prepared to ride out to the Mainline. Now this was probably only the second or third time that I had ever switched this firm; but I was watching Rod and I expected him to have the engine crew slow down and stop so that he might reapply the derail…but NO, NOT ROD!!! Instead he continued to hang on the side of the car and reached down with his trailing right foot and flopped the derail back into the derailing position without even stopping!

I couldn't believe it…I had never witnessed anything like that before, ever in my railroad career! I hollered at him, "Rod, are you nuts!?! What if that derail had jammed? It would have yanked you right off the side of the car!"

Rod just looked at me and replied very calmly, "It wouldn't! That one flops really easy and I do it all the time."

After that, we just went on to Greenville serving all of our customers. Now remember, those were still 16 hour days and on that trip, we just managed to make it back to the crossovers at the west end of the yard at Durand, where we waited for a ride. We finally tied-up and went off duty at 7:10 A.M.

Years later, whenever I would see Rod, I would still mention that technique to him…to this day I cannot believe what he did!

But to Rod, IT WAS STILL NO BIG DEAL!

C&O (former PM) view of Boardman Yard's enginehouse and yard office in Traverse City, MI on August 7, 1976.

My Trip from Traverse City to Manistee and back on the C&O When I was a Young and Foolish Kid!

By: Jim Harlow

I spent the summer of 1970 at Interlochen, Michigan attending the *National Music Camp* for the 8-week session, and my family stayed for the 2-week "post camp" session afterward.

I had "cabin fever" bad, and had the itch to do something different; so I got the hot idea to see if I could cab-ride the southbound freight on the Chesapeake & Ohio that went through Interlochen. It ran south from Traverse City (TC) to Manistee, and then returned to Boardman Yard in Traverse City. (Boardman Yard took its name from the river and lake where the yard was located.) So I gave my folks a load of BS as and excuse for being away (I have forgotten just what) and took off on my bike...biking the 18 miles from Interlochen to the yard! I knew when the crew went on duty there to take the morning freight to Manistee, and I was in luck...the engineer was real friendly! He said that he had seen me giving him the "highball" at Interlochen on the evenings that I could steal away from the group to see the train go through town when he was on that run. He said, "Sure. You can ride in the cab of the trailing unit." So, I got on board and away I went on the train, thrilled to the core because I had NEVER ridden in a locomotive before!

When we arrived at Manistee, I was dead tired! The personnel in the railroad's office let me "hang out" there until the northbound freight to Traverse City departed; but there were no chairs to sit in anywhere in the crew room. For the first time in my life, I found out I could sleep standing up! No Fooling!!!

Anyway, the northbound freight's departure was to be at about 4 P.M.; so, when that crew boarded the train, *that* engineer said, "Nope!" when I asked him if I could ride in the second unit. And then he wagged his index finger at me and said, "And don't let me see you hopping in a car!"

Naturally, I took that to mean if he didn't see me, I *could* ride in a car to get back to TC.

I quickly scoped out the train and saw that it had several boxcars in it with the doors open on a couple of the empties. The train was about to leave; but I found I could not climb inside a boxcar…they were much too high for me! The train had a couple of gons in it; so I grabbed the ladder on one of them and quickly scampered up and inside of it. I found it was full of heavy scrap metal…such as junk car engine manifold blocks or things similar to that. I figured they were so heavy that they wouldn't shift around as the train was moving…so, I sat squatting in the corner of it. In a matter of minutes I was on my way back to TC on the train!

Well, I only had a light jacket on and I had forgotten how cold that country got during the night, even in late August…so, when riding in the open at about 5 mph, I nearly froze to death!

At one point the crew had work at an on-line industry to do enroute and they had to run their engines around the train in a siding at this point. I remember sticking my head up to see what was going on…and when the engines came by on the siding, there was the engineer wagging his finger at me again!!! It was like he was saying, "You naughty kid…I see you and I warned you NOT to let me see you if you got on my train!"

Fortunately, I did not get set-out at that industry and nobody came up to the gondola to tell me to get off of it!

Shortly I was on my way once again after their work was finished.

It All Starts Here and Other Railroad Stories

On the approach to Boardman Yard, I figured I'd better get off the gon before they stopped and could hold me for the cops or something. So, I got off the train, which at that point had slowed down to about 8 mph or so. I kept myself hidden in the weeds as I made my way back to my bike, got on it, and made my way back to Interlochen. And so, no one was the wiser…or at least I hoped so!

Stupid, foolish railroad nut kid! You can bet I NEVER did that again!!! But I sure enjoyed the trip! I'll never forget it!

Sadly the old Pere Marquette (C&O) line between Manistee and Traverse City was pulled out by the CSXT in 1982.

(Jim, I'd love to know how you explained your absence to your parents!?!---Chuck Geletzke)

I Just Wanted a Railroad Career!

By: James Harlow

I absolutely hated to practice my viola; whereas, my brother always seemed to like to practice his instrument! Plus, I hated orchestra rehearsals…the conductors had to spend a great deal of time having certain instrument sections run through different passages of the music to get it right…this was way too boring for me to endure! Sometimes I would actually nod off while this was going on…

I went to the *University of Michigan* (U of M) in Ann Arbor for one semester (fall 1970 just to satisfy the "push" of my parents, who had steered me that way while I was in high school) and found that to be traumatic! I couldn't handle the pressure of it. I actually still have nightmares once in a while, to this day, about trying to get to classes on time, if you can believe that!?! One class (a beginner's class learning to play the string bass) I actually skipped, because I kept forgetting to attend it! (And not only that, the teacher was a friend of my Dad!!!)

A couple of my classes were held in auditoriums; you know…with a hundred students crowded in there…and try to hear what the professor was saying above all the ambient noise…particularly the noise of the students crinkling or turning their papers…I couldn't hear anything above that in a room that was made to perform music in, acoustically! (I have Very Sensitive hearing…Even Now…even though I've developed Tinnitus over the years. I can still hear subtle sounds before anyone else can hear them!)

And, Plus the pull of the Railroad was just too much! Even though my folks were paying for a room on the North Campus for me, I was actually living out of the depot (which had a baggage room at that time)! Even practicing my viola there sometimes (when I could make myself practice it!)!

When Thanksgiving came around that fall, I decided to tell my folks I'd had it! There was NO WAY I was going back to the U of M for a second semester!!! I was going to work for the railroad!!!

After I started working for the railroad, I discovered there was a library at the U of M (the 3rd floor of the Transportation Library on the main campus) that had ALL KINDS of technical books on signaling, trackwork, railroad transportation in general, a complete section of all the railroad annual reports for the railroads in Michigan going back to the beginning of their time, etc. If I had discovered that while I was there that semester, I swear that NOBODY would have found me for a LONG, LONG TIME!!! Nobody ever told me that one could take courses on Transportation in college!

Conversely, IF I could have made a living playing the music of J. S. Bach, I would have done that! In my old age today, nearly every time I hear his music, I get "blubbery!" It actually brings me to tears sometimes, it's so beautiful!!! But that was totally impractical; there are Very Few Musicians in the World that are that good to do that!

So, it's complicated with me; but if one lives in "Harlow's World," it's Completely Understandable!!!

Those that know me well, all say that I was born 100 years too late to retire directly from railroad employment! My folks, who I disappointed to no end when I made my decision to quit college, always knew that. But eventually, I think they understood they couldn't control my passions!

I was actually warned by the first block operator I broke in with, that I would never retire from railroading…technology was coming to take operator's and towermen's jobs away. I was way too passionate ABOUT RAILROADING TO BE TALKED OUT OF IT! And as True as that turned out to be, and as hard as it was to make a living after the towers were all "done," I'd do it all over again…if I had to!!!

And by the way, my brother is just as passionate about playing his cello as I am about railroads! He swears he's going to keep playing in the *Philadelphia Orchestra* as long as he can still "hold a bow," even though he was eligible for full retirement about a year ago!

Probably Milwaukee's Finest!

By: C. H. Geletzke, Jr.

Let's see, it was on the morning of May 16, 1971 and I was called at 3:45 in the morning to report for duty at 5:45 A.M. at the Grand Trunk Western Railroad's new West Tower in Pontiac, Michigan to work as Flagman on Trains 416 and 415. This through freight ran east out of Pontiac Yard over the Pontiac Belt Line and Romeo Subdivision about 48 miles to the little farm town of Richmond, and then headed north (actually railroad east) to Port Huron a distance of approximately 20 more miles. There we would yard our train of mostly finished automobiles and auto parts out of the Pontiac assembly and stamping plants destined for Canada and points east. After yarding our train, we would pick-up our westbound train, made-up of mostly similar empties to go back to those same plants and returned by way of the reverse route. This job ran seven days a week.

On this day, we had the regular Engineer, Carl Neimi…one of the best on the system. Additionally, our Conductor was Craig Freshour and the Head Brakeman was Archie Straub…Archie had way more seniority than me; so I cannot figure or recall why he happened to be working the headend??? For power we had two GP9's the GTW 4139 and 45When we returned to Pontiac we were greeted with a big surprise! Apparently, a loaded piggy-back trailer out of Milwaukee had turned-over and fell off its flat car near the west end of the yard! As we rolled through a clear track Switchmen and Car Inspectors were pointing toward the trailer and holding up bottles of beer all over the yard! Believe me, they had beer stashed everywhere…even in the underground boxes between Tracks 6 and 7, which were designed to store new air hoses! Yes, I'll bet that automobile trunks were packed with beer and that there was a party in Pontiac that night!

Oh yes, we tied up at 1:15 P.M

J.G. TYSON

Trainmaster/RFE

Duluth, Winnipeg & Pacific Ry. Co.
Ranier MN 56668
Box 235
(218) 286-3521

CN (GTW) Conductor, Larry Williams is seen later in his career on April 22, 2010 working at East Yard in Hamtramck, MI.

A Real Tiger's Fan!

As told by: GTW-CN Conductor, Larry E. Williams

Chuck H Geletzke, Jr.

If you are a longtime baseball fan like our storyteller, Larry Williams (and me), you will recall the era before ticket scalpers basically took over the sale of game tickets in virtually all professional and Division One college sports raising the prices for big game tickets and through hugely inflated prices generally stopping the ability of "the average fan" to acquire tickets for all major games. If you don't believe me, look at the serious fans today on televised games who are able to scrape together enough money to take their family to a normal game during the regular season...but come the playoffs or the World Series, just look at the number of ticket purchasers sitting right behind home plate...playing video games or talking on their phones, and not paying any attention to the game! To me that is really sad; but as we all know, "Money talks and BS walks!"

Conductor Larry Williams and I worked together frequently for a huge portion of our railroad careers...both on the road and in the yard. During the regular baseball season baseball was certainly one of our daily topics of conversation.

One day Larry told me the following two stories, which I found not only sad; but UNBELIEVABLE!

When "our" Detroit Tigers found out they had a good chance of playing in the World Series in 1968, my (Larry's) brother, a friend, and I each mailed away for a random draw lottery to receive two tickets each for the World Series. I was the only one who won the draw. My two tickets were for Game five of the World Series. As it would happen, five days before the game I was inducted into the U.S. Navy! My brother and our friend used the tickets. At that time, the Series was still played during the afternoon and at 1:00 P.M. E.S.T. I was in Great Lakes, Illinois being checked-in at the U. S. Navy Boot Camp having my head shaved as Game 5 was being played on the television! I told the barber that I had tickets for that game! He sympathetically let me watch some of the game. Adding insult to injury, my friend caught a foul ball in the stands hit by a St. Louis player. That should have been my ball! Sadly, I never received that opportunity again! (Oh yes, the Tigers won the game beating St. Louis 5-3. Detroit won four games of the seven game series.)

In 1971 it was announced that the All Star Game was going to be played in Detroit on July 13, 1971. My friend and I drove down to Tiger Stadium at about 10 o'clock at night to get in line for All Star tickets, which were to go on sale at 9 A.M. the following morning. Before the tickets went on sale we got in line and patiently

105

waited our chance to purchase tickets for the Game. Because we had a good idea what to expect, we took along folding lounge chairs, food, and drink and settled in for the night. Once in line, we just set-up our chairs and waited for the line to begin moving ahead. The following morning we watched the sunrise. At about 8:45 A.M. someone hollered, "THE TICKET WINDOW IS OPENING!!!" With that, people jumped out of line and started running ahead of us and many others too! By the time we were able to gather up all of our belongings; over a thousand people had gotten ahead of us! Sadly, we never obtained seats for the game…perhaps the new system via the phone and computer is an improvement???

p.s.

Right now in May of 2024 rampant inflation is a big topic in the news and it just so happened that I received a text from Larry Williams. My son, Justin, who lives in Dallas recently attempted to purchase 4 All Star tickets for the family…the game, which will be in Dallas this year. He opted out because it would have cost $3200.00 for not too good of seats! Some tickets were selling for $3000.00 each! It reminded me of the World Series tickets I bought in 1968 for $14.00 for two tickets. That's not a typo! Us poor folk have to watch it on tv!

Chapter 5

Now a young Manager

The Missouri Pacific (MP) depot and Freight Office at Angleton, Texas as
seen on October 28, 1973.

Movie Posters

By: C. H. Geletzke, Jr.

I have told you before how in 1973 I worked as an Assistant
Trainmaster for the Missouri Pacific Railroad (MP) in both Freeport
and Angleton, Texas. Because Freeport was the site of Dow
Chemical's largest plant (with 54 miles of track just within their
fences) and the amount of revenue they generated for the railroad;
Freeport was the highest revenue producing station on the entire
Missouri Pacific System!

I normally began my shift at midnight and generally worked
until around 3 o'clock P.M., spending the preponderance of my time

at Angleton. My major responsibility was to marshall and build two major eastbound freight trains and one westbound every morning in a little four track yard...basically with three useable tracks! Thankfully I had a wonderful yard crew, terrific clerks and agent, and we just worked together to move the freight...of which, over 80% contained hazardous commodities!

Sometimes in the morning I might spend several hours sitting at the operator's desk (we only had an agent on days) and we did not have any yardmasters; so basically, I was the guiding force! At the desk I would talk to the crews on the radio, to the dispatcher in Houston over the Dispatcher's Line, and to the various businesses on the bell phone...this was years before it would be referred to as a "landline!"

One other task that I have neglected to mention was the fact that at that time the railroad was still handling LCL (Less than Carload) freight, except that it was actually LTL (Less than Truckload) freight because it was transported in piggy-back trailers. These were small individual freight shipments such as those handled by United Parcel Service (UPS) or Federal Express (FedEx) today. In our case, at Angleton, our little old wood frame depot would receive a daily trailer load of packaged freight, which would be stored and sorted in the freight house portion of the depot, in the rear. After the shipment was received and sorted it would be delivered by a contracted drayman, in his own pickup truck, to various consignees throughout the area. Similarly, he would pickup shipments, which these individuals and corporations wanted shipped.

I will never forget, it was early on a Saturday morning in September of 1973 and I was pulling my hair out, trying to get Trains "Double-A" (the hottest train on the entire railroad) and Trains 860 and 859 out of town. I had the Dispatcher's phone to my ear and was talking on the radio, when all at once the "landline" rang. I calmly told everyone to hold-on and I answered the phone. It turned out to be the owner of the Beacon Theatre in Angleton and he asked if I would check to see if a package of movie posters for an upcoming movie to be displayed on the front of his theatre had arrived? I asked him to hold on too, and ran back into the freight room and rummaged around looking for a package of what I would estimate to be movie posters. Miraculously, I located them fairly quickly, and ran back to the office and told the gentleman that I did indeed have his posters! He was thrilled and asked if he might come right over to pick them up.

Chuck H Geletzke, Jr.

Following our conversation, I returned to the business of getting trains "out of town;" but isn't it funny, here it is over 50 years later and I can still recall just how happy that man was because I had found his posters…and to him, I am sure that those items were every bit as important as those hundreds of chemical cars trying to work their way in all directions out of Freeport! Yes, that was the end of an era in railroading and I was fortunate to be a part of it!

Form 20055

MISSOURI PACIFIC RAILROAD COMPANY
THE TEXAS AND PACIFIC RAILWAY COMPANY
CERTIFICATE OF EXAMINATION

BLOOMINGTON, TEXAS   AUG 13 19 73

This Is To Certify That CHARLES H. GELETZKE JR.
has been examined upon the Rules pertaining to position of
ASSISTANT TRAINMASTER

Examining Officer

RULES EXAMINER

Title

Signature of Holder

Chapter 6
Back to the Ranks!

GTW Train 651 with passenger GP9 4919 was working at Ionia, MI on
April 8, 1983. (Lawrence R. Bolton photo)

My Last Trip to Grand Rapids

By: C. H. Geletzke, Jr.

Considering I had a 45-year railroad career, most of which
was on the Grand Trunk Western (GTW), you cannot believe how
frequently I am asked if I would post photos that I took on the Grand
Rapids Subdivision over the years. What most of these
individuals do not understand is that I only worked out of Durand,
Michigan as a road brakeman in 1969 and 1970 before I entered the
Marine Corps…and the crews that

Chuck H Geletzke, Jr.

normally manned the Grand Rapids Sub. trains were all based out of Durand. Of course there was one other major factor, which entered into this equation…freight trains 451/450
from Durand to Muskegon and return ALWAYS ran at night!

After "tours of duty" on the Delray Connecting Railroad and the Missouri Pacific I returned to the GTW as a Locomotive Fireman and re-established seniority on November 9, 1973. For those of you who were around then, you might recall that late in November was the beginning of *The Fuel Crisis* and since that time in American History we have watched American Industry wither away into the sunset, if you know what I mean?

As you no doubt know by now from my previous stories, I was always a hard worker and took little time off. So, when I was furloughed for four consecutive weeks in 1974 I began to question whether I had made a good move. But, that was nothing compared to 1975 when I was laid-off on the third of January…not to be permanently recalled until the middle of January 1976! Oh sure, I was "called in Emergency" to work the Milwaukee Jct. Hostling job on 3-30, 5-4, 5-17, 5-18, 5-22, and 5-23. Well, guess what? On June 20th I was recalled to work and assigned to the 3:00 P.M. Hostling Job…but then, on June 23rd, **I was furloughed again!** On June 25th, I was used again in Emergency! Then, on June 30th I was once again recalled and managed to work 6-30, 7-1, 7-2, and was furloughed on July 3rd. They called me again to work the hostling job in Emergency again on July 5th and 6th…yes; it was a roller coaster ride!

Oh yes, please do not feel too sorry for me; because as I have stated before, my brother and I had a semi-tractor and a small fleet of construction equipment and went right to work hauling perishable freight throughout the Continental United States…that said, the hours and time away from home were **WAY WORSE THAN ON THE RAILROAD!**

Now, hold onto your Kromer Caps…while I was working the afternoon hostling job on July 6th, I happened to walk over to the Milwaukee Jct. yard office to get a cup of coffee and to talk with my good friend and Crew Dispatcher, Joe Dooley. While I was in the Crew Dispatching Office with its huge board displaying all of the jobs and crewmen manning all of those assignments, Trainmaster, Ty Gorski entered the room and asked, "Hey Kid, how'd you like to be a brakeman again?" He often called me "Kid."

Naturally, I responded in the affirmative and was told I'd be "marked-up" as a brakeman at the completion of my shift. (As a side note here, let me add that in the event that I was recalled as a fireman, I would then have to make a choice as to which craft I would pursue.)

By this time of the summer I was no longer driving "Interstate" and had my semi-tractor leased to a local outfit, *Kubach Cartage*, and since my brother was off for the summer from school, he just took over hauling the freight.

So, at 11:00 P.M. I completed my tour as an Emergency Hostler and my Name Tag was placed on the Road Brakemen's Extra Board...I would be rested to work and available at 7:00 A.M. Don't you know that at 1:30 A.M. they ordered and ran the *American Freedom Train* with the former Reading 2102 from Detroit to Ada, Michigan (on the Grand Rapids Subdivision). And what did I get to work? I was ordered for Trains 5555/5556 not just a work train; but a Weed Sprayer, from Detroit to West Pontiac and return, on duty at 7:45 A.M. I always wondered what breathing in that spray back in those days did to us...and what about the guys who worked for the spraying contractors and how long did they live???

All was not necessarily a bed of roses for the Trainmen either...on July 27th, I was furloughed as a brakeman (and was still furloughed as a Fireman)! Only four days later, on July 30th, I was back on the Extra Board as a Brakeman.

By now you are no doubt beginning to observe what an uncertain life a railroader might encounter during their "formative" years. On July 9th, I was furloughed for one day and recalled the next!

After ten paragraphs, I guess I should now get to the reason that I wrote this story. Earlier I mentioned my friend, Joe Dooley. Now I had never met Joe's wife Cindy; but apparently she had a childhood friend from Philadelphia, who was going to be visiting over the coming weekend...and Joe wondered if I would be willing to come over and go out to dinner with all of them on Saturday evening, October 18th...a blind date!?! I recall thinking to myself, "Well why not; I'll probably never see her again anyway!"

On October 16th I was called for Train 435, with engines 5903 & 5920 (two SD40's), a layover job to Battle Creek with Engineer, Jerry Krall; Conductor, Kenny Powers; and Flagman, Paul Schenck. We went on duty in Detroit at 7 o'clock P.M. and off duty in Battle Creek at 2:45 A.M. on the 17th. I thought we'd probably be ordered back out sometime later that evening; but gradually I began

Chuck H Geletzke, Jr.

to wonder if I would make it back in time for my date? Oh well, Joe would understand, after all, he was from a family of railroaders!

Early in the morning of October 18th we were finally called for Train 434 to be on duty at 3:15 A.M. Yes, I should make it home in time. On this trip we had the 5910 (SD40) and a pair of GP9's the 4552 & 4439. The trip went extremely well and we went off duty at 9:50 A.M. That would mean that I would be rested to work again at 5:50 P.M.; so I had to watch my position on the board very carefully!

I washed my car, took a nap, and arrived at the Dooley's apartment at 7:00 P.M. In only a few minutes I was introduced to this cute young lady, Leslie Price, who certainly did not sound like she was from Philadelphia! We then climbed into my thankfully clean car and drove to a restaurant in Auburn Hills.

In the restaurant, at first, it was mostly me talking with Joe and Leslie having a discussion with Cindy. I recall thinking to myself, "This is not going very well." But, that was only until I stuck my menu in the butter and wiped it across my slacks and one disaster led to another and soon Leslie was really laughing! When our desserts arrived, they were ice cream sundaes, each with a cherry on the top. That's when I announced, "Remember, you always have to save the cherry for last!" That did it; I really think she started to like me. We then drove back to Joe and Cindy's and it was decided that we would meet for brunch at Noon on Sunday. Then, Leslie and I just sat and talked until 5 A.M. when I headed for home.

As you can imagine I was watching the Extra Board closely and it actually looked like I might possibly even "lay-in" all day and not be called. I got up and went to church with my Mom, Dad, brother, and sister. I then headed directly for Joe and Cindy's, knowing that I would be a little late. (Again please remember that this was still close to 15 years before most people would have cell phones.) When I did not arrive on time, Joe called my parent's home and asked where I was? My sister, Laurie stated, "He should be there any minute, he is coming right from church."

Years later, Leslie reminded me of that day and stated that at first she was upset that I did not arrive on time; but the fact that I would get up and go to church…after staying up until five in the morning, definitely increased my credibility!

Well, Leslie was supposed to fly out of Detroit and back to Philadelphia at 5:00 P.M.; somehow her plans changed. We went to brunch at a local Drayton Plains restaurant (right around the corner from HO model railroader and King of Signals, Mike Burgett's

113

future home) and had another wonderful day. When we got back to the Dooley's home it was decided that Leslie was going to postpone her flight until Monday, which I thought was great! What I didn't know until much later was that she called her mother and not only stated that she was staying an extra day; but that "she met the man she was going to marry!"

If I recall correctly I stayed there and talked until about 6 o'clock in the evening then said good bye…and that we would talk and possibly arrange a third date!?!

Early the next morning (October 20th), I was ordered for 6:45 A.M. to deadhead to Durand in order to work Train 653, on duty at 8:15 A.M., the "Grand Rapids Local." I worked with Engineer, Jack Mowen; Conductor, Rod Baker; and Flagman, G. O. Potter…I always called him "G. Naught!" On this trip we had the engine GTW 4920 a passenger GP9, and we worked most of the towns along the way…Owosso, Ovid, St. Johns, Fowler, Pewamo, Ionia, Saranac, Lowell, Ada, and then yarded our train at Grand Rapids. We tied-up at 6:45 P.M., which because it was in excess of twelve hours, required us to have ten hours rest.

This was the first and only time that I ever laid-over in Grand Rapids in my railroad career. After cleaning up, all of us walked to a restaurant for dinner and then I walked back to the hotel and wrote my first ever letter to Leslie. From then on, she was on my mind!

The next morning, we were back on duty on Train 652 at 7:45 A.M., with the same locomotive and worked our way back to Michigan's railroad capitol. Looking back, I am guessing that my thoughts were just not on railfanning…I did not take any photos along the way…and I did have my camera! Apparently I had other thoughts on my mind…

I continued working as a brakeman until October 30th when I was again furloughed. Leslie and I talked on the phone almost every evening…interestingly, before she met me, she never knew anyone who did not work Monday through Friday or Saturday, 8 to 5!?!

On November 13th I reestablished my position on the Brakeman's Extra Board (history shows that that was the final time that I was ever furloughed…even though I was still laid-off as a Fireman) and continued working there until I was able to take my two week vacation, which turned out to be my third date with Leslie! Actually, it was a third date, which lasted 12 days, when I drove out to Philadelphia and spent Thanksgiving with her and her Mom.

Chuck H Geletzke, Jr.

Our fourth date occurred on December 31st, as Leslie flew out to Detroit. I arranged to pick her up at the airport and while there, I asked her to Be My Wife!?!

Yes, she accepted and 363 days from the day we met, October 16, 1976 we had a Bicentennial Wedding in Philadelphia! That was 47 years ago today and like most of you, we have been through thick and thin together…just imagine a born and raised nine to fiver raising three wonderful children and being married to a railroader for thirty-three of those wonderful years!?! Looking back, I don't believe that either of us would change a thing…and do you know what both of us believe? Our date on October 18, 1975 had God's finger prints all over it!!!

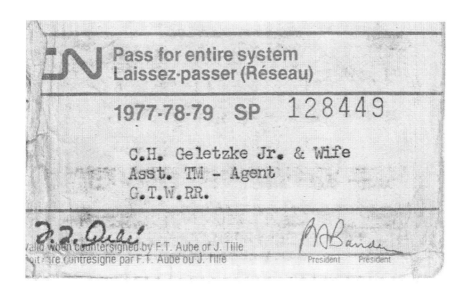

Chapter 7
Management...again!?!

A view from the cab of northbound GTW Train 471 "The Salt Line" with GP9 4134 meeting the daylight Saginaw, MI yard engine, GTW 7229 an SW900 at the Saginaw Frt. Yard on March 24, 1967. The tracks on the left belonged to the NYC and would eventually be acquired by the GTW on April 1, 1976.

Saginaw's Yard Limits

By: Charles H. Geletzke, Jr.

I will never forget, it was in late 1975 and very early 1976, the train dispatchers and yardmasters (particularly in Detroit) on my railroad, the Grand Trunk Western (GTW) got into a huge confrontation over who had control of the main tracks within Rule 93 or Yard Limit territory! Now let me state, there was never an

Chuck H Geletzke, Jr.

issue on the Holly Subdivision where First Class Trains were operated under timetable authority; no, instead the problems occurred over the operation of the Mount Clemens Subdivision and Highline where Extra Freight Trains and yard engines intermingled all day long. The major issue was that traditionally, the yardmasters had controlled this territory by basically directing the territory as a "Terminal Dispatcher," and in turn, keeping the train dispatcher informed as to what they were doing. The problems stemmed from the fact that the train dispatchers really did not have a good understanding of the layout of the terminal and its daily operation and secondly, the train dispatchers were often so busy, that it might take "forever" for the yardmaster to get through to them to get permission to make a move! Thus over the previous forty or fifty years, the General Yardmaster (who was actually a Trainmaster) served basically as a Terminal Dispatcher. All of this seemed to work extremely well until (I am guessing) certain members of the Train Dispatcher's Union decided that they wanted to "call all of the shots!!!" This slowed the operation down dramatically! It may have been safe; but it was extremely slow!

For me, I became aware and involved in this skirmish in April or May 1976 when I was working in Bay City, Saginaw, and Midland, Michigan following the GTW's acquisition of the former Penn Central trackage in that area as an Assistant Trainmaster. In short order I found that I was spending the preponderance of my time in Saginaw directing the operation of two daylight yard engines, because the terminal (which was all in Yard Limits) did not have yardmasters.

At about 8:00 A.M., trying to follow the rules, I called the Train Dispatcher, and asked for permission for one of my yard crews to bring their locomotive out of the Engine Servicing Compound and go to work. Now I knew, from my experience as a road brakeman, that the running time from Durand to Saginaw, if a train did not have any local work to perform in route was one hour and fifty minutes. I also knew that Train 471, "the Bay City Local" or "Salt Line" was just departing Durand! That meant that we would not see the Salt line for almost two hours; but TD#2 was not going to let my crew set foot on the Mainline!

I then asked the Dispatcher what the purpose was for having Yard Limits (which essentially permitted crews to occupy the Main Track with permission, clearing scheduled trains on time and being able to stop within one-half their range of vision short of any obstruction)? And we did NOT have any scheduled trains on this subdivision. With that he got mad at me, started screaming, and said, "You just keep your engine in the clear until Train 471, Extra _____ North goes by, and then give me a call!"

At that point in time, we had a tremendous number of customers in Saginaw, which translated to a great deal of yard and firm work…in a limited amount of space. I could not begin to visualize how my crews (which were both tremendous) were going to accomplish their missions that day; but now I was furious!

TD#2 and I wound up yelling at one another (which was totally out of character, at least for me) and we were overheard by my boss, Trainmaster, Gene Shafer, himself a former Train Dispatcher. At that point in time, he told me to settle down…and then sent me home for the day.

Here it is 48 years later and I still cannot begin to understand how a yard crew is supposed to keeps its customers happy if they have to "sit in the clear" for a train that at a minimum is still over two hours away!?!

Sometimes, wearing bib overalls was much easier…but then, I always wanted the railroads to have as much business as possible!

Westbound Amtrak Train 365 is seen arriving on Conrail (former NYC, PC) at Kalamazoo, MI on January 15, 1977.

Making-up Time

As told by: Leslie E. Geletzke

I've written before about how my wife, Leslie and I were transferred by the Grand Trunk Western Railroad (GTW) from Port Huron, Michigan to Kalamazoo only 12 days prior to Christmas 1976 when we had only been married for a total of two days short of two months!

Because the *Fisher Body* Plant, which was the GTW's largest customer in Kalamazoo was shut down for the holidays, and because the man I was replacing, Keith Charles, was still there, I was permitted to return home to our apartment in St. Clair, Michigan for the Christmas Holiday and for New Year's Eve.

On Monday, January 3rd I drove back to Kalamazoo and went back to work. On Wednesday the 5th, Leslie rode Amtrak Train 65 from Port Huron to Kalamazoo and I met her at the depot. We then spent the next six days apartment hunting…in actuality, Leslie did much of the "hunting" by herself, while I was learning how to keep *General Motors*, *Checker Motors*, three major paper mills, and a myriad of smaller firms happy!

Tuesday evening I drove Leslie to Amtrak's former New York Central passenger station in Kalamazoo, so that she could catch Amtrak Train 364 back to Port Huron at 7:05 P.M. It turned out that the train was running a little tardy and my new wife was concerned about what time the train would actually arrive in Port Huron…it was due to arrive there at 11:20 P.M.! I stated that the train would make up time once it got on the Grand Trunk at Battle Creek. I could tell that she was skeptical about driving home all by herself that late at night!

Before too long the train arrived, I kissed her good-by, and put her aboard the train, which happened to be one of the new Amtrak *Turboliners*! I then headed back to my motel.

At that time Conrail was still supplying the train and engine crews for the Amtrak trains operating over their railroad and the GTW was doing the same. In the case of the GTW, the engine crew originated in Battle Creek and the train crew was based out of Port Huron.

Number 364 was scheduled to depart the old New York Central station in Battle Creek at 7:40 P.M. and the crew change was made there. From that location, it was only a distance of about one-half mile to Nichols tower where the train would become Number 64 and would enter GTW trackage at 7:45 P.M. and complete the final 157.6 miles of its run.

Naturally, the Conductor came through the train and checked or collected everyone's ticket who boarded at Kalamazoo. Following the change of crews at Battle Creek the GTW Conductor came through the train checking the final destination of each passenger and punching the tickets of those who boarded at Battle Creek. When he and the brakeman got to my wife they immediately noticed that she was riding on a pass and started asking her a number of questions. Of course the entire crew knew me as I had previously been an Assistant Trainmaster at Port Huron. To this day she says that they could not have been nicer!

I am guessing that it was after the stop at either East Lansing or possibly Durand, the Conductor asked Leslie if she would like to come up to the "headend" and sit next to the Engineer in the Fireman's seat and of course she readily accepted! By this time, that train was FLYING!!! I don't believe that she ever knew the train's exact speed; but I guess at one point either the Engineman or Conductor said to her, "Now don't you tell your husband just how fast we've been running!?!"

She turned to them and said, "Oh, don't worry…he told me you'd get us in on time!"

(A little side note per retired GTW Locomotive Engineer, L. R. Bolton. Interestingly, in the Amtrak Timetable these trains were listed as Numbers 365 and 364 and used these numbers on Conrail; but in the GTW Employees Timetable, they were billed as Trains 65 and 64…so who knew!?!)

On April 15, 1978 we see GTW 7014 an SW9, the regular engine on the KSR "Kalamazoo Switch Run (Train 521) spotted on the Freight House Track while the crew went to dinner. The author's office was located just to the left of the front door and the room in our discussion was just to the immediate left of the locomotive cab.

What if!?!

By: Charles H. Geletzke, Jr.

I believe that I may have covered a portion of this story once before???   One evening, in 1977, shortly after I assumed the position of Assistant Trainmaster/Agent at Kalamazoo, Michigan for the Grand Trunk Western Railroad (GTW) I was sitting at my desk in the freight office, all by myself, when a thought popped into my mind! From my desk I could look out my office door and in the far right rear corner of the freight office I could see a portion of an interior storage room. Occupying nine square feet of floor space within that cubicle was our big black office safe and all at once it occurred to me ...that I did not know or have the combination!?! What if someone barged into the building one night and demanded that I open the safe? What would or could I do?

Actually the contents of the old security storage unit were probably inconsequential! Truth be known, I had no idea what its

121

contents were! I knew there were papers inside, and oh yes, our coffee fund, which I am guessing at that time may have totaled $40. But what if an armed bandit demanded that I open the safe not believing that its contents were not of much value and definitely not buying my story of a lack of knowledge!?!

The next morning I approached Myrna Wallace our Stenographer, aka "my secretary" and inquired about the combination. It was not a problem. She wrote it down for me and I inserted the paper into my wallet. Myrna then gave me a demonstration of how to actually open the safe and showed me its contents…the items were exactly what I would have expected. I immediately felt better!

Fortunately, I never encountered any problems with burglars and in the two and one half years that I worked there, I probably only had occasion to open the safe myself, two times at most!

More about that little room…

Only weeks before I departed Kalamazoo for my new position as Trainmaster on the Detroit & Toledo Shore Line Railroad in Toledo, Ohio, one afternoon a GTW painting gang just showed-up and announced…"Were here to paint the interior of your office!"

Believe me; we had no prior knowledge of their project!

The foreman of the gang, which was headquartered in Battle Creek, then stated, "We are only going to deliver and unload our tools and equipment here today. We'll begin the actual work tomorrow!"

"Hey thanks for the advance notice!" I was now worried, we had paperwork and records stacked everywhere.

The head of the crew then explained exactly what they had in mind and how they would do their best to work around us. I began to feel a little better.

At that point the foreman asked me if I knew when the office was last painted and I stated that I had no idea.

Following that short discussion, he led me into that little storage room and pointed out that way up near the top of the room's 16-foot ceiling in an obscure corner was a small area of different color paints that I honestly had never noticed before. That paint chart actually documented the various colors and dates illustrating every time the building's interior was ever painted! It was amazing! I am

Chuck H Geletzke, Jr.

guessing that every other GTW structure probably had a similar historical record located somewhere within its interior!?!

Oh yes, on the entranceway wall that formed one of the walls of my office was a bulletin board. On its frame to the left and right, were two hand painted *Grand Trunk Railway* insignias, which had to have been as old as the building itself…I loved them! I immediately told the foreman that I did not want them to paint over those! Thankfully, he masked them right away and stated, "We'll take good care of those!"

p.s.: I don't know exactly; but I believe that the office was officially closed only about one year later. It was kind of sad, I never even was able to meet or train my replacement!

I have no idea what may have happened to that bulletin board??? I think the building may have sat vacant for a number of years and then about ten years ago, it was gutted and turned into a Sushi restaurant. It the process they even removed the interior's second floor where we stored all of our records…I am guessing that all of those went into the trash!?!

Well, we did have one break-in!

Sometime in 1978 our freight office was actually broken into! It occurred during one night while we were supporting the *Kalamazoo Division of Fisher Body* and our regularly assigned clerk on the night shift was performing his/her assigned duties out at Kilgore Yard.

The perpetrator broke a window, unlocked the front door, and entered the freight office. While there they apparently found the need to remove our relatively huge microfilm reader (I cannot imagine what use they would have had for that? I have a feeling that they may have thought that it was actually a computer…we will never know for sure!). Additionally, they took several smaller items that I no longer recall and our office railroad radio. The radio was one of the earlier "portable" models, which had a sling to loop it over your shoulder to transport it and required 24 "D" cell batteries to hold a charge! An operator would have to be independently wealthy just to keep the unit charged and with useable batteries!

When our Chief Clerk, Marv Mock discovered the break-in at approximately 7:00 A. M. he immediately reported it to the *Kalamazoo Police Department* and they sent a team of investigators

123

over to examine the scene of the crime. To the best of my knowledge, a culprit was never found.

On the other hand, we were immediately issued a replacement radio and for the next several weeks we would hear mysterious non-railroad transmissions being sent over the airwaves. As I said, they stopped after the next several weeks as I am guessing the batteries lost their charge and were never replaced. We all surmised that the radio probably wound up somewhere in the bottom of the Kalamazoo River.

A GTW Maple Leaf needle point made as a Christmas present for C. H. Geletzke, Jr. by Leslie Geletzke in Kalamazoo, MI in 1977.

My Maple Leaf

By: C. H. Geletzke, Jr.

Chuck H Geletzke, Jr.

Following my wife's and my marriage in 1976, I discovered that one of the things that she loved to do in her free time was to Needlepoint.

Now initially I knew little about that craft; but being a lifelong model railroader and woodworker, I quickly discerned that there was a tremendous amount of skill and patience involved in completing a needlepoint project! Going along with this, I have always admired everyone who has a hobby or special interest...as long as it is of a positive nature!

I explained how in December 1976 we were transferred by the Grand Trunk Western Railroad (GTW) from Port Huron, Michigan to Kalamazoo. Once we were settled in our apartment I noticed that Leslie would often spend her evenings doing her needlework and normally, she would work on these projects while we were watching television together. As time went on I was amazed at the amount of time and skill involved in each project...and she seemed to love it!

Interestingly, as the year 1977 progressed and we passed Labor Day and approached Thanksgiving and Christmas, I noticed that she did not seem to be devoting anywhere near the time in her projects that she had previously. One evening I finally asked her, "What's the matter? Why have you stopped working on your needlepoint projects?"

Leslie retorted with, "I don't know, I guess maybe I am losing interest in it."

Then I went on to tell her that I thought that was a shame and stated that I missed not seeing how each of the projects progressed.

Every evening that I was home I noticed that only on a rare occasion would she get out her latest canvass and only stitch for what usually seemed much less than an hour. I tried everything I could to encourage her to continue. Finally one evening she even said, "I don't know; I guess I just don't feel like it!" And it went on that way all the way until Christmas morning.

Naturally, each of us placed our gifts under the tree on Christmas Eve and on Christmas morning awoke to see what Santa may have brought also.

When it was my turn to open a present, I rapidly started slitting the paper on an interesting looking package. As I opened the end of the long thin item I exposed the end of a needlepoint canvas. As I continued opening the item, I immediately noticed that it was a hand stitched needlepoint of a GTW Maple Leaf insignia sewn in all of the proper colors and ready for framing! I was so excited!

That was when Leslie gave me the details. Apparently she had my good friend, model railroader, and GTW Brakeman, Larry Bolton draw a perfect GTW herald on a piece of needlepoint canvas. Then everyday, while I was at the office, she had been sitting home stitching, trying to finish the project before Christmas morning! Believe me, it was beautiful!

Leslie, then said, "After stitching all day, now you know why I never felt up to stitching during the evening! Just so you know, I still love the hobby!"

Only a few days later we took the project to a local Kalamazoo frame shop and had it custom framed. Here it is 46 years later and it still occupies a place of honor on a wall to the right of my desk where I do all of my writing.

Thank you Leslie and thank you, Santa!

The Culverhouse Track

By: C. H. Geletzke, Jr.

Until Illinois Central Management took over the operation of the Canadian National Railroad and changed the method of operation, the former Grand Trunk Western Railroad (GTW) was always an East-West railroad, with the exception of three subdivisions. The Cass City Sub. was north-south from Pontiac to Caseville, the Saginaw Sub. from Durand to North Bay City was also north-south, and lastly, the Kalamazoo Subdivision from Pavilion to the north side of Kalamazoo was the third north-south line.

Much of the GTW trackage on the Kalamazoo Subdivision dated back to the original owner, the CK&S or Chicago, Kalamazoo & Saginaw Ry. By the 1920's all of this trackage within the City of Kalamazoo became jointly used by both the GTW and the New York Central (later Penn Central [PC] and Conrail [CR]). All of the single track portions through town were maintained by the GTW and where there was double-track, the western portion was GTW and the trackage on the east NYC. Most of the industries served directly off of this trackage were additionally served by both carriers; but there were several exceptions!

Chuck H Geletzke, Jr.

On the single track portion of the line, on the west side and just north of Lake Street (Milepost 9.6) was a double-ended track known as the Culverhouse Track, which at least during my time as GTW Assistant Trainmaster-Agent there from December 1976 through May 1979 was strictly used for storage. I tried to do a little research and determine just how this siding obtained its name without any luck. It did become quite apparent that the Culverhouse name was an old family name in Kalamazoo that went back at least as far as the 1890's; but that was the best I could do. Interestingly, there was only a small building located on the west side of the track at the extreme south end facing Lake Street. North of there, the land dropped down a fairly steep embankment on the remainder of the west side and it did not appear that there was ever any rail served industry located there. That said, I have no idea why that little track was ever actually constructed there!?!

One day in the spring of 1978 I was working out at Kilgore Yard on the southeast side of town when we received a radio call from the conductor on the KSR (Kalamazoo Switch Run). Apparently, per their switch list they and their locomotive (the GTW 7014) headed north, had just reached into the south end of the Culverhouse Track and were getting ready to "dig" three or four cars out of the track, which had been stored there for several weeks. They tied on, coupled the air, and began to pull. All at once the train's fireman spotted workers, on his side, running around and waving their arms frantically! Naturally, he immediately yelled at Engineer, McCall to stop the move! When the dust settled, the conductor and the two brakeman crossed over to the fireman's side of the train and walked north about three car lengths. There they spotted a now mangled-up conveyor-unloader now twisted out of shape and hanging pathetically out of a boxcar door! It was quickly determined that these men were in the process of unloading a boxcar load of shingles and now their conveyor belt had been rendered totally useless!

At this point the conductor and his two brakeman, who were regularly assigned on the job began discussing the placement of that loaded car. Because they had all been working the job regularly for at least the past three or four weeks, all of them knew that they had NEVER placed a loaded car in that track!

I immediately drove to the location of the incident.

127

Following our discussion and a radio call to Chief Clerk, Marvin Mock, we quickly determined that WE, the Grand Trunk Western Railroad, never spotted that loaded car in that track!

It turned out that the car was placed there for unloading by Conrail and that one of their crews cut the car in between the other cars that we had stored there. Now let me state that this was not the end of the story…you see the Culverhouse Track was one of the few tracks in the terminal that was NOT open to Reciprocal Switching, and that technically, it should have been interchanged to us, and we should have spotted it there! And because the roofing company did not have a "Side Track Agreement" with either railroad, it had no right to ask to have the car spotted there in the first place! It should have been delivered on a Team Track.

Fortunately, the preponderance of the shingles and other roofing material had already been unloaded at this point; so the workers were able to manhandle the remainder into a truck allowing our crew to pull the cars that they needed. As stated, the conveyor was a total disaster!

Several days later I arranged a meeting with the owner of the roofing company, Tom Burke our Customer Service Representative, Don Dwyer, the Conrail Trainmaster, and our Freight Claims Agent. Going into the meeting, it was already decided that we would agree to replace the conveyor as technically, our crew should have made sure that "no one was in, on, or about those cars before they pulled them!" But right from the start, the roofer became so belligerent and nasty and totally unwilling to discuss the cause of the accident and the principal of Side Track Agreements! We finally just gave-up, grabbed our belongings, and left his premises! In the end, Conrail lost a customer and possibly so did we…but it is impossible to deal with an individual when they are totally unwilling to listen not to mention have a civil discussion.

On September 20, 1979 author Geletzke caught the D&TSL's "B&O Puller" with GP7's 50 & 42 on the Toledo Terminal RR crossing the Maumee River on the Upper River Bridge. The train was enroute to the B&O at Rossford, OH. The crew would leave the entire train, including engines and caboose there and then taxi back to Lang. The train crew would then make a second trip over to the N&W's former W&LE Homestead Yard, aka the creation of the slang term, "double-dip!" Sadly, this bridge burned in 1981 and was never repaired!

"Double-Dip"

By: C. H. Geletzke, Jr.

No doubt most of you have seen lists of railroad slang in various railroad publications over the past decades. Not seen on these lists however are assorted terms, which are unique to individual carriers and regions of the country.

One of my favorite railroads, The Detroit & Toledo Shore Line (D&TSL) even though it was incorporated in 1899 and interchanged with over 13 different carriers in Toledo, Ohio never physically delivered to or pulled from any of these other railroads (except the Toledo Terminal Ry.) until November 16, 1960, when under the leadership of C. J. MacPhail, began delivering to the Toledo & Ohio Central (T&OC) a subsidiary of the New York

Central (NYC). It was not until June 13, 1965 that the Shore Line negotiated the right for its crews to begin delivering to the other Toledo railroads!

Now on most days after this significant date D&TSL crews would run "Pullers" to the NKP (former W&LE), PRR, C&O, NYC, and B&O. All other interchange within the terminal was handled by the Toledo Terminal Railroad. Following the establishment of this agreement, D&TSL crews would deliver to the various foreign roads using their own locomotive and caboose. After making the delivery they would return to Lang Yard in North Toledo, Ohio "cab lite." All of the other railroads delivered in the same manner.

When this agreement was established on the Shore Line, it was agreed that D&TSL train crews (these were road crews) would make one delivery, return to Lang, and if time permitted, a second delivery could be made. You will recall that through December 31, 1970 railroad crews were permitted to work up to 16 hours before requiring rest.

Enginemen, under their contract, however, were only permitted to make a single trip!

Over the ensuing years it became generally established that a single Shore Line crew would make the delivery to PRR, C&O, and NYC, again returning "cab lite." However, the B&O Puller was a "horse of a different color" and generally the hottest of all of the Pullers handling a block for the B&O's hot train, "The Dixie!" On the B&O the "Dixie Puller" as it was sometimes called, would take a train from Lang on the north side of Toledo to the B&O's Rossford Yard on the southwest side of town. Remember, at that time, Toledo was the third largest railroad center in the United States…behind Chicago and St. Louis. Once they yarded their train at Rossford, they would leave their engine and caboose there and taxi back to Lang. (Later in the evening a B&O crew would run their Shore Line Puller to Lang using the Shore Line's engine and cab.) After arriving in the taxi back at Lang, the Shore Line enginemen would go off duty and go home. The train crew, on the other hand, would work with a newly called engineer, and a different engine and caboose and take a second train, the "Wheeling Puller" (following the merger it became the "N&W Puller") to the former Wheeling & Lake Erie Railroad's Homestead Yard on the east side of Toledo. After making the delivery, they too would return to Lang with their engine and caboose. Over a short period of time, this second trip, or the act of handling a second train, became known as **"Double-Dipping!"**

Chuck H Geletzke, Jr.

Thus, a train crew would be called daily to "work a B&O Puller and 'double-dip' to the Wheeling."

There is a Part Two to this story…when my children were little and I was working out of Lang, they would hear me talking about crews "double-dipping" to the then N&W. One day one of my son's had to let our dog out to go to the bathroom.

When the two of them came inside, my wife asked him if the dog "Did his business?"

Without any hesitation at all, my son replied, "Yes, he DOUBLE-DIPPED!" You never know what our children think they hear us talking about…

D&TSL SW9's 119 & 121 derailed at Edison Ave. in North Toledo, OH on August 6, 1980 when they ran out of track!

END OF TRACK!

By: Charles H. Geletzke, Jr.

The Nickel Plate (former Wheeling & Lake Erie) had several ways of interchanging with the Detroit & Toledo Shore Line (a road in which the NKP had a 50% interest) prior to its inclusion in the Norfolk & Western merger on October 16, 1964. The Wheeling & Lake Erie would take its cars for the Shore Line, which were assembled either at Homestead Yard or Front Street Yard in Toledo and prior to 1952 or 53 would head across the Maumee River and upon receiving a favorable signal indication negotiate the interlocking at Manhattan Jct. and head toward the Wheeling depot on Cherry Street (additionally it is quite possible that they may have also made this maneuver as a shoving movement). When the tailend of the drag was clear of the Manhattan Jct. interlocking a member of the crew on the caboose would stop the train using the conductor's valve. Upon receiving the proper signal indication and the correct route the conductor or fieldman would signal for the interchange movement to "back-up" and this assignment would shove across the PRR-Ann Arbor diamond toward the D&TSL at New York Avenue. From there they would shove about one mile north into Lang Yard crossing the Toledo Terminal Ry. at the Manhattan Boulevard interlocking.

After 1952 or 53 the track arrangement at Manhattan Jct. was changed, which allowed the Wheeling to head all the way into Lang Yard and eliminated the reverse move previously required. This change saved a great deal of time.

The Nickel Plate or former Clover Leaf also participated separately in the interchange at Lang, only they would run between their yard at MC Junction to Gould tower and then via the Toledo Terminal Ry. to and from Lang in either direction as directed by the Toledo Terminal train dispatcher. Generally, they would operate by way of the double-track on the "Backside" of "the Terminal" crossing the interlockings at Nasby, Vulcan, Tower K, and Hallett to Manhattan Boulevard (or Shore Line Crossing as it was called in the TTRR timetable) where they would make a left-turn and enter the Shore Line via the "Long Wye." This move was discontinued some time after the 1964 amalgamation of the NKP into the N&W and this portion of the Toledo Terminal was "single-tracked."

Unlike the other Toledo railroads and most of those nationally, the Shore Line contrary to the provisions of the *National Interchange Agreement*, was not allowed to deliver to the other carriers within the Toledo Switching District (except the TTRR) prior to 1960. Until this date all of the other roads "delivered and

Chuck H Geletzke, Jr.

pulled" at Lang with the exception of those roads that utilized the services of the TTRR. The Shore Line brotherhoods began protesting this fact in 1924; but it was not until November 16, 1960 that the Shore Line finally was given the authority to begin delivering to the New York Central's subsidiary the Toledo & Ohio Central (T&OC) at Stanley Yard on the southeast side of Toledo. And if 36 years was not enough, Shore Line crews did not receive the ability to deliver to the other Toledo carriers until October 13, 1966!

Thus we can see that shortly after 1964 all interchange within the Toledo Switching District between the N&W and the D&TS took place via the original route and connection of the W&LE. This all worked fine for many years; however as cars began to increase in length and loads became heavier and track maintenance was deferred problems began to occur. This then sets the stage for our story...

On Sunday, September 16, 1979 the N&W's "Shore Line Puller" derailed 11 cars in their train while negotiating the curves at New York Avenue in North Toledo while attempting to make a delivery to the Shore Line. The track was taken out of service for two days and interchange between the two roads was accomplished by routing their pullers over the TTRR between Ironville and Shore Line Crossing.

Monday, April 7, 1980 saw the N&W again coping with the derailment of several cars when the road's "Shore Line Puller" experienced cars leaving the rails at New York Avenue. Apparently the series of tight reverse curves was not able to accommodate the newer longer cars. The cause listed on the N&W's Derailment Report was listed as: "change of super-elevation," i.e. improper previous repair!

On May 8th a Thursday, we witnessed still another derailment when just a single car in the middle of the N&W's Shore Line Puller derailed at New York Avenue. This time track damage was minimal and the track was okayed for operation the very next day.

Would you believe that in the very next delivery, eight empty tank cars in the middle of the Shore Line Puller not only derailed; but turned on their sides right on New York Avenue! By this time both railroads had had enough and the tracks were never repaired nor replaced. For the next several months, interchange moves were once again routed via trackage rights over the Toledo Terminal Railroad between Ironville and Manhattan Boulevard (Shore Line Crossing).

After several months of planning and engineering on the part of the N&W they decided that they would build a new connection to

133

the Shore Line using the abandoned right-of-way of the former Pennsylvania Railroad connection from Manhattan Jct. to a point on the Shore Line just north of the intersection of Bassett and Sciota Streets perhaps .2 miles north of New York Avenue. Demolition, grading, and construction commenced in late August 1980.

As any of you know who may have been railroaders, it is almost impossible to make plans to do anything that involves entertainment. On the evening of Tuesday, August 5th I had planned to attend the regular meeting of the Detroit Railroad Slide Group at Kenny Borg's home in Dearborn, MI. Oh yes, I was the Shore Line's Trainmaster and I was stationed at Lang Yard. While eating supper I received a telephone call from the Lang Yardmaster, the late Lenny Tomanski, informing me that a gondola loaded with scrap had derailed going over the hump and it had the entire north end of the yard tied-up! I should state here that prior to the construction of the hump at Lang, four yard assignments per shift handled all of the switching. With the hump's completion in 1968 one yard assignment with two locomotives could handle the work on each trick. Back to our story...I told the yardmaster to have the No. 5 or afternoon yard job head to the south end of the yard, complete their switching there, and then double-up the two northbound's, Train 400 "The Tunnel Run" for Port Huron and Train 421 "The Flint." Meanwhile, I quickly gobbled my supper, jumped in my company car, and headed for Lang...taking my slides with me just in case we were able to re-rail the car without too much effort.

As I drove through the gate toward the yard office I quickly learned that I would not be attending the slide session that evening..."Houston we REALLY have a problem!"

Aside from the derailed car tying up the hump at the north end of the yard everything was going quite normally. Yardmaster Tomanski had followed my instructions and was in the process of having the No. 5 afternoon yard assignment double-up the cars for Train 400 at the south end of the yard. The yard crew had ahold of about 100 cars and was pulling them out onto the "Heavy Side Lead" at the south end when trouble struck again! You see no one, myself included, took into consideration that today was engineer Don Harlow's first day to work at Lang Yard in about two or three years. While Don had a reputation as an excellent engineman, he had been working the two locals and Engineer's Spare Board out of Edison Yard in Trenton, Michigan 33 miles to the north and had not even been to Lang in that length of time.

Chuck H Geletzke, Jr.

Additionally, all three Lang Yard assignments traditionally worked with two SW9's mu'd together (coupled for multiple-unit operation) and coupled "nose to nose." Thus the engineer generally operated from the cab of the northernmost unit, which alleviated many "run-through switches" by improving visibility considerably. Since the crew was now working at the south end of the yard and thirty-three years have past, I have to say that I no longer recall which unit the late Mr. Harlow was operating from.

Anyway, Mr. Harlow pulled the long string of cars out the south end of the yard, received a restricting signal to cross the diamond of the Toledo Terminal Railroad at Manhattan Boulevard and headed toward New York Avenue at restricted speed (at that time defined basically as a speed that would permit stopping within one-half his range of vision and short of any obstruction). He was probably running between 10-15 mph when he noticed people in their backyards waving frantically at him and yelling at the top of their lungs. **"THE TRACK IS OUT!"** At first Don was not sure that he was hearing correctly, so he throttled down and stuck his head out the cab window…but now it was too late…way too late! He looked ahead, his eyes growing as large as a pair of headlights and he immediately threw the automatic brake valve into EMERGENCY! All he could do was hang-on to the control stand as the two units, SW9's #119 and #121 flew off the end of the dismantled track bouncing along the indentations where the ties had once been, until the units settled in the dry sand and cinder ballast of the sub roadbed. Oh-oh, now what?

This was just about the time I drove into Lang Yard.

I immediately drove the mile and a half…as the crow flies, to Edison Ave. in North Toledo and took a look at the situation. Surprisingly, only the two units were derailed; but they were both completely beyond the end of track! I got on the radio and called Lenny Tomanski and had him call Glen Thomson the Chief Mechanical Officer and Bill English, the Chief Engineer, so that they could arrange to clean-up this mess.

Jeffers Crane Rental was called and supplied two heavy cranes to perform the re-railing; and as I recall, we were all there most of the night and most of the next day too. I made arrangements to get the yard crew on another pair of engines and we re-railed the derailed gon at the north end of the yard and got the pair of northbound trains out of town. As you might guess, they did not depart with their complete trains; but that is railroading.

135

Now you're probably all wondering who was to blame and who was found at fault? Believe it or not, no formal investigation was ever held. When we managers looked into the chain of events, it was determined that in fact Shore Line Superintendent, C. L. Border NEVER issued a Bulletin declaring the track out of service at Edison Ave.; in fact, there were never even any barriers, flags, signs, or derails put in place. Apparently Mr. Border just assumed because the Shore Line was such a small railroad that everyone knew that the track there was Out of Service...but you all know what happens when you assume!

The new connection using the old PRR right-of-way was completed and put into operation in early September 1980 and the problem with derailments in this area was eliminated.

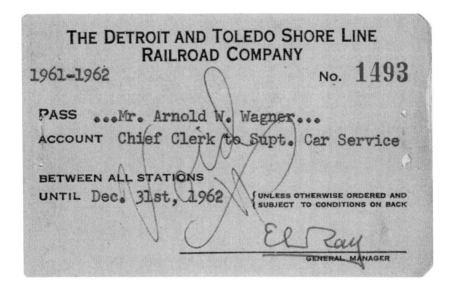

Chapter 8
Others' Tales

Vern...

By: L. E. Batanian, retired Santa Fe, BN, BNSF Locomotive Engineer, and Amtrak Road Foreman of Engines-Rocky Mt. District

Vern...I think I got the name right; but will change it if any of the Needles' boys disagree. There were anywhere from 30 to 45 pools on the West End of the Santa Fe out of Needles, California and about five less on the East End. They were set by mileage...the way it ought to be...this Trip Pay sucks...they own you! So, it's hard to remember everyone's name, because you did not work with them all the time like a Conductor and his crew.

Vern was another 40's hogger I liked to work with. He would let his Fireman run...that fact alone ought to make me remember his name! I recall that Vern wore starched khaki shirts with his bib-overalls, along with his *Hamilton* 992B pocket watch. He was a pretty thin man...I think all the tobacco he chewed may have had something to do with that! The funny thing about Vern was, when it came to brands of chewing tobacco he was an expert...and a collector, you might say! Vern carried pouches of tobacco from all over the United States, North, South, East, and West. He had a bag from EVERYWHERE in his grip.

Like I said before, I did not chew...not that I did not try...I just think there are better ways to die than gagging to death!

Vern had them all...from *Beechnut* to the *Chattanooga Chew*...whatever flavor they made, he had it! Pouch or Plug...it did not take me long to figure out why my father-in-law, Gus, got along so well with Vern. Chewing tobacco wasn't the only thing Vern collected...I remember one night I got out of Needles firing for Vern. Right off the bat, I was in the Engineer's seat and he was digging in his grip humming to himself..."Ahhh, here they are," sez he...as Vern held up a pair of wire cutters and his flashlight. "Do you fish, Leon?"

"Yes I do," I replied.

137

"I'll be back!" And out the door he went.

Most hoggers let you check the power over as you left town and started up the hill to Goffs. When you got back up to the headend, then you got in "the seat"…if they let you…not all; but most! It's uphill for 31 miles from Needles to Goffs. If you made it to the TOP in and hour…you had a "Smoker!" A "Good Train," an hour and a half…"a Dog," two or more hours depending on if you had to head-in to clear anyone. Two hours was only 15 mph or so…I'm thinking the coal train or the 408…a well known "DOG"…old Vern had been gone quite a while and I was getting a little concerned. I looked back and I could see his flashlight as he made his way through the units…he seemed to take awhile in each unit and I could see his light bobbing around as I looked back on the curves. I thought to myself, "I wonder what he is up to back there?" So, we ground our way up through Java and on to Ibis as I kept looking back to check on Vern. He was not taking a nap…that's for sure! Soon Vern opened the cab door and the roar of the five "big jacks" got my attention! He dropped his wire cutters in his grip and came over next to the control stand and opened up two pouches of chew…I thought he was offering me my choice of the tobacco…I could smell it as he extended his hand toward me…that is until he shined his flashlight into the pouches, which he put right in front of my face. Inside the empty pouches were ALL the electrical wire seals from the trailing units! "These things make the BEST fishing weights, Leon!" Sez Vern. "I melt them down and cast my own weights."

It was all I could do to keep a straight face and from busting out laughing! Next thing I knew, Vern was back in his grip…out he came with a pouch full of casted fishing weights…"Here you go, Leon…let me know how you like them!?!" And, on we went up the Hill to Goffs. Vern gave me more than fishing weights that night…he gave me another memory of working with a 1940's Hogger. You can't make this stuff up…It was Railroading!

Paper towels…

By: L. E. Batanian, retired Santa Fe, BN, BNSF Locomotive Engineer, and Amtrak Road Foreman of Engines-Rocky Mt. District

Chuck H Geletzke, Jr.

Paper towels…there is no doubt about it…hands down, the Santa Fe Railroad had the best paper towels money could buy! Each locomotive had a paper towel holder bolted to the electrical Cabinet in the cab. When a locomotive was serviced, the Laborer who serviced the cab with drinking water also filled the towel holder. Additionally, he checked the tools, swept the cab, and washed the windows while he was at it. Believe me, I know! Before I went into Engine Service I too worked as a Laborer.

The paper towels were tan colored. I think it may have been a natural color…they were unbleached…like the paper filters for my coffee maker. Not only were these towels great to wipe your hands with or to use as a pair of "gloves," and when the need came up…**they made the BEST BACON EVER**…I kid you not…don't ask me how they got there; but while frying bacon at home a few of these on a plate and goodbye grease! Believe me, they could suck up more oil than the Valdez Oil Spill…they were really that good!

I got out of Needles, California late one night with my father-in-law, Gus, hot on my tail…we worked back to back on the board as much as we could. As my train came around the 50 mph curve at Pisgah, the sun was rising in my rear view mirror and I noticed that there were cardboard boxes along the right-of-way every so often. I wondered what the heck this was all about. When I got into town, I took my power to the house and went to the Crew Room to tie-up. Gus soon came in and we were shooting the breeze and I asked him, "Did you see all of those cardboard boxes out by Pisgah?"

Gus replied, "Yes," and that "a boxcar door more than likely slid open and out they came."

I didn't think anymore about it and after making a "Dead Day" (being paid for waiting there over 24 hours and not being used), we both got out on our turns. On this trip, as I got to Pisgah, I noticed that there were still those big boxes lying along the north side of the right-of-way…and there were allot of them!

Once Gus came into Needles we developed a plan to hop in my truck and head back to Barstow. On the drive back our conversation turned to the boxes at Pisgah. We hatched a plan to get on the old road at Ludlow and swing by Pisgah and see what spoils might be laying along the right-of-way…what better way to break-up the 175 mile drive and maybe have some fun doing it! We had picked-up a few "cold ones" and when we left the highway soon we were making our way along the 36 poles per mile on the adjacent Santa Fe's dirt road. No sooner had we cracked open the refreshments and low and behold we passed a Santa Fe Track Inspector with cardboard boxes stacked on top of his little buggy as he putted by and waved. I down-shifted my 71 *Jeep* pick-up, which I'd recently bought from my friend, Leo, as we wound down into a dry wash and up the other side. This was getting interesting! Soon we found the spoils...cases upon cases of paper towels! We felt like Pirates as we started loading the Jeep pick-up. We would load a few and then have a cold one...load a few more and have another...we stacked them so high, they were above the cab and had to tie them down with a rope. At that point, we cut-off the cold ones, not wanting to have too much of a glow on us, as we made our way back to Barstow on the old road. I swung by Gus's house to drop him off and to split-up the "Bounty"...*Bounty Paper Towels*! My Mother-in-law came out as we were stacking their share on the porch..."What have you two been up to?" was all she could ask. I took our share back to my home and unloaded and stacked them on the back porch...we did not buy any paper towels for months and months after that!

That said, I want you to know that I still used Santa Fe Brown ones for my BACON!!! Hey, if it ain't broke, don't fix it! You can't make this stuff up...it was Railroading!

Here's a short one for you...

By: Joseph DeMike

As for people at grade crossings, there is no way to fix stupid!

I learned very early in my career on the Erie Western Railroad flagging a crossing means SPEED UP to some motorists! We were making a backup move late one night in Decatur, Indiana. The cut was moving and about a car length from the crossing. I was standing about two feet on the pavement with a lit red fusee. This car came flying and about hit me! Without even thinking, I flung the fusee after the speeding car who then hit the brakes...while I caught the cut and went on my way. From then on, I flagged from the sidewalk...

Let me add that Joe DeMike had quite a railroad career working on the Erie Western; the Chicago & Indiana; Prairie Trunk; Chicago, South Shore &

Chuck H Geletzke, Jr.

South Bend; and later as Operations Manager for *Ringling Brothers* managing the nationwide operation of their two circus trains. I think he would qualify as a real "Boomer!?!"

RI 424 was photographed at Blue Island, Illinois on February 24, 1980. (Jack G. Tyson photo)

The Rock Island that I recall

By: Mark A. Hinsdale, C&O tower operator; GTW Trainmaster; and CSXT manager and General Manager

When I worked as Trainmaster for the Grand Trunk Western Railroad at Blue Island, Illinois during 1976 and 1977, transfer practices between railroads in Chicagoland generally called for each road to deliver interchange cars, and then return cab light to their home terminal (I believe this was referred to as the National Interchange Agreement.). A few arrangements were in place for one railroad to deliver and pull for a specified period of time, such as six months or a year, and then the task would revert to the other involved carrier. GTW and Rock Island (RI) were big interchange partners at the "Island of Blue," and at least two trips were made by each railroad every day to handle the volume between us. Occasionally, RI would use a pair of these center-cab Alcos when

141

they brought traffic to us from their Burr Oak Yard, also in Blue Island. I was able to grab a couple of pix of them on their home rails; but did not engage in photographing them while in the terminal at Blue Island. I was too afraid of being admonished for doing so, although I was likely placing too much concern on who would actually care.

Shortly after my assignment to "The Island of Blue," I discovered the Rock Island's Burr Oak Yard, which this power is sitting at the west end of, was 100% ballasted with brake shoes. They were everywhere! Without any paths for carmen to access trains being inspected, I guess they found it easier to just leave them laying around to be available at every turn, rather than haul them in.

The Colonial Colliery was seen in the "patch" of Sagon, PA where it was jointly served by both the PRR and Reading Railroads. (Date & photographer unknown; R. K. Nairns collection)

Your Details Should Be Correct!

As told by the late Robert K. Nairns

Chuck H Geletzke, Jr.

My good friend, Bob Nairns lived in Shamokin, Pennsylvania and loved the two railroads of the Shamokin Valley…the Pennsylvania (PRR) and the Reading (RDG). Bob was also a very fine modeler and very active in the *Shamokin* (PA) *Railroad Model Club*. On the club layout, one of the things that Bob specialized in was the modeling and construction of HO Scale anthracite coal mines and the "patches" or mining towns, which surrounded them.

Back in 1995 the club was having an open house for the public and Bob who had grown-up in the Hard Coal Region just loved when older members of the community would browse the perimeter of the layout and he would see how his models evoked memories from these residents who too spent their youth and formative years growing up in the patches! He recalled people looking at his mining layout and saying, "Oh, that's not right, for our patch did it this way, or, my father built it this way for 'The Company!'" Bob said his favorite though was stated to him by an old lady in her eighties, whose father was Mine Boss at *BEAR VALLY COLLIERY*. She said, "YOUNGMAN (Bob was probably in his late fifties at the time)! OUTHOUSES WERE BACK TO BACK AT THE PROPERTY FENCE IN A PATCH! THAT WAY, THE COMPANY ONLY HAD TO PAY TO DIG ONE HOLE!" Would you believe that she returned the following year to see that I'd changed it!?!

Preparing for the future!

Philadelphia—Shamokin—Williamsport

Effective November 15, 1941

Subject to Change

READING
Railway Lines · **SYSTEM** · Motorbus Lines

Reading Lines

Time Tables

Shamokin Division

Schuylkill Valley Branch

and

Little Schuylkill Branch

RECLINING CHAIR CARS
without additional charge

between Philadelphia and Shamokin on trains Nos. 6, 9, 92, 97, 2003, 2008, 2012

between Philadelphia and Williamsport on trains Nos. 5, 11, 12 and 14

also between New York and Williamsport on trains Nos. 11 and 14.

T.T. 3   (68-B) 3rd Ed.   Ct.   6-22-42   (Printed in U.S.A.)

Reading Shamokin Division Passenger time Table dated November 15, 1941

Below is a suggestion from the Reading Railroad on the last page of the above time table. It is interesting that this took effect only 22 days before the United States was attacked by Japan!

VICTORY and VACATION

You'll be helping your country wage a victorious war by taking your vacation early—before the midsummer rush period, or late—after the rush is over. Plan to use midweek trains to avoid weekend congestion.

AVOID WASTE—KEEP THIS FOLDER

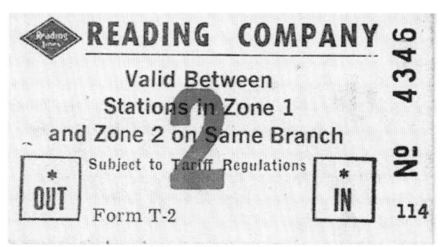

A Reading Commuter Ticket, which I purchased in 1975 and never used!

Chapter 9
One More Time...

GTW eastbound Train CO-55 with DT&I 219-GTW 5816-58__-58__ has just passed Byron Babbish's home in Bloomfield Hills, MI, just around the curve to the left, and is now headed to the former Consumers Power Co. Whiting Electric Generating Plant located in Erie, MI on August 31, 1983. (Jack G. Tyson photo)

Four Toots...

By: C. H. Geletzke, Jr.

Yes, I realize that Operating Rule 14 (j) o o o o (four short blasts of the whistle) is defined as a "Call for signals."

And I am also quite aware that Whistle Signal 14 (g) o o (two short blasts of the whistle) is an "Answer to any signal not otherwise provided for."

Thus when I was operating a train at almost any location and someone (railfan or just a friendly person) would wave; I would almost always acknowledge their wave with two short blasts of the locomotive's whistle (or horn) and a friendly wave of my own. But, what if I merely wanted to attract the attention of a non-railroad employee, what operating rule would cover that situation?

Two appropriate stories…

When my good friend and Grand Trunk Western Railroad (GTW) Locomotive Engineer, the late John N. "Jack" Ozanich built his wonderful home and outdoor railroad, just east of Battle Creek Yard at Milepost 184 on the north side of the Flint Subdivision, I would always blow four short toots as I past his home whether going east or west. If he happened to be home, he would usually acknowledge my signal by waving a highball with a red flag. At night, no matter the hour, he would flash his porch lights two times. We did this for years until I retired. But, Jack was a fellow employee; so technically I probably could justify my "call for a signal!?!"

Now in my second case, I wonder if upper management would have condoned the use of the whistle had I been caught in the act…particularly with former Illinois Central management.

I am going to guess that it was probably in the late 1970's that I noticed a Detroit area railfan and member of the *Michigan Railroad Club*, Byron Babbish, had began writing a series of articles on the GTW in their monthly publication. In time I noticed that many of the photos that he included were stated to have been taken along the GTW's Holly Subdivision, with many behind his home in Bloomfield Hills, Michigan. Now in 1976 I entered GTW management and left the Detroit area and did not return until late 1980. Meanwhile I continued to see periodic photographs posted under his byline and eventually I determined that this individual must reside in the vicinity of Milepost 20.1 on the Holly Sub. So, having returned to engine service, I decided that whenever I was going to pass my surmised location of Mr. Babbish's home, that I would blow four quick short toots of the whistle while approaching his location…let me state that this was frequently during the night! After the second or third time, someone in the Babbish household began flashing their lights back at me. Once again, let me state that Mr. Babbish and I had still never met and yet this act of friendship continued on until sometime probably after the year 1995 and our acquisition of personal computers. Somehow Byron determined that I was then the regularly assigned engineer on the GTW's "Fuel Run," which operated daily between Milwaukee Jct. in Detroit and Pontiac, Michigan. He also knew that I was enthralled by the Detroit & Toledo Shore Line Railroad (D&TSL) and that I was in the process of writing a book on that road. Somehow he contacted me via computer and arranged for us to finally meet at the Pontiac roundhouse and eventually sold me a brass HO scale D&TSL Mikado that he had acquired. From then on, the tooting continued when passing his home until I retired. Following my retirement, it was Byron who taught me how to self-publish my own railroad books, for which I am eternally grateful! Eventually I learned that Byron is a truly accomplished violinist and my wife and I have accompanied him and his wife and family to a number of fabulous concerts! In the end, who would have ever thought that two railfans would meet and become friends because one of them signaled a Rule 14 (j) while passing the other's home!?! You can't make this stuff up!

GTW Locomotive Engineer, Richard O'Leary's "Green Cooler!" (R. J. O'Leary photo)

Chuck H Geletzke, Jr.

A Tale about the Green Cooler

By: Richard J. O'Leary

My family had a little gathering for me on Sunday last, for my 75th Birthday and I pulled out this old cooler to set out by the campfire. Nicked up, beat up, and quite old as coolers go, I chuckled about how this came to live here.

While working the Engineer's Extra Board out of Durand, Michigan in the mid-eighties, I was called for freights Number 414 and 411, Durand to Dearoad (in River Rouge, Michigan) a distance of 73 miles each way. There was no fireman called and I believe that the head end brakeman may have been Rod "Home Run" Baker. After 40 odd years, the identity of the conductor and flagman are lost to me.

The train was nothing remarkable leaving Durand and all went according to plan...Durand to Pontiac. A large pickup at Pontiac changed the complexion of things. We departed there...Pontiac...with 100 plus cars and a questionable trainline. And, it had turned foggy...I mean really foggy! The Holly Subdivision being ABS (Automatic Block Signaled) territory, helped to alleviate some anxiety over visibility and the run down the hill to Milwaukee Jct. went smoothly, although the trainline continued to be of some concern. We snaked around the Highline Wye at "the Junction" onto the Highline and headed for West Detroit and Delray. Poking along at 10 mph was about all I felt safe with considering the conditions. Things were lined up and we slipped by West Detroit and started down the grade to the split-rail derail and stop signal for Delray and the bridge. As visibility was almost non-existent, I was unable to see the signal light for the derail; but being familiar with the territory, I was confident. We crept slowly down toward the signal until able to make out the stop indication and ground to a stop about a half-car short. The bridge tender was notified of our location and both the brakeman and I let out a long exhale! Just then the remaining slack ran in...with a huge THUMP! Well now, that was a bit surprising and more than a little embarrassing. Upon a hasty inspection we found one wheel on the lead unit was indeed past the signal and on the ground! It was at this point that a few "work words" seemed appropriate and were employed to attempt to remedy the situation…all to no avail. Both Mr. Baker and I knew that before long the radio was going to start, gentlemen with neckties on, carrying flashlights, were going to show up, and we or at least I was going to have to do some fast talking! It was time to get to work.

Baker and I, having worked rerailing jobs, suspected that with a bit of luck and our expertise that we could get this thing back where it belonged. Scrounging around the scene we found enough scrap lumber to make an attempt. It seemed that the only joker in this play was the aforementioned slack. With three units we had plenty of power; but with one wheel on the ground and a leaking trainline, we were still attempting to shove more than 100 cars uphill. What could possibly go wrong!?!

By this time the tail-end crew was aware that something was amiss; but were put at ease by their engineer's confident albeit vague assurances. As things turned out, there was a little bit of slack left in the train and when the power was applied, we jumped right back on the rail…brilliant!

As Rod and I were "high-fiving," the radio came alive with a call from the train dispatcher (I believe it was JRM John McKinnis) in Pontiac asking if everything was alright. I replied that everything was okay and then he slipped in a comment about the fog calling me by my first name, which always seemed to me to be a verbal wink-wink nod! He said that the bridge operator was ready for us and to have a good trip.

The fog lifted as daylight approached. We turned at Dearoad, picked up our return train, and headed for home. Surprisingly, we had no work at Pontiac and made good time on the westward trip. Sailing along at track speed we passed Gaines (the last town before Durand) and received yarding instructions from the Durand Yardmaster. I was feeling pretty good about the way this trip had turned out considering how it could have gone, when the radio fired-off again! This time, it was Trainmaster, Larry Wizauer and he wasn't calling Train Number 411! He was calling Engineer O'Leary, and he asked if, when I had the power put-away and my paperwork done, I would "join him in his office." Good feelings, high fives, and all the rest went right out the window at 40 or 50 mph and I prepared myself for what was certainly lying ahead.

With my duties complete, I headed up to the Grocery House to take my spanking. I knocked on Mr. Wizauer's door and he signaled me in as he was on the phone. Wrapping up his call, he turned to me with a big grin, stuck out his hand to shake mine and

Chuck H Geletzke, Jr.

said, "Congratulations! You've won this month's Safety Award!" He then reached down behind his desk and came up with a brand new Coleman Cooler. That's the story of "The Green Cooler."

GTW Locomotive Engineer, Richard O'Leary, returning to his engine, GTW 7018 at Flint, MI after eating lunch at the Atlas Coney Island in 1984 or 1985. (R. J. O'Leary collection)

Sadly, I wrote the above story with Richard's assistance on May 17, 2024. Today, June 5th, I learned of Richard's passing on June 3rd. He will be dearly missed by all who knew him.

With that said, let me include one more story about Richard, which I never intended to write or publish. Only today I found out that Richard was only six months older than me; but because he was born prior to December 1st of the preceding year, he was one year ahead of me in school. All of you who have read my previous books know that it was always my intention to go to work for the railroad upon turning 18 and graduating from high school. Well, one day I happened to be in downtown Royal Oak, Michigan when I saw one of the Grand Trunk Western Railroad (GTW) commuter trains zip through town…seated in the fireman's seat was a young fellow, whom I perceived to be younger than me! Boy was I jealous! Several months later, when I was working as a Laborer in the Pontiac, MI roundhouse, on that day we had an Extra Hostler…it happened to be Richard O'Leary, and I immediately recognized him as the "kid" firing that commuter train! After introductions we became friends and worked together many times over the years, particularly while I was a brakeman. Interestingly, I only told Richard of this story about three weeks ago. Richard you will be missed by all of your friends and me!

Retired GTW Locomotive Engineer and modeler, Larry Bolton operating on the late Jack N. Ozanich's famous Atlantic Great Eastern model railroad in Battle Creek, MI on December 20, 2010.

THE ICEBREAKER

It All Starts Here and Other Railroad Stories

By: GTW-CN Locomotive Engineer and Supervisor of Locomotive Engineers,
Lawrence R. Bolton

When I began my railroad career in the mid 1970's, the industry was male dominated. Women were working only in clerical positions at my employer. Beginning in the 1980's, the company endeavored to diversify its workforce by hiring women as brakemen (even the job titles were masculine). Once exposed to working conditions few of the new-hire women stayed. The long hours and odd hours required by the job, and a general lack of acceptance by the old heads caused most to abandon railroading as a career.

One of the new brake (persons) men became quite indignant with me for laughing at her shirt. It boldly stated, "I live for weekends." I told her if she was going to work as a road freight brakeman, she would probably need a new shirt that said, "What is a weekend?" This particular new-hire had a very short railroad career.

A few of these women did stay and eventually were promoted to the position of Conductor. One of these new conductors was a young black woman that I would occasionally be paired with as a train crew. These train trips seemed especially long as conversation was limited to the minimum required to do the job. The cause of this communication barrier was having so little in common. Age gap, race and gender differences all conspired to limit interaction with one another. She spent much of her idle time on the job reading fashion magazines. During delays I would read a book or a Mustang magazine. One day, while working with this conductor, I was reading the current Mustang Monthly magazine and noticed a report that one of the cosmetics companies had introduced a line of nail polish available in all the colors of the new Mustang cars. When I asked if she knew anything about that, she said, "No;" but was immediately interested. I gave her the magazine so she could read the article. That started a conversation about the Mustang hobby, which led to talking about other topics. While I cannot say that we became best of friends, we had a much-improved rapport from that day forward over the chance convergence of our interests.

Chuck H Geletzke, Jr.

GTW Conductor, Frank Samul is seen shoving into East Yard in
Hamtramck, MI on May 6, 2001.

A different form of Precision Railroading

By: C. H. Geletzke, Jr.

This will be a short one! One day in the late 1980's I was in
the Grand Trunk Western Railroad's (GTW) locker room at B.O.C.
Yard in Hamtramck, Michigan getting dressed for work. Right down
the aisle was Switchman, Frank Samul…a guy whom I must say was
always a true professional! I always enjoyed working with Frank!
Anyway, I looked over at Frank and he was in the process of sliding
a carpenter's folding ruler into the side pocket on the right pant leg
of his bib-overalls. With a sense of complete curiosity I just had to
ask, "What's that for Frank? Are you doing carpentry during your
"spot time?"

Frank got a big smile on his face and said, "No, I use this to
spot the tri-levels at the *General Motors Corporation* B.O.C. (Buick-
Oldsmobile-Cadillac) ramps." Frank then went on to elaborate that
when they shoved the empty tri-levels into the various ramp tracks
the distance between each car had to be fairly precise. If the cars
were too far apart, the "bridges" that were placed between each car
that the new autos were driven over, would not reach from one car to

another. And, if the cars were shoved together too tightly and all of the slack compressed, this would create another problem…thus, the allowable distance between each car at each dock had to be between a certain acceptable range. All of the other guys that worked these jobs…just estimated as best they could. Not Conductor, Frank Samul…he would measure the distance in between each pair of cars (I cannot recall; but I think six or eight cars were spotted in each of the eight loading ramp tracks). Believe me, when Frank placed them for loading, it was ALWAYS done precisely and the tracks never had to be "re-spotted!"

Frank Samul was a REAL Railroader!

The Importance of Straw

By: the late Robert K. Nairns

All mines and washeries used straw and kept it on hand for hopper cars. I just saw a car two weeks ago (this was in November 1990) in Port Clinton, Pennsylvania with straw filling a tear in the side sheet. The straw was used to fill any holes; but was used mostly, in my time, in the pocket doors. During the winter the doors would freeze up…some collieries had fire pits to "unfreeze" them (this was also done at steel mills and coke ovens); but this warped the doors badly and in some cases made the cars unsuitable for loading. Here in Shamokin, Pennsylvania, the *Glen Burn Colliery* used gas fire pits, which burned the bottoms out of a large number of Pennsylvania Railroad cars…naturally; the railroad charged the mine fore the damage. (From editor, Chuck Geletzke: When I worked for the Delray Connecting Railroad on Zug Island in Detroit, Michigan, we encountered a huge problem with our largest customer, the *Great Lakes Steel Corporation.* They would place loaded hopper cars carrying varying type of materials into their Thawing Shed and then basically forget about them! When the cars were returned to us, we often found that all of the gaskets in the entire airbrake system had been burned out of the car and needed replacement! In 1970 and 1971 this averaged about $2,000 to $3,000 per car!)

Sledge hammers did not help either! Another thing once common was seeing ice sickles hanging from the pocket doors. These often presented huge problems for local coal dealers located in

Chuck H Geletzke, Jr.

northern small towns. Often, only using a partial stick of dynamite was the only way to dislodge the car's contents.

Independence Street Crossing 1949 by artist, M. T. Zyla.

Gift of a Reading Steam Print

By: the late Robert K. Nairns

Merry Christmas (1990)!

It is with a very great pride that I send you this print as a Christmas present and also for so much you sent me in the past! There is so much of Bob (Wark) in this print…had to be loved to see it, as without his reminiscences of firing (Reading passenger trains) 6 and 97, all the do's and don't and little details of the "READING WAY" as he called it, this would just be another steam print.

The Print depicts the first run of 6 & 97-KING COAL as a named train instead of a numbered one in 1949…I will let Bob's words explain it.

The G3 class engine was kept in the engine house between runs. Around five in the morning the hostler brought the engine out of the engine house. She was gone-over, moved out to the coaling dock where she was coaled and watered and cleaned. Meanwhile the fireman and engineer reported in, grabbed a quick cup of hot coffee and a sandwich from the two colored dining attendants on 6 & 97's diner.

A final check of the engine by her crew, she hooked up to her train and pulled up and over onto the Eastbound Main. The yard switcher hooked onto the hind end car (the engine was pointed west out of town) and a final topping-off of water. It is now after seven and after a final check on inbound traffic the switcher towed our train down through town past the station, across the lower Independence Street road crossing to the east West Cross-over Switch. After clearing the switch, the switch engine cut-off, the switch was opened and now we waited for the signal to pull across to the Westbound Main up to the station to load for our 8:30 A.M. departure. Meanwhile the switch engine would come over the cross-over where her fireman would reset and lock the switches, and then hold the Main. At 8:30 we'd "whistle off" and start to pull with the switcher following us up to the yard. There she would return to her yard duties.

"Safety at all times, always be a minute or two early if you can; but never be unsafe!" (Robert Wark)

So, here you have the 211 pulling across the lower Independence St. crossing up (to the depot) to load. I was nine years old that year. Mr. Zyla (the artist) kept the original and Print No. 1. He gave me Print No. 2 of 950 prints. I understand yours is numbered in the low hundred's (I didn't want to unroll it from the mailing tube). Inside is a Certificate of Authenticity signed and numbered as is the print also…by Mr. Zyla. If you frame it, the certificate is pasted on the reverse of the frame. Mine was placed in an envelope attached to the frame as he was unsure I'd like the frame (WHAT ME!)…Who'd think a year ago I'd be doing this!?!

I am going to try to send this by UPS through our plant, where I work…let me know how you receive it?

Once again, Merry Christmas from all of us, yours, Bob

158

Westbound GTW Train 21 is seen at Clay Ave., having just departed Milwaukee Jct. in Detroit, Michigan in 1959 with 4-8-4 Northern 6327. The train is running "with the current of traffic" on the Westbound Mainline; but if another train operating in the same direction, was required to run on the Eastward Main, it would be required to comply with Whistle Signal 14q.   (Fred Furminger photo)

Michael T.

By: C. H. Geletzke, Jr.

Before I go on any further with a discussion about Operating Rule 14q, let me tell you a little about a Detroit & Toledo Shore Line Railroad (D&TSL) Conductor, the late, M. L. "Mike" T. Now I know that we are not supposed to speak ill of the dead; but let me state that Mike was truly a great guy and well liked by the majority of his fellow Shore Line employees; but let me just say that Mike was unique in the industry.

It All Starts <u>Here</u> and Other Railroad Stories

      I first met Mike in May 1979 when I was transferred to the D&TSL as Trainmaster in Toledo, Ohio from the GTW in Kalamazoo, Michigan. When I was first introduced to this Conductor, who was about my age, I could not believe how big he was! Just guessing, I would estimate his weight to have been somewhere between 400 and 500 pounds! He probably stood about 5'10". The entire time that we worked together I could never imagine how he passed the railroad's physical exams!?! I never once mentioned this to my superiors as I assumed that they were fully aware of Mike's condition. Let me state that on the plus side, Mike did show up for work every day for every assignment!

      Since I just explained the basics of the D&TSL's "Universal Seniority" system, I still marvel at the way most of the senior trainmen worked together with Mike, basically recognizing his "disability."

      For an example, Mike was so large…he would not fit through the cab doors on any *General Electric* locomotives! I always wondered what he would do if he ever had to get off a train in a hurry!?! This was years before many railroads banned getting on and off of moving equipment, and Mike could not do that if he had to! In addition to his grip and lunch (which we'll talk about shortly), Mike carried his own step-stool…with a rope attached; so after stopping he could lower it to the ground and later lift it aboard the train after he boarded.

      I recall working the Shore Line end of the "Flint Run" (Trains 421/422) as the regular engineer back in March 1991 and Mike was the regular Conductor. We would take Train 421 north out of Lang Yard in Toledo, Ohio until we met our counterpart, GTW Train 422, which originated in Flint, Michigan. We would always meet somewhere between Dearoad Yard in River Rouge, Michigan and Pontiac Yard…always in an area with multiple tracks. In making the meet, both trains would stop with their locomotives side by side, adjacent to one another. Once stopped the Engineer and Head Brakeman would secure their belongings and then we would swap trains. Once headend crews had changed, one or both trains (depending upon the location and the length of each train) would pull ahead until the two cabooses were side by side…then they would stop. Let me state that all of us endeavored to stop the cabs perfectly parallel to one another; but just ask any Locomotive Engineer that stopped a little too soon or perhaps a little tardy, requiring the tailend crews to walk an extra car length or two…may God help them after

Mike T. finally climbed aboard! Mike wanted and expected a perfect stop! Once stopped, he would lower his step stool, climb down very carefully, carry all of his belongings to the other caboose including his stool, climb aboard, and then pull the stool up on one of the end platforms using his rope. As I've stated, I just could not believe that railroad management condoned him working in this manner!?!

Now let's talk about Mike's lunch. While the majority of us always carried a normal average size lunch…generally enough for two meals, Mike carried a fully packed shopping bag…on EVERY trip! Even if it was a job that was normally allowed time to go to a restaurant, such as the unit coal trains taking the loads up to the *Detroit Edison Monroe Power Plant*, having to wait for the cars to be unloaded, and then return with the empties…it did not matter, Mike ALWAYS started each trip with that full shopping bag! Let me state also, that it was always empty by the end of the trip…I am sure he considered an extra trip to a restaurant a bonus! I have been told by a number of crew members that on many trips, Mike's shopping bag would be empty after only two or three hours on duty.

On at least one occasion, while switching the *Consumers Power Whiting Power Plant* in Erie, Michigan, Mike was sitting up in the cab with the engineer and not only ate his own lunch; but polished off the lunch of one of his fellow trainmen who was out on the ground doing the work! I was amazed an issue was never made of that and that an investigation was not conducted.

Mr. T. had three major interests that I was aware of. He was a "big time" gun collector, a hunter, and a model railroader. Mike always drove a full-size pickup truck and one year he went on a hunting trip to West Virginia. Now because of his size and lack of mobility he would usually hunt right from the back of the truck or the side of the road. I don't know whether he had friends accompanying him or if he just hunted alone? Anyway, after he returned from one of these outings, I will never forget him telling everyone in the Lang Yard office about some of the excitement he encountered on this journey. Apparently he was hunting along the side of a dirt road way back in the woods all by himself. All at once he realized that he needed to go to the bathroom. Being an experienced hunter, he carried a small portable potty in the rear of his truck. He removed it from the trucks cap enclosed bed and set it on the ground right behind the truck. Mike had no sooner got seated when all at once a school bus pulled up alongside of him and stopped…just imagine, ALL of the kids ran over to that side of the vehicle, pointed at him, and started laughing! What a sight that must have made!!! As I stated, Mike told us all about it!

Mike had a young son, also named Mike, who too hired out and was promoted to Conductor in 1995. When I first met him he appeared to be in excellent physical shape having played football in high school; but after several years he qualified as a yardmaster and in time was on the way to surpassing his father in girth. Sadly he passed away shortly after his father at the age of only 35!

Now let's tie this into our story…

I guess that this was what totally amazed me! On every division, in every craft, on every railroad I was ever around, seniority was everything! As an employee moved up the seniority list he or she was enabled to hold a better job, which was usually better paying or at the very least had better working conditions. So just imagine on the Shore Line senior employees voluntarily taking a lower paying position requiring more physical labor to allow a junior grossly overweight employee to collect more money sitting on his posterior!?! In some respects I can see where it may have been the good Christian thing to do; but then I used to wonder, were they in fact contributing to his problem of obesity? In the end, Mike passed away too at a relatively young age and never reached retirement…very sad!

Rule 14q

By: C. H. Geletzke, Jr.

Rule 14.   **ENGINE WHISTLE SIGNALS**

Note: Engine whistle signals must be sounded as prescribed by this rule. The signals are illustrated by "o" for short sounds; "—" for longer sounds. Each sound of the whistle should be distinct, with intensity and duration proportionate to the distance the signal is to be conveyed.

Rule	Sound	Indication
14(q)	--o	When running against the current of traffic:
		(1) At frequent intervals and approaching stations, curves or other

Chuck H Geletzke, Jr.

> points where view may be obscured.
>
> (2) Approaching passenger or freight trains and when passing freight trains.
>
> (3) Preceding the signals prescribed by (d) and (e). (NOT RELEVENT TO THIS DISCUSSION.)

Now let me tell you how Mike T. fits into this story.

Operating Rule 14q is one of those rules that fell out of use after the railroads began utilizing radios. I would venture to say that today and even back as early as the late 1970's, unless a locomotive engineman was really up on his rules, most would not even know the purpose of this rule or ever actually apply it.

Thus, when I was appointed Supervisor of Locomotive Engineers in 1993, whenever I conducted Rules or an Engineer Promotion Class, Rule 14q and its use was one that I would stress and encourage engineers to use.

Beginning in my first class, I developed a favorite way of explaining and teaching the rule. I would say, "Just imagine, you are the engineer on a northbound train on a dark or foggy night and you are about to come off the Highline at Milwaukee Junction and proceed around the Highline Wye onto the Holly Subdivision. As you proceed cautiously around the wye, way up ahead, you spot the markers on the tailend of a caboose, on a train occupying the Westbound Mainline. But, you have been instructed to run 'against the current of traffic' on the Eastward Main Track. As you ease onto the Eastward Track, you blow a long and a short blast (Rule 14q) using your locomotive's whistle. Now what you don't know is, that Michael T. is the Conductor on that train on the Westward Track and he is lying on one of the bunks in the caboose, and all at once, he spots a beam of light as your headlight illuminates the interior of his caboose! But, rather than jump up in a panic, Michael T. knows his Operating Rules, and when he hears that Long Blast of the whistle, followed by a short, he knows that you are going to be running on the other track and that he can roll over and just relax!" This fictitious story never failed to fill the classroom with laughter!

One more Rule 14q Story

By: C. H. Geletzke, Jr.

163

I guess it was in the late 1980's and I was holding the GTW Engineer's job on one end of 439 and 438 between Flat Rock and Battle Creek, Michigan. This job worked seven days a week, departing Flat Rock one evening, working its way to Battle Creek a distance of 187 miles, laying over in the hotel, and then returning the next day.

Larry Williams was my regular conductor and one night we were ordered late out of "the Creek" on our eastward trip. Now because another eastward train was having a problem on the Eastward Main Track somewhere between McAllister Road (at the east end of Battle Creek Yard) and Charlotte, the Train Dispatcher issued us orders stating that we "had right over opposing trains on the Westward Track McAllister Road (M.P. 181) to Mill (M.P. 216.1)."

As we pulled out of the yard and approached the Restricting Signal at McAllister Road I blew a long and a short blast on the whistle. Once our entire train was out on the Westward Mainline, I increased speed. But, let me state that there are a tremendous number of curves between this area and the town of Charlotte. As I approached or entered each curve and at other points, I blew Whistle Signal 14q on the diesel's horn. Oh yes, additionally I blew Whistle Signal 14j (four shorts) as I passed fellow locomotive engineer, modeler, and railfan, Jack Ozanich's home, located high on the hill on the north side of the tracks at approximately Milepost 183.5...this I did traditionally on EVERY trip! I continued blowing Whistle Signal 14q where necessary all the way to Mill on the west side of Lansing, our state's capitol. From there, Larry and the rest of our crew and I just worked our way back to Flat Rock.

You would think that this would be the end of this story; but not quite! On our next trip back to Battle Creek a day later, I was informed that I was to see the Trainmaster upon arrival in the Cereal City." As I entered the supervisor's office, he asked, "Just what the hell were you doing last night?"

I replied, "I have no idea what you are referring to!?!"

The Trainmaster, John Robertson,who once actually worked for me, went on to say that last night he had received a telephone call from another Locomotive Engineer's wife, complaining about an eastbound train that passed her home at about two o'clock in the morning..."blowing the horn excessively!" He then asked, "What was that all about?"

Chuck H Geletzke, Jr.

I then responded, "I was just complying with Operating Rule 14q."

At that point, the Trainmaster had to confess that he did not have a clue as to what Rule 14q was; so we got out the rulebook and had a "mini-rules class." Following our discussion, the relatively young official admitted he had never heard of Rule 14q, and agreed that I was indeed complying with it explicitly; but then he concluded the discussion with, "in the future, perhaps you can ease off the whistle a little a mile or two east of the yard!?!"

End of story.

Oh yes, after I told Jack Ozanich what had occurred he laughed and said, "I knew that was you, and I knew exactly what you were doing! The only two other guys on the entire system that would have done the same thing were Larry Bolton and Jack Tyson and I knew that neither of them were in the area!"

GTW Train EM-12 with the BN 5042-7152-____ at Battle Creek, MI on October 18, 1993 in route to Detroit Edison in Monroe, MI. (Jack G. Tyson photo)

Once Again We Violated the Federal Hours of Service Law!

It All Starts Here and Other Railroad Stories

By: Charles H. Geletzke, Jr.

Okay, I will admit that what I did was against the law...and wrong!

On Tuesday, March 2, 1993 I was called by the Grand Trunk Western Railroad (GTW) crew dispatcher in Troy, Michigan to be taxied from our yard office in Hamtramck, Michigan 125 miles west, to Battle Creek to work Train EM-66, a loaded Detroit Edison coal train that had originated in Montana and was destined for their Monroe, Michigan power plant. Our train was ordered for 12 o'clock noon. On this trip I was working with Conductor, Paul Henson and Brakeman, Conwell Avery, two experienced railroaders. We climbed in the cab and left town at 12:10 P.M. We arrived at "the Creek" at 2:00 P.M. Upon our arrival, the yardmaster informed us that our train, powered by the BN 7132-BN 7210-BN 7913 (three SD40-2's) had died under the Federal Hours of Service Law at Marcellus, Michigan (Milepost 135.5) and 43.5 miles west of Battle Creek! Apparently the train had three "kickers" near the rear end of the train. Kickers were problems with the air brakes on an individual car, which, when the air was applied, would cause the entire train to go into EMERGENCY! Apparently a Relief Crew had already been sent out from Battle Creek Yard (Milepost 181) and they finally arrived with our train at a little after 6:00 P.M. I am sorry; but my notes do not state whether the three "Bad Order" cars were set-out at Battle Creek, or if the problems were rectified. Never the less, we departed at 6:40 P.M. with 116 loads of western coal.

We had a straight shot over to Durand (M.P. 253.3) and pulled to a stop west of the diamond at 8:50 P.M. where we encountered Train 200 (a hot piggy-back train) ahead of us; and both of us had to meet westbound Train 439 coming off the single track Holly Subdivision. Our signal finally popped up and we departed at 9:35 P.M.

At the little town of Holly, Michigan we crossed the C&O diamond and headed-into the C.T.C. (Centralized Traffic Control) Siding (M.P. 46.7) to meet Train 207, a hot merchandise train for Chicago. We pulled to a stop at 10:20 P.M. and started to pull at 10:35 P.M. We now only had one hour and twenty-five minutes remaining to work...our goal was to make it to Detroit, where we would be relieved by a former Detroit & Toledo Shore Line (D&TSL) crew...it was going to be close!

Chuck H Geletzke, Jr.

We got back up to our maximum allowed speed of 40 mph (for mineral trains) and pulled through Pontiac Yard (M.P. 27) with about forty minutes remaining to work…then we encountered a red Stop signal at M.A.L. Crossing (M.P. 25.4), stopped and started pulling after receiving permission from the Train Dispatcher to pass the red signal. Then at Milepost 24.2, Yellow Cab we encountered another Stop Signal. Again we received permission that after stopping for the red signal we could proceed on the South Track…we later learned that this dispatcher HAD THE C.T.C. SYSTEM LINED-UP IN THE WRONG DIRECTION! By now we had about fifteen minutes remaining to work and we encountered Restricting Signals all the way down the Hill to Birmingham!

Our tailend cleared Opdyke Road (M.P. 22.2) at exactly midnight. We were now officially "DEAD!" Here was where I made a "managerial decision." I knew that if we stopped here that the cab driver that was being sent to pick us up would have a next to impossible chance of finding us…particularly in the dark of night! Instead I pulled down to the depot in Birmingham (M.P. 17.8) and rolled to a stop at 12:20 A.M. We never told the dispatcher exactly what time we arrived over the radio. We just said, "Send our ride to the Birmingham depot."

Miraculously, our ride with the Shore Line crew was there waiting for us and after changing crews, we departed in the cab and arrived back at Hamtramck at 12:45 A.M. and tied-up at 1:00 A.M. Miraculously, we never heard another word about our violation! If this same event occurred only as short a time as three years later, we would all be spending a minimum of one year "on the street!"

"So Chuck, if you went to work at noon, got off at 1 o'clock the next morning, when did you go back to work again?"

I worked with the same crew again at 9:00 P.M., March 3rd on Trains 433/432 to Battle Creek.

What's That?

By: Charles H. Geletzke, Jr.

On March 7, 1993 Grand Trunk Western Railroad (GTW) Conductor, Joe Ferro, Brakeman, J. C. Self, and I were returning from Battle Creek, Michigan to Detroit on Train N-080, a National Steel Corporation steel train. For power we had the GTW 5724-

167

5732-5833 (three GP38-2's) and our train was made-up of 45-empty NSAX coil steel gondolas. We had previously arrived in Battle Creek on westbound Train N-087, tied-up at 11:15 P.M., and went to the hotel for rest. On this, our return trip, we were ordered for 7:15 P.M., having had exactly eight hours rest.

Our eastward trip was turning out to be exceptional and believe it or not, we only made one stop, and that was at Gaines for only five minutes at 10:00 P.M. From there we shot right down to Detroit, right over to West Detroit where we stopped for only ten minutes beginning at 11:50 P.M., over the N&W's Wabash Old Mainline, and then we were held-out of Flat Rock yard at Ecorse, by the Flat Rock Yardmaster from 12:30 A.M. to 12:50 A.M.

We finally were given the okay to proceed on into Flat Rock Yard; but unbelievably, the yardmaster never bothered to mention that he had an empty Detroit Edison (all DEEX hoppers) unit train being held out between Fort Street and Allen Road…just east of the yard, and it did not even have a marker on the north end!! Now picture this, at this hour of the morning, it was dark…really dark; but thankfully it was not foggy. We passed Conrail's FN tower and then rounded the curve approaching Fort Street. All at once, J. C. Self shouted out, "WHAT'S THAT???" He stated that he had spotted a mere glimmer of our headlight's beam reflecting off metal objects up ahead! We were only running 20 mph and I immediately brought our train to a safe stop…but what if it had been foggy, or J. C. had not been on the ball? Yes, we were working in yard limit territory; but sometimes we all appreciate a little help! Thank God!

After a rather unpleasant discussion with the yardmaster over the radio, we finally proceeded into Flat Rock Yard, yarded our train, took our units to the house, and waited for a ride. Our ride picked us up at 1:40 P.M., we were driven back to Hamtramck and tied-up at 2:45 A.M.

I was called off the Engineer's Extra Board to work again at 5:00 P.M. on Train N-091, a loaded coiled steel train later that same day.

New Personal Record!

By: Charles H. Geletzke, Jr.

On March 15, 1993 Conductor, J. C. Self, Brakeman, T. D. Klein, and I were called to report to the B.O.C. yard office in

Chuck H Geletzke, Jr.

Hamtramck, Michigan (a suburb of Detroit) at 5 o'clock in the morning to bring Train 222, a "Hot Stak-Pak Train" from Battle Creek to Flat Rock, Michigan. The van arrived to pick us up and drive us the 125 miles to Battle Creek and we departed at 5:15 A.M. We arrived there at 7:15 A.M.

The train consisted of only four loaded stack-packs and was being pulled by the GTW 5826 (GP38)-5721 (GP38-2)-4624 (GP9R) a total of 5,750 horse-power!

We departed the Cereal City (Milepost 178.6) at 7:55 A.M. and rolled through Durand (M.P. 253.3 on the Flint Sub. and M.P. 67 on the Holly Sub.) at 9:10 A.M. That was 74.7 miles in one hour and ten minutes.

From Durand I showed our time arriving at 9 Mile Road (M.P. 10.8) the northern border of our Detroit Terminal at 10:16 A.M. That equaled 56.2 miles in one hour six minutes, or a total of only two hours and sixteen minutes for our total of 130.9 miles...definitely my Best Trip Ever! We continued rolling on down to Milwaukee Jct. (M.P. 4.6) and encountered a red signal at 10:25 A.M. The Conrail towerman held us for fifteen minutes and we got underway once again at 10:40 A.M.

From this point on our trip reverted to normal. We pulled down to the Conrail diamonds at West Detroit and stopped at 11 o'clock. We sat there for twenty-five minutes and got underway again at 11:25 A.M. From there we ran the rest of the 27 miles to Flat Rock Yard arriving at 12:05 P.M. and were held out of the yard for 25 minutes. Once released, we pulled into the yard at 12:35 P.M., yarded our train, and took our engines to the house.

We then were taxied back to Hamtramck and went off duty at 2:55 P.M. As you can see, a total of nine hours and 55 minutes for the entire trip was nothing spectacular; but two hours and 16 minutes from Battle Creek to Detroit's Yard Limit Board, that was a new personal record for me! Oh yes, and the sad part was that I wasn't even really trying from Battle Creek to Durand!

The next morning after writing the above story, it occurred to me that I should probably give you an idea of what approximate eastbound running times were for freight trains from Battle Creek to Detroit. On a normal trip I used to figure from Battle Creek to Lansing took 50 minutes, then, one hour from Lansing to Durand. On the Holly Subdivision running time from Durand to Pontiac was about one hour and down the hill from Pontiac to Detroit about 30 minutes. Westward running times were essentially the same with the

169

exception of tugging trains up the hill from Ferndale to Pontiac could easily add one hour to the trip depending up the length and tonnage of the train. Summing it up, a normal eastward trip from Battle Creek to Detroit should be about three and one-half hours and an average westbound run should take about four and one-half hours excluding stops and work enroute. Now if the trips originated or terminated in Flat Rock, you could generally add two hours in each direction.

Another Good Trip!

By: C. H. Geletzke, Jr.

I just completed writing the preceding story when I ran across the notes for an even better trip that occurred on Saturday, August 7, 1993.

On the day previous, Conductor, Paul Henson; Brakeman, H.R. "Home Run" or "Rod" Baker; and I had a twelve hour trip from Flat Rock to Battle Creek aboard GTW Train 439. We were then relieved at 1:00 A.M. outside of "the Creek," and taken to the hotel, where we spent the next eight hours.

At 7 o'clock in the morning our phones rang and naturally, it was the crew caller calling to inform us that we were marked for Train 438, on duty at 9:00 A.M.

About thirty minutes before our on-duty time a crew driver pulled-up to the hotel and drove us to the store for groceries, and then on to the West Tower. This day our train consisted of only 18 loads and 13 empties and on the "business end," we had six units, the GTW 5714 (GP38-2)-6201 (GP 38)-6415 (GP40)-5831 (GP38-2)-4704 (GP9)-6252 (SD38). Rod Baker and I immediately went to the Locomotive Shop, inspected and prepared our units, and with the permission of the yardmaster, tied on our train. We departed at 10:30 A.M.

On this day it turned-out we had a straight shot right across the Flint Subdivision over to Durand, where we passed right through the Chicago Wye at 11:55 A.M. From there it was an unbelievable non-stop straight shot down the Holly Subdivision to Milwaukee Jct., and from there the final 24 miles to Flat Rock Yard was also made without any delays! I believe this was the first and perhaps the only trip I ever made from "the Cereal City" to "Level Pebble" without stopping! We pulled into a yard track there and stopped at

Chuck H Geletzke, Jr.

2:00 P.M. **That made it a 3-Hour 30-minute trip!!!** Most crews only get one or two of these in their entire careers on a busy railroad!

Where I learned to Railroad!

As told by: PC-CR-DT&I Conductor, and GTW-CN Locomotive Engineer, Judson Targett

When I first met Jud Targett in 1993 he was an Engineer Trainee in my Locomotive Engineer Training Class at Flat Rock, Michigan. Jud began his railroad career in Columbus, Ohio as a Trainman shortly after the formation of the Penn Central. He continued working the road out of the various Cincinnati and Columbus terminals into the transition to Conrail and then on April 1, 1976 transferred to the Detroit, Toledo & Ironton (DT&I) working out of Springfield, Ohio. When the GTW acquired the DT&I in 1980, Jud became a GTW Conductor. After the "Judster's" promotion to Locomotive Engineer in 1993 we became good friends and still are to this day.

As I got to know Jud, I learned that he was from a railroad family. His mother was a telegrapher and tower operator for the B&O, generally working in the Columbus area. She worked the preponderance of her career as a tower operator in the Alum Creek tower where the B&O crossed the PRR. One of Jud's brothers had a career in management for the N&W and later the Norfolk Southern. Jud's sister became an NS Locomotive Engineer, his brother-in-law was a machinist in the NS shops in Columbus, and a second brother, the only non-railroader, had a thirty year career in the U. S. Army.

Jud told me that his Mom primarily worked second trick at Alum Creek and during the summer months would frequently take Jud or one of his siblings to work with here…consequently, they all grew-up learning how to railroad.

In one of our conversations, Jud recalled how right to the end, Alum Creek tower, which was only 3.2 miles from Columbus Union Station, was heated by a coal furnace. Jud stated that during the winter months his mother would always shovel coal into the furnace's firebox to insure plenty of heat before she climbed the stairs to the tower's third floor at the beginning of each shift. Similarly, she would generally walk down the stairs before the end

171

of her day and heave more coal into the furnace to insure that her relief too had a warm office when he began work. Jud said that he never forgot how dimly lit the downstairs furnace room of the tower was, with its single light bulb…covered in coal dust. The only time it was clean was when it was replaced; and that only lasted for several hours at best!

Recently Jud sent me a Bob McCord photo of Alum Creek, which he found in a group of photos in the John Fuller collection. Jud's comment regarding one of the shots was "Why does Alum Creek tower have that huge pile of coal next to it lying on the ground?"

I replied, "No doubt, that was for your Christmas stocking!!!"

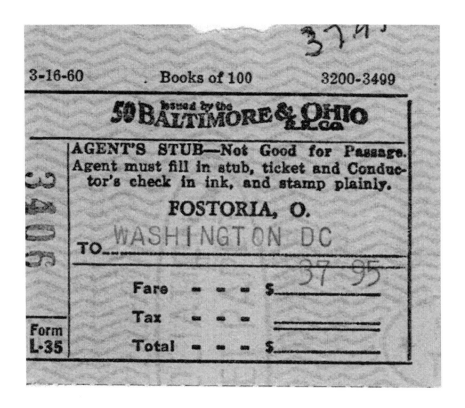

Chapter 10
The Last Time Back in the Craft

An eastbound GTW piggy-back train is seen rolling through the Chicago Wye at Durand, Michigan enroute to Detroit on August 25, 1979. (Robert J. Wise photo)

Rolling the Dice...with the FRA!

By: C. H. Geletzke, Jr.

I am hoping that by now enough time has elapsed so that I will not get into any trouble telling this story!?! As a side note please allow me to begin by stating that only two months prior to our story I resigned my position of Supervisor of Locomotive Engineers at Flat Rock, Michigan and exercised my seniority as a Locomotive Engineer.

On May 16, 1995 I was called off the Grand Trunk Western Railroad's (GTW) Engineer's Extra Board at Hamtramck, Michigan (a suburban community within the city limits of Detroit) to work Train 255 to Battle Creek. My crew of Conductor, Ray King and Brakeman, Jerry "Mushroom" Maslonka, and I tied up at 9:30 P.M.

Exactly eight hours later, at 5:30 A.M., we were back on duty, heading back home aboard Train 438. For this leg of the trip, we had GTW 6423 (GP40)-EMD 406 (SD40)-GTW 6401 (GP40) for power and we would be tugging on 31 loads and 36 empties for a total of 4,445 gross tons. After clearing eastbound Train 274 we departed Battle Creek Yard (Milepost 180.6) at 7:10 A.M.

We pulled to a stop at Lansing Yard (M.P. 217.5) at 8:05 A.M. where we were instructed to pick-up 14 loads and 1 empty. As we began pulling our "pick-up" back to our train on the Mainline, a man climbed aboard and I immediately recognized him as F.R.A. (Federal Railroad Administration) Inspector, Bill Spry. We had met several times before and knew him to be a decent guy; but one who was "All Business!" I did not have any problem with that. We tied back on our train, completed the proper Intermediate Terminal Air Test and departed at 8:50 A.M.

In no time at all we cruised right over to Durand (M.P. 253.3), pulled up to a red signal, and stopped at 9:45 A.M. It was at this point that we received a rare request from TD#2 the Holly Subdivision Train Dispatcher…he instructed us to pull around onto the Holly Sub. and pick-up 3 loaded piggy-back flat cars out of the South Siding. Doing as we were told we pulled around to the east end of the South Siding, stopped at Pitt (M.P. 65.5), where the Ann Arbor Railroad diverged from using joint trackage on our Mainline, and made our pick-up. It was at this point where things began to get interesting! Many of you will recall that at this time, in the mid-1990's, FRA markers (Federal Rear End Devices or "Fred's" on some roads) and RDU's (Receiver Display Units) on locomotives were still fairly new technology wise. Up until now I knew that our FRA marker and RDU had worked perfectly all the way over the road. But here at Pitt, I was guessing that we were in a "Dead Spot!?!" You see; after picking up the three cars and re-coupling the air hoses, we should have received an electronic reading from the marker on the tailend telling us that we had sufficient air pressure on the rear of the train. In the event that we could not establish the correct pressure, one of the trainmen, technically, should have walked all the way to the last car, verified the air pressure with me over the radio, observed the set-up and release, and then walked all the way back to the locomotives…that would have been the proper way to do things. Anyway, there I was sitting in my seat and looking across the cab at Inspector Spry, who at least so far was still sitting in the Fireman's seat, and I was just praying that he would not get up and walk across the cab to look at the air gauges! Now normally, at least at that time, as air pressure would increase on the tailend, in

Chuck H Geletzke, Jr.

various increments, a little bell would ring on the RDU and so far, this was not happening! So, periodically, I would reach up and every so often press the manual bell button, which too would ring the same bell making the appropriate sound. Up until now at least, Mr. Spry was not taking any exception to anything I was doing...I prayed a little harder! When I thought that we probably had sufficient air pressure on the tailend (this was from years of experience), I just reached up, grabbed the Automatic Brake Valve Handle, and applied the brakes. Mr. Spry was still sitting contentedly in his seat. After the air stopped exhausting, I waited 50 seconds, while Brakeman Maslonka observed that the brakes applied on all three of the cars that we just added to our train. Then, I released the brakes and "the Mushroom" physically observed that the brakes on those three cars released too. Still Mr. Spry was sitting in his seat. Oh yes, then as the air came back up in the trainline, once again I rang that little manual bell every so often...believe me, I knew that I was treading on thin ice here! Once I thought that the brakes had probably properly released on the entire train, I informed Conductor King that I thought we were ready and released the Independent Brake on the locomotives and opened the throttle. Would you believe that we didn't roll much more than one car length and the proper air pressure popped-up on my RDU, that little bell rang, and I began feeling much better...NO, that's not the end of the story!

No sir, just after the rear car began to wiggle, over the radio I heard, "Assistant Superintendent, Lewis to Train 438, the Extra 6423 East. Over."

Conductor King immediately answered and responded, "This is the headend of GTW Train 438 the Extra 6423 East answering. Over."

With that, Mr. Lewis stated that they had been observing the Marker on our tailend (which back there worked perfectly) and told us that he and Superintendent Ty Gibson were performing an ET (Efficiency Test) and that we had done everything perfectly in accordance with the rules!

I couldn't believe it! Until the trip was over, I never even told Conductor King or the Mushroom what I was doing...and Praise the Lord, Mr. Spry apparently had no idea either!

With that we departed at 10:35 A.M. rolled right down to Pontiac (M.P. 27) and set-out the three cars. Let me state that Mr. Spry did have me slow down to a crawl at West Pontiac (M.P. 30.4) where he detrained.

175

Once he was off, I told Ray and Jerry what I had done. We than ran down to Flat Rock, arrived at 3:10 P.M., yarded our train. Bussed back to Hamtramck and tied up at 5:00 P.M.

That was a trip I will never forget!!!

A southbound CN (former GTW) train with the CN 9509 & 96__ is seen passing through the Delray interlocker on the southwest side of Detroit enroute to Flat Rock, Michigan on June 10, 1993. (Jack G. Tyson photo)

A TIGHT Trainline!

By: C. H. Geletzke, Jr.

It just dawned on me that I certainly cannot publish another book without including at least one "close call" story!

The date was September 8, 1996 and GTW Conductor, Larry Williams and I were returning from Battle Creek to Flat Rock, Michigan on Grand Trunk Western (GTW) Train 458…our regular seven day assignment. We had earlier tied-up at Battle Creek (M.P. 178 on the Flint Sub.), the previous evening at 10:00 P.M., after working westward on Train 255. Now, having had nine hours rest we were ordered for 7 o'clock A.M. On this morning we had plenty of

Chuck H Geletzke, Jr.

power…the GTW 5850 (GP38-2)-6407 (SD40)-5721 (GP38)-6202 (GP38)-6412 (SD40 "dead in tow")…that's 9,000 horsepower, not counting the dead SD40. After setting-out one Bad Order empty, we completed our Initial Terminal Brake Test and departed at 8:30 A.M. with only 20 loads and 24 empties for a total of 3,034 tons.

At our state's capitol (M.P. 217) we stopped at 9:20 A.M. and picked up an additional 13 loads, giving us a total of 4,044 tons. We were underway at 9:50 A.M.

On this trip, we passed right through Durand (M.P. 253.3 on the Flint Sub. and M.P. 67 on the Holly Sub.) and then had to stop at Gaines (M.P. 62.7), the first community on the Holly Subdivision, where from 10:50 until 11:00 A.M, we waited for westbound Train 243.

Our next stop was at the terminal of Pontiac (M.P. 27) at 12:15 P.M., where we were instructed to pick-up 12 loads and 5 empties, which now gave us 45 loads and 29 empties, a total of 74 cars. With our work completed we departed at 1:00 P.M. and rolled straight down to Delray, a tower on Detroit's southwest side and stopped at 2:20 P.M., a distance of 29.8 miles. As was quite common, we sat there for 15 minutes departing at 2:35 P.M. Now, unbeknown to us, while we were standing there, something happened to our train! It turned out that one of the local kids "angle-cocked" our train! That is to say that one of them closed the angle cock on the rear of our 43rd car…and because we had an exceptionally tight train line, with virtually no leakage, the air pressure NEVER declined on the rear 74th car of our train!

After receiving a Restricting Signal at Delray we pulled right down to D&I Jct. at Flat Rock, a distance of another 14.8 miles, where we planned on stopping at the north end of the yard. As it turned out, a Flat Rock yard job was switching on the north end of the North Yard and their engine, the GTW 4702, a GP9, was sitting right on the first switch that we would encounter. As I approached the yard I began drawing off air…guess what…there was no reduction on the tailend! I drew-off more…still nothing…THE PRESSURE ON THE GAUGE NEVER DROPPED! I then panicked and put the train in EMERGENCY and started blowing my horn in a continuous series of short blasts!

It was then that I saw the 4702 stop…RIGHT ON THE SWITCH…and Larry and I watched as engineer, Danny Tarter abandoned ship!

Praise the Lord; we stopped two car lengths short of hitting the locomotive! It was at that point that Larry began walking back toward the rear of our train and discovered the closed angle cock. While my Conductor was walking the train, I too got off and went over and apologized to the former DT&I engineman. Being a great guy, he was not upset at all; but was glad he was able to get off, and that we did not hit his engine!

What is amazing to me to this very day is the fact that we still had 43 cars on the headend of the train with properly operating brakes and 31 cars with the air "bottled," and the fact that the brakes on those 43 cars were not even close to being sufficient to safely stop that train! It goes to show, you cannot be too careful!

Once the air was restored and Larry was back aboard the headend, we pulled into the yard, yarded our train, and then taxied back to Hamtramck, where we tied-up at 6:00 P.M., an eleven hour day…that thankfully ended safely. That said, being experienced railroaders, Larry and I will always wonder, WHAT IF? And, we will never forget!

Three years earlier, Abby, Chip, and Travis (the Pirates fan) and I watched the Pirates beat the Cubs at Wrigley Field on August 5, 1993 (5 v 2) in a game that only lasted two hours and 27 minutes.

Anything for the fans…

By: C. H. Geletzke, Jr.

Surely I have mentioned before that my twin boys, daughter, and I are all baseball fans! As for my wife, she has always been pretty tolerant of our interest… That said, in 1996 I planned one of the best baseball adventures ever! Well, that was assuming the railroad cooperated!?!

Our outing was planned for June 19, 1998…the summer before my boy's started the 7th grade and my daughter was to become a high school sophomore. At that time, I was working as the regular engineer on Grand Trunk Western Trains 384 and 387 from Hamtramck, Michigan (we actually manned our train at Flat Rock) to Sarnia, Ontario. Once we arrived in Sarnia, we would taxi to Port Huron, go to the hotel for rest, and then return with Train 387 to Flat Rock, after which we would be bussed back to Hamtramck to tie up. That was a seven day a week job!

On this particular day everything seemed to be going fairly normal and hopefully we would be ordered early enough that I could get in, tie up, and pick-up the kids.

Just to fill in the blanks, on Thursday, June 18th, my Conductor, R. P. Brown, who was an extra man and I tied-up at Port Huron at 8:45 A.M. and went to the hotel. We were not ordered out for Train 387 until 8 o'clock P.M. For power we had the GTW 4907 (GP38-2)-5860 (GP38-2)-CV 5801 (GP38) with 44 loads and 7 empties a total of only 2,803 tons. We departed at 12:30 A.M. At Detroit we picked-up 35 more loads out of Farm Track #1, departed at 2:55 A.M. and headed for Flat Rock. After yarding our train we were bussed back to Hamtramck, where we tied-up at 7:10 A.M., which was already seven hours and ten minutes into my Personal Day!

I then drove the 61 miles home to Temperance, Michigan arriving at about 8:30 A.M. and picked up the kids who were anxiously waiting. I then grabbed a really quick breakfast and then we took off for our destination…Chicago!

Upon entering Chicago, we drove straight to Wrigley Field (Well, not exactly. My daughter just reminded me…first we had to stop on the way and purchase Chicago Style Hotdogs!!!) where the Cubs (with a record of 41x30) were to start against the Philadelphia Phillies (their record was 34x35) at 2:20 P.M. C.D.T. Let me state, this was an exciting game…it was all tied-up in the ninth at 8 runs each. At this point in addition to worrying about my Cubs; I was questioning the time…as it turned out the game went 12 innings and sadly, after four hours and 19 minutes of outstanding baseball seated in their fabulous Bleachers, our Cubs lost to the Phils 9 v. 8! But, don't worry, all four of us were real baseball fans, and we just happened to have tickets to see the White Sox play Minnesota!

Chuck H Geletzke, Jr.

So, with our first game over at 6:39 P.M. E.D.T. we headed south to Comiskey Park, where our second game was set to begin at 7:05 P.M. Fortunately, traffic was not too bad going in that direction and we arrived, parked, and found our seats during the first half of the first inning. In this game the (28 x 42) White Sox were competing against the (33 x 37) Minnesota Twins. Since none of us were really fans of either team, no one was sad that the Sox lost 10 to 6. This game only lasted three hours and 11 minutes; so we were on our way headed back to Michigan by about 10:45 P.M. (That would be 11:45 P.M. Michigan Time!)

By then I have to admit that it had already been one long night and one really long day! In all honesty, I was getting tired! Rather than endangering my children or myself, we elected to stop in Michigan City, Indiana and find a motel where we could sleep for several hours. The one we located was right down the street from the Chicago, South Shore & South Bend Railroad's shops. After getting some rest and eating a good breakfast, we once again got underway driving straight home.

Because I had taken the Personal Day on the 19th, I naturally had to miss the return trip on Train 387 on the 20th...for this I would not be paid.

Once home on the 20th, I was able to spend a nice day with my wife and did not have to go back to work until ordered for Train 384 once again at 9:30 P.M. on June 21st.

Such was the life of a Dad, a railroader, and a group of real baseball fans

Temperature Could Be Critical!

By: Octoraro Railway Conductor, Jack Barnett

As a very young newly minted conductor for the Octoraro Railway in Pennsylvania we used to get reefer (refrigerator) cars of potatoes in for the *Herr's Potato Chip* plant in Nottingham, PA. Our Trainmaster showed me the finer points of these cars, which old heads will remember as being very beaten and rotted SPFE or UPFE cars with very unreliable Detroit Diesel engines. I learned very early to despise these cars...

Brad, the Trainmaster, said, "Okay now listen, we are going to restart this junker and the first thing to know...at least it's not 20

181

degrees and snowing…oh, and it's not 1 A.M.!" As both of us
shoved the motor compartment door aside…it took two of us
because the door was so bent and warped, it didn't want to move. I
was instructed to climb into the very narrow space between the
motor and wall only to find out Brad thought it was funny to see me
do it and slip and slide on the oily floor for his amusement!

After a good laugh, for him, I proceeded to hit the Prime
Button and pull the Start Switch. The motor started, ran for 30
seconds and died…tried again…same result. Brad then said, "You
did check the fuel…correct?"

"Yes I did. It had 200 gallons when we picked it up."

Then Brad went to the fuel gauge and tapped on it…it went
from 200 right to zero!!! The temperature gauge was indicating the
load was still warm enough and would hold until the next morning
for delivery. I was so happy when those old cars were scrapped…but
also sad…the newbie's will never know the joys of dealing with
those old clunkers, and yes, later in my career I did deal with them at
1 A.M….in the snow…and rain…

More Abbreviations to Learn!?!

By: Octararo Railway Conductor, Jack Barnett

Again as a newbie I was doing a Car List for interchange on
the move. The card contained spaces for reporting marks and car
numbers; also the kind of car {Gondola=G, Reefer=RBL,
Boxcar=X}. There was one space that stumped me…a space called
LorE…

Puzzled, I asked my engineer, "What's lore?"

He looked at me with the same look I got from my father
when I told him I wanted to be a circus clown and he said…"IT
MEANS LOAD OR EMPTY YOU IDIOT!"

And he and I remain good friends to this day…36 years later!

CN (GTW) Conductor, Donald G. Swarbrick has climbed aboard a newly arrived switcher at the former D&TSL car shop at Lang Yard in Toledo, OH on March 18, 2003.

Those are ten-centers!

Conversation between Donald G. Swarbrick and C. H. Geletzke, Jr.

Many of you readers may recall in my last book, *"Soak It!!!;" and Other Railroad Stories* I told about how when I was nine years old I collected and returned empty soda (pop bottles in my part of the world) and beer bottles in order to earn enough money to purchase my first issue of *Model Railroader* Magazine in November 1958. Well let me state that being the son of parents who survived the Great Depression, I have always been shall we say, "rather frugal!" Secondly, the story did not end there…several nights ago I received a telephone call from one of the retired Conductors that I used to frequently work with…Donald S. Swarbrick. I believe that Don and I have been friends since about 1968 or 1969 and I must say that we worked as a pretty good team, both in the yard and on the road!

During our conversation Don said to me, "Do you recall how you used to take my empty pop bottles home?" I thought about it for a few seconds and then we both started laughing! Don said, "Yeh, I used to bring along two or three bottles of pop for each leg of our trip." At that time we were working a freight run from Flat Rock, Michigan to Sarnia, Ontario and after our arrival we would be bussed back over to Port Huron and sent to the hotel for at least eight hours before returning home. When we were ordered out of the hotel, the crew driver would take us to the local Super K-Mart and we would purchase groceries for the trip home (basically our breakfast and lunch) and once again, Don would procure several more bottles of soda. We did this seven days a week for weeks on end!

One day it occurred to me that Donald was throwing away roughly 60 cents a trip, which amounted to $2.10 a week. Thus we began a discussion on economics, which evolved into me basically giving him hell for the amount of money that he was just throwing away! I recall saying, "Don, do you know what my kids could do with that much money!?!" From there things progressed and eventually, I was carrying six empty pop bottles home to my children at the end of each trip…let me state that they greatly appreciated it.

Yes, I realize this kind of a story sounds totally ridiculous; but you must understand that when one has a degree in Economics, has three young children, and spends close to 12 hours a day in the cab of a locomotive with the same guy day after day, things do become crazy.

Let me conclude that yes, I was concerned about the $2.10 per week that Don was throwing away; but can you imagine the discussion we might have had if we had discussed the cost of the packs of cigarettes that he smoked each week!?! Just think of the money that he could now have invested!!!

Mislettered Unit

By: C. H. Geletzke, Jr.

On the morning of August 28, 2003 I was ordered, along with Conductor Donald G. Swarbrick, for our regular assignment, Train 384 from Flat Rock, Michigan to Sarnia, Ontario. We went on duty at 6:30 A.M. After reading the Bulletin Book I immediately walked out to the Fuel Dock to inspect and prepare my units for the day. In the consist we had the CN 6024 (SD40)-LLPX 3202 (GP40M-2)-CSXT 8663 (SD50). After stowing my gear in the lead unit, I immediately detected two problems with the two trailing units!

Chuck H Geletzke, Jr.

First of all, the CSXT unit was equipped with a feature known as *Smart-Start*, which was supposed to shut the engine down when not in use, and then automatically re-start when the Reverser of the controlling unit was placed in either the *Forward* or *Reverse* position. In theory, a wonderful fuel-saving feature…but like everything else, they needed to be maintained! I then walked over to the Fuel Dock office to find an electrician to possibly correct the problem. He and I walked over together and he simply cut-out the feature…so much for saving fuel!

I then resumed my inspection. At this point I encountered a problem, which I had experienced twice before…to varying degrees. My second unit was supposed to be the LLPX 3202; but it was lettered **St. Lawrence & Atlantic**!!! I then entered the engine's cab and stenciled above the Engineer's front windshield was: **SLR 3202**. Hmm??? At that point I examined the unit's "Blue Card" or *92-day Locomotive Inspection and Repair Record* (The final and ULTIMATE authority) and it and the *Daily Inspection Record* declared the unit to be the LLPX 3202 (LLPX is the railroad abbreviation for *Locomotive Leasing Partners LLC*)! Surprisingly, at that time, nowhere on the exterior of the unit could I locate the initials LLPX!?! Now just imagine if you were operating on a single track railroad and you as a knowledgeable and experienced railroader were given instructions to "Meet the Extra LLPX 3202" and the SLR 3202 showed up? What would you do? Personally, I would not turn a wheel and would contact the Train Dispatcher! So, on this day, that's exactly what I did…even though it was the middle unit in my consist and would not present significant operating problems…unless it wound-up as a leading unit. I considered this to be a violation of FRA (Federal Railroad Administration) Rule 229 and technically the unit should not be used as it was currently stenciled!!!

The Train Dispatcher instructed me to, "Take the unit as it is!"

Okay, the problem was now out of my hands.

From this point it became a normal trip. We doubled-up our train and departed with 37 loads and 45 empties, totaling 5,666 gross tons and we were only 5,547 feet in length. We arrived at East Yard in Detroit at 12:25 P.M. where we set out two "Bad Order" cars and picked-up 5 loads and 31 empties. Our train then consisted of 42 loads and 76 empties with 7,204 gross tons and was 8,398 feet in length. Following our departure at 1:50 P.M. we arrived at Modeland at the extreme east end of Sarnia Yard at 4:50 P.M., yarded our train and changed crews. We then taxied back to Port Huron and went off duty at 6:26 P.M. an 11 hour and 56 minute day.

We then went to the motel and waited for the call to work our way home on Train 383…when the call came, we were ordered for 2:45 A.M. Yes, tell me about normal sleep cycles; but that's another story!!!

My (first and only) visit to a Psychologist!

By: C. H. Geletzke, Jr.

If memory serves me correctly, I believe that I was involved in eight fatalities during my 45 year railroad career. Now you may detect a little uncertainty in that number. That's because during the early days on the job, if an accident resulted in a serious injury, the victim was transported immediately to the nearest medical facility, and with the differences in the forms of communication, if the accident did not evolve into a lawsuit, we often never heard the results or the final outcome of the injured person. I know that this sounds extremely cold; but in some instances, this probably helped maintain our sanity.

As an example, without going into specifics, on one trip we had a woman who failed to stop for the flashing lights at a grade crossing and drove right into the path of our train. When the dust settled, my conductor and brakemen found that her car was filled with cases of beer and she was on her way to the nearby tavern, which was less than 100 yards away! The location and date are not important; but after she was rushed to the hospital, we never were informed on her outcome…either way, it was a terrible event and just like all of the others, one that I will NEVER forget!

Let me state that every one of these accidents are documented in my timebooks and notebooks; but believe me, I have never compiled a total list. These are just incidents that occurred, that never go away completely, and all are ones that I would rather forget…unfortunately, it never happens completely. The only saving grace was that I knew in my heart that I was doing everything in the proper manner and in compliance with the rules at the time of the accident.

186

Chuck H Geletzke, Jr.

Again, without going into the specifics, early one dark and rainy Sunday morning in 2004 my new young conductor and I happened upon a woman out walking along the tracks...she was facing away from us. All at once, at what was probably the last possible second, she turned and faced us...looking me right in the eyes and jumped over directly in front of us and disappeared under the front of our locomotive! If this was not bad enough, I had just been a participant in a similar event only 24 days earlier!

Now throughout the earlier years of my railroad career I guess it was just expected that following an event such as this we would continue working and complete the trip...and then report for duty again the next day; but that was in the "old days," and perhaps in some respects it may have been beneficial...I'll leave that to the experts to discuss.

But, interestingly, the next day was my scheduled off day and then I received a call from a railroad manager instructing me to take the following two days off (with pay) for "Trauma." Additionally, the carrier had made an appointment for me to visit a Counselor/Psychologist on that coming Wednesday in nearby Toledo, Ohio.

This was to be my first ever visit to a counselor and I truly had no idea what to expect. While there, the young female practitioner asked me to explain in detail, exactly what occurred at the incident. Then, she proceeded to ask a multitude of detailed questions about the event. I guess I was there about an hour. At the conclusion of my visit, she stated, "You seem to be handling this quite well; but I have one more project that I would like you to complete. When you get home, perhaps this evening, would you sit down and write out, in your own handwriting, every detail about the event that you can recall...no matter how small or seemingly insignificant? Then I want you to just put those notes away somewhere. In fact, you don't have to look at them ever again if you don't want to."

It was at this point that I told her that I had been recording notes about every day of my railroad career from the very first day until the present.

She then stated, "Perhaps that is why you seem to be coping with this issue fairly well." The lady then stated that it would not be necessary for me to return; however if I had any psychological issues in the future dealing with this event, to please make an appointment with her.

It All Starts <u>Here</u> and Other Railroad Stories

Interestingly, here it is now over 19 years later and one other similar item has resulted from this discussion. When I began writing the stories for this series of books beginning in 2012, I noted that my memory was literally flooded with ideas for stories! Sometimes, even now I will waken in the middle of the night and a potential story will pop into my mind. I have since learned, that if I get an idea for a story, I'd better write down a few notes about it immediately…as I may not be able to recall it again in the morning. So, each time I get an idea I add it to my list…this was Story Number 832 and so far, I have published over 560 of them! Now you may wonder what on earth does writing down stories have to do with the details of a terrible incident on the railroad? Since I began my writing, as the psychologist suggested, once I have a story recorded, it literally seems to disappear from my memory!?! Try it!

CN (GTW) Conductor, Larry William is seen standing in front of the boarded-up B.O. C. (Buick-Oldsmobile-Cadillac) Yard Office in Hamtramck, MI on April 27, 2010. On this very day, Larry; Trainmaster, James Korn0as, and I pulled the last of the stored cars out of the yard. For years after the building was closed, you could still see the glowing lights of the remaining *Coca-Cola* machine through the window in the door on the left and its mate on the building's opposite side.

Chuck H Geletzke, Jr.

Quick, Lock the Door!

By: C. H. Geletzke, Jr.

In the early 1980's the *General Motors Corporation* elected to build a new assembly plant in Hamtramck, Michigan (a community completely encircled by the City of Detroit). The facility was to be called the *Buick-Oldsmobile-Cadillac Poletown Assembly Plant* and it was to be served by both Conrail and my employer, the Grand Trunk Western Railroad (GTW). (For complete details on the opening of this plant, see my story, "First Job to Switch Poletown" in my book *Go Ahead and Backup and Other Railroad Stories.*

Interestingly, I was the first Locomotive Engineer to switch the brand new facility on October 18, 1985 using the engine GTW 4902.

Sadly, due to a multitude of reasons, the railroad ceased serving the plant and the adjacent yard, rip track, and yard office, which were owned by the State of Michigan, on September 5, 2008. Following the shutdown, the yard office was completely boarded-up, with the exception of two tiny windows in each of several doors, which were considered way too small for anyone to access.

Until April 27, 2010 the GTW continued to store miscellaneous cars in the yard, which had nothing to do with the *GM Plant.* Believe it or not, I was called to be the Engineer on the final GTW job to pull all of the cars out of that yard that day!

Now here is the great part of the story…when the railroad closed the yard office and boarded up the building, they left a *Coca Cola* machine plugged in and still running in the lobby or Book-In Room on the ground floor of the structure. At night, anyone who passed could see the glow of its lights advertising its wares through the remaining tiny glass windows in the doors.

When I retired over three years later, and passed that red brick building on my final trip on December 3, 2011 that machine was still telling the world that it had *Coca Cola* products for sale! I have no idea who owned the machine or who paid the electric bill!?!

It could have been bad!

As told by: the late CN (GTW) Conductor, Archie D. Anderson

DCON 836 delivering to CN at East Yard on March 9, 2020. Note:
Air Compressor Shanty in the background.

     I want you to look at the little white shanty in the above
photo at the east end of Canadian National's (CN) former Grand
Trunk Western (GTW) East Yard in Hamtramck, Michigan. One
afternoon near quitting time, my good friend, A. D. "Archie"
Anderson was working the Utility Brakeman ("UB") job here at this
yard…I believe that it was in 2009 or 2010. The UB job was created
in order to assist trains and yard jobs that were changed to
"Conductor Only."

     Apparently things were relatively slow and Archie drove his
personal vehicle to the east end of the yard to await the arrival of the
next train he was to help. Now Archie always took pride in his
vehicles and kept them in immaculate condition! On this particular
day he was driving one of his smaller four-wheel drive vehicles.
While waiting and not wanting his truck to get dirty, he backed it
into the small Air Compressor Shanty, where it just fit. You see,
Illinois Central management, which had recently taken over the
operation of the former GTW deemed the air compressor irrelevant
and an unnecessary expense and had it disconnected and removed.

Chuck H Geletzke, Jr.

They left the empty shanty standing.

Being a hot humid day, Archie pulled down the overhead door and while trying to stay cool, fell asleep. After only a short nap, he awoke and peeked out through a small hole in the wall. Looking up the East Lead he spotted a *Ford Expedition* painted in CN colors and being driven by high ranking CN managers…and it was approaching his shanty! Archie told me that he went into a state of panic debating just what to do! In the end he elected to stay put and say nothing.

As it worked out, the managers drove down the Lead as far as the Mt. Elliott Bridge, turned around, stopped on the Lead and chatted with one another for a while; but apparently Archie was living right that day, as the four or five managers in the vehicle never got out of the *Expedition* and never even looked in the shanty!

Archie called me later that evening and told me what had occurred. He said, "Imagine what would have happened had they opened that door!?! What would I have said? I just thanked God that they eventually went on their way!"

He also told me later that he would never do that again!

One more A. D. Anderson story

CN Conductor, Archie D. Anderson grew up in Mississippi…I believe one of eleven children.

Archie told me that when he turned 16 and obtained his Driver's License he signed up for a program and passed the test to be a School Bus Driver!

Living on a farm in an extremely rural area, Archie stated that he kept the bus at his home every night and on weekends. Beginning his Junior year, every morning he had an assigned route and would drive the bus to school, picking up students of all ages, and delivering them to their school. At the end of the day, he would drive them all home.

Could you imagine that happening today? I don't care how great a driver they are, would you permit a 16, 17, or 18 year old kid to drive your child back and forth to school and special events???

On January 7, 2010 Conductor, Archie Anderson and I have arrived at Norfolk Southern's Oakwood Yard in Allen Park, MI. Before we tie onto our train, we will have to run "lite" out to Delray and turn our unit on the wye.

Annual Engineer Evaluation

By: C. H. Geletzke, Jr.

Let's begin with the first portion of the trip and then we will get into the point of the story…

On January 12, 2010 I reported for duty at the former Detroit, Toledo & Ironton Railroad's (now Canadian National) yard in Flat Rock, Michigan at 12:25 P.M. I was working with my regular Conductor and good friend, Archey Anderson and we were working Train 144, the *Road-Railer*, which handled Norfolk Southern (NS) *Triple-Crown* truck trailers from the NS Oakwood Yard to Toronto, Ontario. Our portion of the trip would only be from Oakwood Yard in Melvindale, Michigan to Sarnia, Ontario, a distance of about ninety miles. For motive power on this day we had the CN 2577 a GE C44-9W.

Chuck H Geletzke, Jr.

After signing in and reading the Bulletin Book I walked over to the Fuel Dock and inspected my unit. Only a few minutes later, Archie climbed aboard the unit, stowed his gear, and we left the dock at 1:00 P.M. and pulled up to the north end of the yard. Normally on the assignment we would run "lite" up to the NS at Oakwood Yard; but today was different...we were instructed to tie onto South 5 Track, which we did at 1:50 P.M. Next we were told to set the head six cars over to South No. 6 and then to return to our train of 6 loads and 1 empty in Track 5. This gave us a train, which was 600 feet in length. Now here was where things got interesting! With all of the work completed and as a Car Inspector was completing our Initial Terminal Air Test, a company vehicle came driving up alongside of our locomotive. All at once, the passenger side door opened and out stepped our Road Foreman of Engines.

Now here let me digress a little if you will. I have explained before that I had been a Supervisor of Locomotive Engineers (SLE) from 1993 through 1995. If I remember correctly, Certification for Locomotive Engineers began in 1992. At that time, each railroad was required to file a plan for Engineer Certification with the *Federal Railroad Administration* (*FRA*), stating how their program would comply with the government's regulations. On the Canadian National in the United States, it was agreed that every Locomotive Engineer would attend a Class and take and pass a written test annually. Additionally, each engineman would have to either be observed operating the Locomotive Simulator for four hours or have a Road Foreman or SLE ride with him or her on a locomotive for a minimum of four hours. Later in my career, additional conditions were added, such as territorial qualifications, which stated that each engineman had to operate over the various different territories annually and if they failed to do so, they would lose their ability to run on that trackage until they requalified. No doubt other changes have probably been instituted since I retired in 2011; but I have not kept-up on those.

Now back to our story...our Supervisor of Locomotive Engineers, Mr. _____ climbed aboard just as we were departing Flat Rock at 2:12 P.M. We then proceeded north on the Dearborn Subdivision 10.2 miles to OJ where we stopped at 2:54 P.M. During the trip Mr. _____ stated that he wanted to ride with me and have me complete my Annual Certification Observation Check Ride. Additionally, he happened to mention that he "had now been an SLE for seven years; but had NEVER been over this territory!"

193

And I recall thinking to myself…"and YOU are here to evaluate ME!?!" Through our discussions, it became very apparent that he had no interest in the job! I am guessing that he had taken the job…just for the additional time off!?!

At this point Conductor Anderson called and obtained permission for us to enter the NS's Oakwood Yard and then lined us through the wye at OJ. We cleared the wye at 2:58 P.M. and headed into Oakwood Yard where we would get our train.

We entered the yard at 2:58 P.M., yarded our seven cars in Track 7 in the Manifest Yard and cut-off at 3:17 P.M. At that point, the CN company vehicle that had previously delivered the SLE to our train pulled up along the Lead. It turned out that it was being driven by another SLE (whom I promoted to Locomotive Engineer in 1994), who all of us workers referred to as "The Chauffer!" Before the RFE climbed down off the engine, he asked to see my Engineer's License and signed the card okaying me to operate for another year. He then said, "You did a good job, Chuck! Thank you for letting me ride with you."

I then thanked him for signing my card and as he climbed down from the engine, I turned and faced Archie and said, "How'd you like that, Arch…a Four Hour Certification Trip, which only took one hour and five minutes, over territory that he had never been over before!?!"

I Must Have Made a Lasting Impression!?!

By: C. H. Geletzke, Jr.

It was April 26, 2010 and I was working my regular job, Number 104 going on duty at East Yard in Hamtramck, Michigan and working with my regular Conductor, Larry Williams. Our on-duty time was 10:00 A.M.

At 11:28 A.M. we were switching at B.O.C. (Buick-Oldsmobile-Cadillac) when our two Supervisor's of Locomotive Engineers (SLE's) came riding in together in one of their company cars. Shortly, the one we referred to as "The Chauffer" asked me to stop and stated that he was "going to ride with me today to conduct your Annual Locomotive Engineer Check Ride."

I climbed down off the engine and told him that his "'cohort in crime, the other SLE riding with him, had already ridden with me on January 12, 2010…and you picked him up at Oakwood Yard at the end of the trip!"

I think they were both embarrassed!!!

A welcome compliment!

By: C. H. Geletzke, Jr.

On January 14, 2010 my Conductor, Archie Anderson and I were involved in a serious and fatal head-on accident on Interstate-94 while being driven back to Flat Rock, Michigan from Sarnia, Ontario. (If you are interested in reading the entire story, see the story "Head-on on I-94!" in my book *With the Slack, That Will Do, and Other Railroad Stories.*

On January 20, 2010 I went upstairs to Assistant Superintendent, Dave Donaldson's office at Flat Rock Yard. The previous day I had misplaced my timebooks and was informed that Mr. Donaldson had them in his office.

While there the railroad officer asked about the ACCIDENT and how Archie and I were doing. He then complimented both of us stating, "I never worry about that job with you two guys on there…you really do a great job! Thank you!"

I replied that I appreciated the compliment.

Even though it was only six days later, he was the first official to ask us about the accident.

GTW 4902 at East Yard in Hamtramck, MI on May 29, 2010.

"Not Who Do You Trust; But WHOM Do You Trust???"*

By: C. H. Geletzke, Jr.

February 6, 2010

Today, Trainmaster, _____ was at East Yard in Detroit, Michigan. Assisting Conductor, J. C. Self on Train 386. Afterward, he climbed up on my engine, GTW 4902 while my Conductor, Archie Anderson and I were taking a break.

I had applied the handbrake and "properly" Isolated the unit when I got off.

When we climbed back on the unit, the handbrake had been RELEASED!

Archie witnessed me both applying the brake and also saw that it had been released.

That guy truly scared me!!!

March 13, 2010

Had a conversation with the same Trainmaster who was involved in the event of February 6th. He said that he "did not" release the handbrake on engine GTW 4902 on February 6, 2010.

I told him, "Gee, that's funny! Archie watched me apply it…and when I pulled the Release handle after we had seen you aboard the unit, the brake was <u>ALREADY</u> released! No one else was on the engine!"

Mr. _____ again stated, "I did not release the brake!"

I then replied, "I'll be watching you in the future!"

- A line from the television show *Who Do You Trust* hosted by Edgar Bergen and later by Johnny Carson between 1956 and 1963.

Perhaps a Miscommunication

Apparently, I was on this Trainmaster's list!

On April 18th I was working Job 104 at East Yard in Hamtramck, Michigan with another good friend, Conductor, Larry Williams and we had the engine GTW 4926. We went on duty at 10:00 A.M. During the day we switched cars at East Yard, ran out to Nolan Yard and Gillen Yard and switched *Cargo-Flo*, returned to East Yard and worked until 8:13 P.M.

Two days later, Supervisor of Locomotive Engineers, Randy Hempton arrived and told Conductor, Larry Williams that he was there to "download" the event recorder "on the GTW 4906," because the above mentioned Trainmaster thought that we were goofing off!

Larry and I just laughed when he could not locate the 4906, he just climbed back in his car and drove away…we didn't mention that we were also using the 4926 that day!

I'm glad that Trainmaster was not a Train Dispatcher!!!

A Similar Story

February 10, 2010

Another Trainmaster, _____ was stopped for "Speeding" by Flat Rock, Michigan Police while hauling a CN train crew. He was arrested for outstanding warrants and was taken to jail!

An Efficiency Test

A northward view of the Tappan interlocking at the west end of
GTW's Tunnel Yard in Port Huron, MI on April 23, 1988. This was
before the construction and opening of the new tunnel in 1995. The
diamond in the left corner is where the GTW crossed the C&O (former
PM). The cars on the right are being interchanged with the Port Huron
& Detroit RR. Just beyond the signals was the Michigan Road grade
crossing, which the author had to pull down to and STOP. I was later
reprimanded for not blowing the horn in compliance with Whistle
Signal for at least 15 seconds and not more than 20

February 16, 2010

Once again, I was working my regular assignment, Train 144
hauling the NS *Road-Railers* from NS's Oakwood Yard in
Melvindale, Michigan to the CN at Sarnia Ontario. I was
working with my regular Conductor, Archey Anderson and we
were rolling along with 76 X 1 (that's 76 loaded trailers and 1
empty), 2,208 gross tons, and we were 4,217 feet in length. My
engine was the CN 5787 an SD75I.

Chuck H Geletzke, Jr.

Being February, it was already dark out as we were approaching the interlocking at Tappan at the west end of Port Huron Yard. We first encountered an Approach Signal and then at the interlocking itself, a STOP Signal. These trains were extremely easy to handle and I pulled right down and stopped clear of the signal. In no time at all, the Train Dispatcher called and said, "CN 5787 I am unable to give you a signal. You may pass the signal at Restricted Speed."

Now because Michigan Road crosses the tracks within the limits of the interlocking, I crept ahead, and observed the crossing signals did not appear to be working, therefore I stopped the train before I reached the crossing…probably twenty feet short of the pavement.

Conductor Anderson walked ahead with a lit fusee and protected the crossing and then signaled me to come ahead with his lantern. Just as I inched the train forward the crossing lights came on and the gates went down. At that point I pulled the whistle or horn lever and signaled two quick long blasts, a short one, and another rather quick long blast (Rule 14L)…there were no vehicles in sight! As I entered the crossing, Archey climbed aboard. We then pulled down to the STOP signal at 16th Street, two miles to the east and stopped at 6:10 P.M.

Oh yes, as we passed the far end of the interlocking at Tappan, Archey yelled over across the cab, "There were two officials hiding behind that signal shanty over there and they appeared to be watching us!"

As you can imagine, the story does not end here. Eight days later, on February 24th, I received a "Letter of Caution" dated February 22nd from the Supervisor of Locomotive Engineers, reprimanding me for "only blowing the whistle for five seconds at 6:01 P.M. on February 16, 2010" when I crossed Michigan Road at Tappan on Train 144.

Interestingly, he failed to state that I had to stop first and then restart, causing the gates and flashers to begin working.

I should also quote Operating Rule 410 (7) here…"At speeds of 60 mph or less, start signal at least 15 seconds but not more than 20 seconds before entering the crossing."

On February 24th I was able to talk with the SLE, who was a friend, and voiced my concerns regarding the Letter of Caution pertaining to the Incident of February 16th. The SLE stated, "He was out doing ET's (Efficiency Tests) with the System Road

Foreman (a former Illinois Central man). The SLE stated that he "did not take exception with what I did…however, apparently his boss, the System Road Foreman was a stickler for the rules (100% compliance)…common sense was not to be used!" (I would refer to this as Modern Railroading!) I also explained that the Whistle Post on the Mt. Clemens Subdivision, approaching Michigan Road had been missing for well over six months and that I had reported its absence to Port Huron Trainmaster, James Lord, many times and that it still had not been replaced! (Apparently 100% compliance was only a one-way street!)

Finally, on October 22, 2010 I was able to have a conversation with the System Road Foreman and was able to state "my side of the story" and requested to have the Letter of Caution removed from my record?

Because he did not realize (they were so busy hiding) that we had actually stopped before entering the crossing, he agreed that what Archey and I had done was proper for the situation. He agreed to have the letter removed from my Personal File.

Oh yes, and additionally during our conversation on October 22nd I asked him about the "poor training," in my opinion that Engineer Trainees were receiving. I told him of my experiences with a certain unnamed Trainee several weeks earlier. I explained the problems that I encountered. The System Road Foreman agreed that there were problems. He also explained to me that Engineers No Longer Need to Check Fluid Levels on Locomotives when performing Daily Inspections! I had not been told this and could not believe it! I told him that I can see that I truly have become a dinosaur and that it is truly a crime…the poor and lack of training that the Engineer Trainees were receiving!

I once again spoke with the RFE on October 29th and again asked when the Letter of caution would be removed from my file, per my discussion with his boss the Senior RFE on October 22nd. The SLE stated that he "would have it removed soon….and that he would take care of it!"

I then enquired if I would receive a letter confirming that it had been removed from my file.

The SLE then said, "No!"

I then asked the SLE how I would confirm that it had been removed?

He responded, "I don't know!"

What a joke!!!

I then told the SLE about the problems that I observed with the Engineer Training Program. I really don't think that he had any idea! I explained…"you watch, one of these guys is going to cause a major wreck!"

I don't think that he had any idea just how little most of these guys knew!?!

Sadly, when I retired 14 months later, the Letter of Caution **was still in my personnel file!!!**

Today (November 3, 2010 at East Yard at approximately 2:45 P.M. the SLE known as "The Chauffer" drove in and went right into the yard office. I was out on our engines, the CN 5547 & IC 2464. After about 15 minutes, he appeared outside and then drove away. Craig Joyce, my Conductor, said that he had a discussion with the SLE (incidentally, a man that I promoted to Locomotive Engineer back in the early 1994) and told him that we did not want any Engineer Trainees with us on our job.

At that point the SLE replied, "Well, I don't know." He then went on to say, "I understand that Chuck (Geletzke) is upset with just about everything (possibly referring to my recent conversations with both the Senior Road Foreman and one of the other SLE's   and I don't know why!?! If he is so unhappy; I don't know why he just doesn't retire!?! (Recorded by Conductor, C. Joyce at 3:13 P.M. on 11-3-2010)

Where's the *Charmin*?

Apparently Trainmaster, James Lord at Port Huron thought that someone was stealing toilet paper at the Port Huron yard office. He therefore hid it all and was rationing it to all employees! This only lasted one day.

Still NOT Qualified!

On December 14, 2010 I was called to work Train 384 from Vickers over the Norfolk Southern to Alexis, and then over the Ann Arbor to Diann, and into Flat Rock Yard. Brian Peacock (another good man that I promoted to Locomotive Engineer back in the early 1990's) was called to be my Pilot as I was no longer qualified over this territory. At the completion of the trip the Trainmaster at Flat Rock said, "Well, now you ARE qualified!"

I responded, "No sir, not yet! I have never had a Norfolk Southern Rules Class!

View (looking east) at Port Huron, MI of the "new" St. Clair Tunnel on January 11, 2022.

"I know, it's Unbelievable!"

By: C. H. Geletzke, Jr.

I found this very interesting…eight years before I retired in 2011, my employer promoted a new Road Foreman of Engines to cover our area of the Canadian National Railroad (CN). What I found especially interesting, was the fact that this man, who was not too far behind me in seniority, and from Port Huron, only ever worked yard jobs! I am certain that at some time he may have worked the road; but personally, I could not recall it or when! In fact,

Chuck H Geletzke, Jr.

one of the "locker room" topics of conversation at the time of this man's promotion was that he had never even made a trip through the St. Clair Tunnel, between Port Huron, Michigan and Sarnia, Ontario…this was the most intimidating obstacle on our entire railroad…and now he was going to train enginemen to run through it!?!

Anyway on August 8, 2010 this Road Foreman contacted me and stated, "I want to put two Engineer Trainees on your job, one day next week, and evaluate them."

I then asked my boss, "Will I get to stay home that day?"

With that, he gave me a real strange look and then said, "No, why would you even think that!?!"

I then replied, "Well you know I am working Train 144, which handles the *Road-Railers* and only ever has just a single unit…meaning both my Conductor and I each have to have somewhere to sit!" (I know that I was a little sarcastic!)

With that the Road Foreman said, "I'll have to get back to you on that."

Oh yes, I never did hear from him!

Not to blow my own horn; but let me state that when Jack Tyson, Larry Bolton, and I were all Supervisors of Locomotive Engineers, we would each ride the entire round trip with Student Engineers on their assigned trains, even on layover jobs in order to evaluate them when they were nearing promotion! As a bonus, we would always call the regular engineer on the job that was assigned to train them, and we would tell him to "stay home" (and still be paid for the trip), just as a little added appreciation and bonus for taking a Trainee on their job.

I'm Afraid!

By: C. H. Geletzke, Jr.

Most of you know that I ceased being a Supervisor of Locomotive Engineers for the Canadian National Railroad on the former GTW, DT&I, and D&TSL in 1995. Since that time, I had just been operating locomotives and running trains.

Now let me state that several of my readers, who too had been professional railroaders have told me that my writing has appeared to get "darker" to them as I progressed toward the end of my career and retirement in December 2011. My guess it was/is because of the changes due to the differences in Illinois Central management and hopefully not a case of "spoiled milk!?!" I think they are probably right and I guess I should apologize and say, "I am sorry."

Tonight while going through one of my old timebooks, I ran across the following notation dated September 15, 2010 and written at 5:57 A.M. All names have been omitted to protect the innocent and the guilty.

I am lying here in the hotel and I cannot sleep due to what I witnessed yesterday. Yes, I had Engineer Trainee, _____ with me on Train 144 (The Road-Railer) from Flat Rock, Michigan through the St. Clair Tunnel, to Sarnia, Ontario. Now I will profess that I have never been a fan of this individual; but he does have redeeming characteristics. _____ can be a hard worker, he is intelligent, articulate, of good moral character, he asks questions, and takes criticism fairly well. _____ pays attention and wants to learn. His biggest fault is that he is a whiner and can be a complainer and at times he appears to lack commons sense. I have not made a judgment of his mechanical aptitude yet. The problem I see with _____ (and I am guessing the others in his class), is a total lack of adequate training, interest, observation, and evaluation on the part of his supervisors! Basically, _____ wants to learn; but has not been given the "hands-on" supervision and instruction that he needs to perform the duties of a locomotive engineer in the proper manner.

_____ is to be promoted to the position of Locomotive Engineer in less than two weeks. In my opinion, he is not even close to being ready!

Now so far, I have only spent one tour of duty with _____, yet I observed the following: he did not know how to perform the proper inspection of the locomotive...he did not even know how to check the oil on the air compressor or even know that the clean clear liquid on the dipstick was oil! He did not know how many fire extinguishers were on each unit, nor did he know their locations!

_____ had never performed a Shop Track Test on the engine. When he got ready to move the locomotive, he had not even noticed that the brakes were cut-out! I explained the importance to him of a proper Daily Inspection, and what you are implying when you sign The Daily Inspection Card. _____ had never filled-out a Work Report Form and did not know its importance nor that it was

Chuck H Geletzke, Jr.

required upon the completion of each tour of duty. _____ did not know proper Whistle Signals nor the proper use of the headlight. _____ did not notice lights that were out upon making an Initial Engine Inspection. _____ has had **no experience** with locomotive trouble-shooting!

So far, at least on Train 144, his train-handling was good. He pays attention and is alert. I hope that we get some varied-size trains to work on his train-handling skills. _____ knows his signals; but does not truly understand their meaning or importance. I tried to explain that the indication of a signal is not nearly as important as knowing what the possible indications of the next signal might be! This comes from proper testing and instruction.

I was also concerned when _____ told me how during his Engineer Training at Lang Yard in Toledo, Ohio, he had trained with Engineer, _____. He stated that Mr. _____ would leave the property for hours at a time, leaving him and the Conductor, to perform all yard switching! I explained to my Trainee that Mr. _____ (who was a former Assistant Superintendent and Road Foreman of Engines) was basically abandoning his post and jeopardizing the jobs of his fellow crew members!

In summary, I feel that _____ has the ability to be a good Locomotive Engineer; however, he is lacking the proper training, instruction, interest and guidance from his supervisors! _____ is doing a good job; but he is **NOT** ready to be promoted to Locomotive Engineer.

Lastly, the SLE's (Supervisors of Locomotive Engineers') should pay far more attention to which engineers they assign students. Effort should be made to assign them to the **BEST**!

Oh yes, _____ also does not know the physical characteristics of the territory that he ran over yesterday. If he is put with a new Conductor who also is unfamiliar an accident could certainly result!

Also, Engineers apparently are no longer required to fill-out Evaluations on the Students and Miles that they run the locomotive and the number of hours are no longer required either!

Signed,
C. H. Geletzke, Jr.
Locomotive Engineer
9-15-2010 at 6:37 A.M.

Wittnessed by:
C. Joyce
Conductor
9-15-2023 (9:42 P.M.)

Lastly, we went back to work again on Train 387 at 9:55 A.M. on September 15, 2010.

An Individualist!

By: C. H. Geletzke, Jr.

I'll bet many of you have read stories describing how back during steam days many locomotive engineers would blow the whistle on their steam locomotive in a unique way so that anyone listening might know who was running that train. In the early days, many engineers even had their own personal whistle that would be changed out when they changed engines! I have read many stories telling how an engineer's wife or girlfriend would hear him coming into town and know that they'd better start preparing supper.

Sadly, most of this disappeared when the railroads converted to diesels.

Well, back in 2010 my daughter, Abby, graduated from medical school and moved out to Hershey, Pennsylvania where she began her surgical residency at the *Penn State Hershey Medical Center*. Periodically, my wife and I would drive out and spend several days with our daughter, her husband, Brian, and our granddaughter, Josie. On our first night out there at around two or three in the morning, I heard a Norfolk Southern locomotive going through town (on the former Reading) and at what I assume was each grade crossing, the engineer would blow two longs and a short to warn motorists and pedestrians. This train must have been a yard job or local and during the next several nights I heard the same whistle signal as the engine worked back and forth through town. On our fourth and final morning there my wife, Leslie, said to me when she awoke, "Did you hear that train going through town? Doesn't that engineer know that the proper whistle signal for a grade grossing is two longs, a short, and a long!?!" That was from my wife...and

Chuck H Geletzke, Jr.

she NEVER worked on the railroad…or at least was NEVER paid for the hours worked!!

Then, before I could even respond to her question, she asked two more excellent questions. "Are their whistle signals different out here? And…"What would happen if that engineer hit a car and he or she was not blowing the proper whistle signal?"

I must say, the second question was very profound!

First of all let me state that as far as I know the signal to be used when approaching a grade crossing is two longs, a short blast, and one long until the crossing is fully occupied…and to the best of my knowledge this rule applies universally on every railroad in North America. Now I will state that some railroad's with the assistance of the *FRA* (*Federal Railroad Administration*) have added other conditions, which in my opinion have taken common sense out of the equation! For example: Some roads (perhaps all) say that the engineer must commence blowing the whistle when the engine reaches the whistle post sign…there is no allotment for the fact that it might be 70 mph territory and due to the train's length and weight the train is only running 10 mph…and maybe it is 3 A.M. in a residential neighborhood! Yes, CN's former IC officials just loved to perform Efficiency Tests (ET's) on this rule! (I'll write a story about that in the future.) It also did not matter if the train was going to stop before it reached the crossing…the whistle MUST be blown…NO EXCEPTIONS! Anyway, I am sure you get the idea!?!

Now let's address my wife's second question. Just suppose our "individualist" engineer had only blown his "two longs and a short" and then hit an automobile, what would be the outcome then? And let's just throw in the fact that the driver, who perhaps did not even stop for the flashing signals, also went around the crossing gates…and was seriously injured or even killed!!! Then what?

And after the fact, let's say that the injured party's attorney went around the scene of the accident or the nearby neighborhood…and found even one or two people who definitively stated that they only heard that particular locomotive blowing "two longs and a short!" At this point I would guess that the case might end up in court and just due to that factor alone, the railroad might be held responsible…just saying???

Looking back on my career I will say that there were times that I may have taken a little latitude with some of the rules; but never when it involved grade crossings!

Before I finalized this story I asked one of three friends who are attorneys in addition to being railfans and modelers for an opinion on this story…here is what one of them had to say.

One point needs to be made, the burden of proof is always on plaintiffs and there is what's called a "but for" test when it comes to tort liability. Put simply, there had to be 1) an injury (or death), 2) a duty of the defendant's part, 3) a breach of said duty, and 4) the injury would not have occurred BUT FOR the defendant's breach. Whether this scenario would go to trial is always specific to the parties, venue, and facts; however, the fact that witnesses (or the "black box" on the locomotive) indicated that the engineer blew two longs and a short, rather than the regulation sequence would not in and of itself lead to litigation. It may be a fringe factor when weighing negligence, if any, against the carrier. Was the driver of the car drunk? Speeding? Radio blasting? Etc…

One of my favorite "but for" scenarios was my sister-in-law's accident on ice. She was admittedly going too fast for the icy conditions and ended up sliding into the back of a stopped box truck on the shoulder, wrecking her minivan. When we talked about it, she said "that truck driver didn't have his orange triangles out! That's against the law!" So if the triangles were out, she would not have slid into the truck? "But for" the lack of triangles? No!

The go to factors when looking to the carrier for signs of negligence are always whether or not the crossing protection was working properly (usually the biggest factor), lights were lit on the locomotive, if the horn was blown at all, and if the brakes were applied timely.

Sadly, when I took the depositions of a Class One railroad's train crew/trainmaster/gumshoe last year, the railroad's own attorneys did not know half of the terminology (!!) and certainly, the Plaintiffs' attorney wouldn't have even known to ask/investigate such a thing as the whistle sequence, let alone that a locomotive does not have a steering wheel! Totally clueless! "So when the Conductor sits at the wheel to drive the train…"

No, the shortened sequence would not itself lead to litigation, but would probably lead to NS disciplining/terminating the engineer. The general public is not as smart as Leslie! You can tell her I said that!

Hopefully this helps.

Chuck H Geletzke, Jr.

CN (GTW) Job 104 working at Moterm in Ferndale, MI with the GTW 4902 on May 5, 2010.

Another Territorial Qualification Story

By: C. H. Geletzke, Jr.

In my previous book, *"Soak It!!!"…and Other Railroad Stories*, in one of my stories titled "Territorial Qualifications," I described how in 1995 I was basically qualified to work every inch of the former Grand Trunk Western Railroad (GTW); the Detroit Toledo & Ironton Railroad (DT&I); and the Detroit & Toledo Shore Line Railroad (D&TSL), plus small portions of other foreign railroads. Following a change in governmental regulations, which required that Locomotive Engineers must work over specific portions of territory at least once each year to maintain their territorial qualifications, over the next several years, the lines on which I was permitted to work gradually melted away. You see, if at anytime more than one year should lapse, we would forfeit our ability to work on this trackage and would have to "requalify."

Early on the morning of January 11, 2011 the crew dispatcher called me and stated that I was being called to work Train 397 from Port Huron to Battle Creek on duty at 6:30 A.M.; now understand, I was the regular engineer on Train 144 from Flat Rock to Sarnia, Ontario and return.

I told the caller that I was "not qualified to work over the Flint Subdivision."

With that, the crew dispatcher asked, "Are you qualified to Moterm?"

I replied, "I am qualified AT Moterm (in Ferndale, Michigan); but you are apparently asking from somewhere to Moterm...where is it from?"

The crew dispatcher then asked the MCO (Manager of Corridor Operations) and he said, "from East Yard (a distance of only about seven miles)!"

With that I responded, "I'm your man!"

It turned out that I was to be on duty at 9: 15 A.M. and only piloting Engineer, Steve Armstrong on Train 529. When I got there, the train was there and the crew was waiting. We had engine GTW 4909 with five loads and no empties. We departed East Yard at 9:48 A.M., stopped for a red signal at Milwaukee Jct. for 16 minutes, and arrived at Moterm at 10:32 A.M. We then set-out our entire train, ran lite back to East Yard where I tied-up at 12:48 P.M., a three hour and thirty-three minute day...NOT BAD!

Here was a new one on me!

By: C. H. Geletzke, Jr.

While working with Engineer Steve Armstrong on the previous mentioned trip, he told me of a recent experience, which I must confess in my 45 years on the railroad, I had never encountered before!

Steve told me that he had recently received an Investigation Notice in which he was charged with: Insufficient Velocity." Apparently meaning not running track speed!

What are the odds???

By: C. H. Geletzke, Jr.

Since I just told the almost unbelievable story about finding a replacement door for my HO scale *Varney* stock car, I hope you will tolerate one more story demonstrating unbelievable odds…only this one will be of a non-railroad nature.

In August 2011 I took two weeks vacation from the railroad and my wife and I drove to Greenville, North Carolina to visit our son, "Chip" and then we headed down to Pensacola, Florida to attend our son, Marine 1st Lt. Travis Geletzke's graduation from the U. S. Navy's Flight School.

On our way south, we stopped for several evenings in Savannah, Georgia to tour the city, see the sites, and visit the wonderful *Georgia State Railroad Museum*. One afternoon during our visit my wife, Leslie, happened to be looking at a Map of the City of Savannah. All at once she spotted Price Street in an area that we were going to be visiting…Price is her maiden name. Then she followed Price Street on the drawing through its wonderful residential district and all at once yelled out, "I don't believe it!"

"What is it?" I responded.

She then said Price Street intersects with Gaston Street!" Gaston was her mother's maiden name!

We then drove to the intersection of the two streets and photographed the Gaston-Price street sign.

Now, here is the question. How many people do you know that can locate each of their parent's last names on a intersecting city street sign? The odds have to be overwhelming!

"It's Possible to Miss Christmas!"

By: C. H. Geletzke, Jr.

He was checked in his transports by the churchs ringing out the lustiest peals he had ever heard. Clash, clang, hammer, ding, dong, bell; bell, dong, ding, hammer, clang, clash! O glorius, glorius!

Running to the window, he opened it, and put out his head. No fog, no mist. Clear, bright, jovial, stirring, cold-cold, piping for the blood to dance to-golden sunlight; Heavenly sky; sweet fresh air; merry bells-oh glorius, glorius!

"What's to day?" cried Scrooge, calling downward to a boy in Sunday clothes, who perhaps loitered in to look about him.

"EH?" returned the boy, with all his might of wonder.

"What's to day, my fine fellow!" said Scrooge.

"Today!" replied the boy. "Why CHRISTMAS DAY"

"It's Christmas Day! said Scrooge to himself. "I haven't missed it. The Spirits, have done it all in one night. They can do anything they like. Of course they can. Of course they can...

(From: *A Christmas Carol* by Charles Dickens 1843)

When I read about the younger railroaders of today, I often hear that they complain about not being able to spend Thanksgiving

Chuck H Geletzke, Jr.

and Christmas with their families. When I started my railroad career in 1967 it was understood that as a younger employee it was imperative that you be available to work on the holidays, so that the older employees might be able to spend the day with their families. It quickly became apparent that as an individual's seniority increased, so would his or hers ability to have special days at home...but, that privilege had to be earned! In my case, as a college student, working my way through college as a railroader, it was expected that I would be available on all weekends and holidays...agreeing with this premise was why the railroad hired me in the first place...in actuality, they were endeavoring to make things better for all of their older workers. And the plus for me...I was able to pay my own way through college and I never expected any help or assistance from the government! HOW ABOUT THAT!?!

Lastly, let me state that as a "youngster," I expected to work those special days; but as I got older, was married, and had children, I soon learned that in order to assure that I would be home on very special occasions, the only way was to sign up for my vacation on each of those weeks! Similarly, there was always a huge number of men who would take their vacations or a portion thereof during deer season...I quickly learned (not being a hunter) that I could earn some of my highest paychecks by just being available during those times!

With that said, I thought that I would go back through my timebooks and notebooks and see, just how many Thanksgivings and Christmas holidays I actually worked during my 45 year career on the railroad...let's take a look.

1967 I was furloughed from GTW Pontiac roundhouse.
1968 Thanksgiving: Brakeman GTW Passenger Trains 165/164 "The Mohawk."
Christmas: Flagman GTW Passenger Trains 169/168.
1969 Thanksgiving: Flagman Passenger Trains 998, 169, 168, & 999 out of Pontiac.
Christmas: GTW Flagman freight Trains 434/433 out of Durand.
1970 Thanksgiving: In U. S. Marine Corps. Reserve.
Christmas: Home from Marine Corps. Booked-up to work on December 28th.
1971 Thanksgiving: Furloughed from Delray Connecting RR.
Christmas: Furloughed from Delray Connecting RR.

1972 Thanksgiving: Missouri Pacific RR. Day off as Management Trainee.

Christmas: Missouri Pacific RR. Day off as Management Trainee.

1973 Thanksgiving: GTW Fireman-Detroit 0800 Chevy Job Cancelled for day.

Christmas: GTW Fireman-Detroit 0730 City Yd. Job Cancelled for day.

1974 Thanksgiving: GTW Hostler-Detroit 1500 Hostler, Job Cancelled for day.

Christmas: GTW Hostler-Detroit 0700 Hostler, Job Cancelled for day.

1975 Thanksgiving: GTW Brakemen's Extra Board-Detroit. One week vacation.

Christmas: GTW Brakemen's Extra Board, Laid-In, all jobs cancelled.

1976 Thanksgiving: GTW Asst. Trainmaster-Port Huron,. 2330-0810 & 2330-0730.

Christmas: GTW Asst. TM/Agent Kalamazoo. 2330-0730.

1977 Thanksgiving: GTW ATM/Agent Kalamazoo. One week vacation.

Christmas: GTW ATM/Agent Kalamazoo. On call… all jobs cancelled.

1978 Thanksgiving: GTW ATM/Agent Kalamazoo. On call…all jobs cancelled.

Christmas: GTW ATM/Agent Kalamazoo. All jobs cancelled.

1979 Thanksgiving: Trainmaster D&TSL Toledo. One week vacation.

Christmas: Trainmaster D&TSL Toledo. On call…all jobs cancelled.

1980 Thanksgiving: Fireman GTW Trains 215/214. One week vacation.

Christmas: Fireman GTW Trains 215/214. Job cancelled

1981 Thanksgiving: Fireman GTW Trains 215/214. One week vacation.

Christmas: Fireman GTW Trains 600/601. Job cancelled.

1982 Thanksgiving: Fireman GTW 0800 All Purpose. Two weeks vacation.

Christmas: Fireman 0700 East Yard. Job cancelled.

1983 Thanksgiving: Fireman 0700 East Yard. Three weeks vacation.

Chuck H Geletzke, Jr.

       Christmas: Fireman 1530 All Purpose. Job cancelled.
1984 Thanksgiving: Detroit Engineer's Extra Board. Laid-In not called.

       Christmas: Detroit Engineer's Extra Board. Laid-In not called.
1985 Thanksgiving: Detroit Engineer 2400 All-Purpose. Job cancelled.

       Christmas: Fireman Detroit 1500 All Purpose. Job cancelled.
1986 Thanksgiving: Engineer Detroit Extra Board. One week vacation.

       Christmas: Fireman Detroit 0700 East Yard. Job cancelled.
1987 Thanksgiving: Detroit Engineer's Extra Board. Two weeks vacation.

       Christmas: Detroit Engineer's Extra Board. Laid-In not called.
1988 Thanksgiving: Engineer 1600 All Purpose. One week vacation.

       Christmas: Engineer 2300 All Purpose. Job cancelled.
1989 Thanksgiving: Battle Creek Engineer Trains 387/384. One week vacation.

       Christmas: Engineer Detroit Combination Spare Board. Booked off!
1990 Thanksgiving: Engineer Extra Board Toledo. One week vacation.

       Christmas: Engineer Toledo Trains 421/420. One week vacation.
1991 Thanksgiving: Detroit Engineer's Extra Board. One week vacation.

       Christmas: Detroit Engineer's Extra Board. Two weeks vacation.
1992 Thanksgiving: Detroit Engineer's Extra Board. One week vacation.

       Christmas: Detroit Engineer's Extra Board. One week vacation.
1993 Thanksgiving: Supervisor of Loco. Engineers-Flat Rock. One week vacation.

       Christmas: Supervisor of Loco. Engineers-Flat Rock. One week vacation.
1994 Thanksgiving: Supervisor of Loco. Engineers-Flat Rock. One week vacation.

       Christmas: Supervisor of Loco. Engineers-Flat Rock. One week vacation.

1995 Thanksgiving: Engineer Detroit Trains 255/458. One week vacation

Christmas: Engineer Detroit Trains 255/458. Two weeks vacation.

1996 Thanksgiving: Engineer Detroit Trains 255/458. Two weeks vacation.

Christmas: Engineer Detroit Trains 255/458. One week vacation.

1997 Thanksgiving: Engineer Detroit Trains 251/258. One week vacation.

Christmas: Engineer Detroit Trains 384/387. Job cancelled 12-24 & 25.

1998 Thanksgiving: Engineer Detroit Trains 384/383. One week vacation.

Christmas: Engineer Detroit Trains 384/383. Two weeks vacation.

1999 Thanksgiving: Engineer Extra Board Toledo. One week vacation.

Christmas: Engineer Extra Board Toledo. Two weeks vacation.

2000 Thanksgiving: Engineer Flat Rock Trains 264/385. One week vacation.

Christmas: Engineer Flat Rock Trains 264/385. One week vacation.

2001 Thanksgiving: Engineer Flat Rock Trains 384/383. One week vacation.

Christmas: Engineer Flat Rock Trains 384/383. Nine days vacation.

2002 Thanksgiving: Engineer Flat Rock Trains 384/383. One week vacation.

Christmas: Engineer Flat Rock Trains 384/383. One week vacation.

2003 Thanksgiving: Engineer Flat Rock Trains 384/383. One week vacation.

Christmas: Engineer Flat Rock Trains 384/383. Twelve days vacation.

2004 Thanksgiving: Engineer Toledo Trains 382/whatever. Six days vacation.

Christmas: Engineer Toledo Trains 382/whatever. Eleven vacation days.

Chuck H Geletzke, Jr.

2005 Thanksgiving: Engineer Toledo Trains 382/383. Six vacation days.

Christmas: Engineer Toledo Trains 382/383. Two weeks vacation.

2006 Thanksgiving: Engineer Toledo Trains 382/383. One week vacation.

Christmas: Engineer Toledo Trains 382/383. One week vacation.

2007 Thanksgiving: Engineer Toledo Trains 382/whatever. One week vacation.

Christmas: Engineer Toledo Trains 382/whatever. One week vacation.

2008 Thanksgiving: Engineer Toledo Trains 382/383. Eight days vacation.

Christmas: Engineer Toledo Trains 382/383. 15-days vacation.

2009 Thanksgiving: Engineer Flat Rock Train 144. One week vacation.

Christmas: Engineer Flat Rock Train 144. Four days vacation.

2010 Thanksgiving: Engineer Flat Rock Train 144. One week vacation.

Christmas: Engineer Flat Rock Train 144. Twelve days vacation.

2011 Thanksgiving: Engineer Detroit Train 144. One week vacation.

Engineer Detroit Train 144…retired 12-4-2011 at 1:14 A.M.

Well, there you have it, how do you like that? In actuality, I cannot even believe it myself! In a railroad career, which spanned just shy of 45 years, I only worked on Thanksgiving five times and Christmas four times! In all honesty, I can't believe it myself! BUT, please remember, we had many more employees then, few other workers took vacation during those two weeks, and I did work most of the other holidays when called to work.

Next Stop

By: Wendell "Wink" West

Retired U. S. Army and Ministry Pastor at Journey Church in
Strasburg, PA

As many of you regular readers know, I recently moved from
Michigan to Pennsylvania where I met and have become best of
friends with one of my neighbor's, "Wink" West. Wink is the author
of a wonderful book titled: *FROM DUSK TIL DAWN* and has
granted me permission to include one of his stories in this book.

Have you ever ridden on a commuter train? I recently retired
from a position that required I commute to and from work on a train
(Harrisburg to Philadelphia and return). I did this for more than a
decade. It was a ride full of all sorts of activities. As a matter of fact,
this book could have been completed long before its publication
from the time I've spent on the train, but there were too many
distractions. Since my commute was approximately two hours one-
way, I had the pleasure of hearing the conductors make various
announcements as we made our journey down the tracks. As we
approached each stop, the conductor would announce where we were
and which doors along the very long train ride would open to allow
passengers to exit and board. Each time we arrived at the end of the
line they would utter, "ladies and gentlemen, the final stop will be
Philadelphia. All doors will open, please watch your step; there is a
gap between the train and the platform. Thank you for riding
Amtrak, we hope you have a great day!" There were times they
would let me announce a stop. It was usually my own. I'm thinking
that was so I would stop talking about how much better I could make
the announcements.

Steve Kaslik talking on the pay phone in Royal Oak, Michigan's Washington Square Plaza. (Steve Kaslik photo)

Unbelievable!

By: Steve Kaslik

It is not often that one is treated to an unexpected surprise where an object of one's youth remains intact and/or is improved against all odds, including the mere passage of time. Especially objects that have not been seen in, well, decades or more and that are also largely extinct in most public places. I am referring to the pay phones, Cellular telephones have largely sent the pay phone the way of the dinosaurs, except for a few places where they hang on.

On December 2, 2023 a group that included myself went out to dinner at D'Amato's, which is located within the Washington Square Plaza Building in Royal Oak, Michigan. It still exists in its late-1990's form, with some modernization here and there, which in and of itself is unbelievable with all the changes over the past 25 years (needless to say). The food is still great, too. After everyone was done eating and the bill paid, I wanted to see the wall where the pay phones "used to be"…the very phones that I used to call GTW TD-2 (Grand Trunk Western Train Dispatcher 2-who dispatched the very busy Holly Subdivision in the late-90's) for a lineup back in the "day."

As I remembered it, the phones were located at the top of a winding marble staircase in the Washington Square Plaza, on the second floor. I did not acquire a cell phone until 2000; so any calls out had to be made via pay phone. Between 1995 and 2000, I would call TD-2, who in the evenings, was typically Erick Facknitz ("EAF" in railroad parlance) for the afore-mentioned lineup. Erick, also a railfan, would look at his computer screens and sometimes peek over the shoulder of TD-3 to see which trains would be coming through Royal Oak within the next few hours. It should be noted that this was in the time before 9/11 and said practice of calling for a lineup was still largely acceptable. Erick would answer the phone in his signature fashion by simply saying "Two." We would update each other on what was going on in life and how our respective families were doing, then get down to the rail action. It this time period, the Holly Sub. was HOT! There were approximately 20-25 trains per day, including Amtrak, between Pontiac and Detroit. Being that I lived near the Mt. Clemens Sub. (in Richmond), we would largely get international traffic to and from Canada, mostly with CN power. The Holly was different, as it hosted a multitude of colorful consists, with motive power from the ATSF, BN, BNSF, CNW, Cotton Belt, DRGW, DWP, GTW, SP, UP, and so forth. With lineup in hand, I would hang the receiver back in the cradle and head downstairs, then to the Amtrak platform to watch the show. It was a great time to be alive!

Fast forward back to December 2, 2023. The group left the table and started up the winding white marble staircase. I had not been to D'Amato's since 2013 and was sure the phones were gone. We reached the top of the staircase and turned the corner on the second floor…not only were both phones still there; but the area was cleaned regularly, light bulbs were replaced overhead, and everything was exactly how it was some 25-30 years ago! I was blown away. I truly expected solid sets of Burdakin Blue when I stepped outside. It's the little things…

Amtrak Train___ is seen arriving at Mount Joy, PA on March 5, 2024.

A recent trip on Amtrak

By: C. H. Geletzke, Jr.

Chuck H Geletzke, Jr.

If you are a regular reader, you know that I began my railroad career in 1967 and that since the formation of Amtrak on May 1, 1971, I have been an Amtrak pass holder. Now without going into a tremendous amount of detail, what many of you probably do not know are the basics of just how that pass works. While working on the railroad and as a retiree, my wife and I (and formerly our children until they turned 18) were/are able to ride "free" over the former Grand Trunk Western (GTW) trackage currently utilized by Amtrak. In our case, that means that we can ride the 158 mile stretch between Battle Creek and Port Huron, Michigan. Additionally, we can ride the 23 miles of track between the depot in Detroit and Pontiac, Michigan…that's it! Not much compared to a former employee who had worked for the former Penn Central or Santa Fe, just for an example. To use our pass on any other trackage served by Amtrak, we are required to pay "half-fare."

Taken at face value, this probably seems quite fair; but, there is one caveat, which pretty much sinks the ship! You see, the problems occur because any and all pass holders are only permitted to make reservations up to 24 hours in advance! So, if we decided that we wanted to ride from Lancaster, Pennsylvania, near our home, to San Diego, departing at 8:00 A.M. on December 22nd, we would not be permitted to submit our reservation request until after 8:00 A.M. on December 21st! Naturally, in most cases, by this time, all of the reservations will have been filled…rendering the pass essentially **WORTHLESS!** Yes, it might work just fine if we only wanted to ride into Philadelphia; but to plan a vacation or long trip, we quickly learned that this was/is out of the question! (Here let me additionally state that having retired as a Canadian National Railroad (CN) employee, my wife and I have a VIA RAIL pass, which we have only ever used one time; but as I recall we could make reservations as much as several months in advance.)

Now let me tell you about my latest trip aboard Amtrak. My wife and I decided to take our daughter and our grandchildren on a train to Philadelphia from Lancaster for the day on October 13th. Naturally, I knew that I would have to pay the full fare for my daughter and half-fare for my two grandchildren ages nine and five. Since we had not used the pass since way prior to Covid, I thought that I'd better ask the ticket agent in Lancaster just in case something had changed.

So, on Monday morning, October 9th, I took Leslie out for breakfast at our favorite diner in the Lancaster area, *The Neptune*

Diner. It is only two blocks from the Amtrak (former Pennsylvania Railroad) depot in Lancaster. After a great breakfast we drove to the huge passenger station and parked in front of the building in an area, which permitted free thirty minute parking. We then walked into the building and waited our turn to speak with the Ticket Agent...the wait was not long. When it was our turn, I presented our Amtrak passes and explained my dilemma...mainly wanting to know if the same 24 hour rule still applied to utilize the pass. The young ticket agent was very friendly and helpful...unfortunately, since Amtrak no longer prints out timetables, it is a little tricky for a novice to determine when and on which trains he or she might like to ride.

I explained that we wanted to ride a train into Philadelphia on the morning of October 13th, from Lancaster; but I honestly had no idea of the departure times of the various trains. The helpful agent then brought up a list of eastbound departures from Lancaster on the morning of the 13th on his computer...apparently the times and trains can change depending upon the day and other uncertain conditions...believe me the day of being able to plan entire trips by looking through the *Official Guide of the Railways* is long gone! We then determined that we wanted to board an eastbound *Keystone Train* (I still have no idea of what that means) on the 13th at 8:42 A.M.

Next the agent wanted to know on which train would we like to return from Philadelphia??? After looking at his computer screen Leslie and I determined that Train 609, departing *William H. Gray III* 30th Street Station (apparently the station was renamed in 2014...so who knew?) at 2:35 P.M., would probably work best for our little group. The Ticket Agent then informed us, "Since you both will be riding on an Amtrak Pass, you will not be permitted to make your reservation until AFTER 2:35 P.M. on October 12th (the day previous to the trip). Now if you arrive a little early, I won't be able to help you purchase the tickets until AFTER 2:35 P.M.! I'm sorry; but that is just the way it works." (Yes, that is the way it has worked since 1971...for the past 52 years!)

I then thanked the gentleman and told him that we would return to purchase our tickets on Thursday, October 12th, after 2:35 P.M.

Thursday afternoon Leslie and I returned to the Lancaster station and arrived at approximately half-past two and once again parked in the Free 30 minute Parking Area. We then walked into the station and climbed the huge flight of stairs to the second floor and waiting area. Again we waited about ten minutes to speak with the Ticket Agent. When it was our turn, he remembered us from the previous Monday and noted that it was now after 2:35 P.M. He then inquired, "I assume you still wish to ride the same two trains?"

"We stated that, "We do." And then he began entering the information to print out the singular ticket that would cover all five of us. The first thing that truly surprised me was that he needed to know the names (and I believe address) of each individual! I am guessing that this is new since 9/11? We then gave him all of the desired information for our daughter and her two children, ages nine and five. The children would be charged half-fare. All of that was very simple. The agent then, once again, asked to see my wife and my Amtrak Pass and he recorded all of the pertinent and necessary information. Let me state that by this time, we had been standing at the ticket window for at least 15 minutes, and there were now several people waiting their turn behind us. All at once the ticket agent who had almost fully completed the transactions, blurted out, "Wait a minute! You and your wife are both senior citizens, and the senior citizen rate is cheaper than what you will pay riding on the pass!" With that he began redoing the ticket, I then presented my credit card, and paid for the round-trip ride for all five of us.

By now I was beginning to feel bad…at this point, we had been standing at the window with the agent for at least 25 minutes. With the transaction completed, we thanked the gentleman and he in turn thanked us. As Leslie and I began to walk away, he said to us, "Remember that for the future…the Senior Citizen rate is generally cheaper than riding on a pass, and **YOU CAN MAKE RESERVATIONS MORE THAN 24 HOURS AHEAD!**"

At that point, I was ready to ride the bus!

The next morning it was raining and all five of us met in the parking lot of the Lancaster, PA train station. Now let me admit, I am certainly not a kid, and I am definitely challenged when it comes to computers; but for the life of me, neither my wife nor I could figure out how to insert all of the required information into their computerized parking system! After getting soaked in the rain, we finally went inside of the depot and requested help. To me experiences like that just elevate my blood pressure and take the fun right out of the trip! I cannot begin to imagine how they handle "long term" parking!?! With the parking situation settled, we walked down the steps to the platform where I took several photos and boarded our first train at 8:42 A.M. It turned out to be an enjoyable trip for all of us; but I did meet one interesting individual.

Somehow the train's young Conductor overheard me talking about the railroad to my grandson, Finn, who is probably a future railfan. The Conductor then entered into our conversation, asked me where I had worked, and then told me that his father had been a locomotive engineer. I then asked him, "Who did your Dad work for, the Pennsylvania Railroad?"

"No not quite." The passenger train's boss then very authoritatively summarized, "First he worked for the Central Penn, then the outfit with the blue and white engines, and later he retired from the NS (Norfolk Southern)."

I tried to correct the young railroad employee and stated, "Your Dad must have started on the Penn Central and then worked for Conrail?"

No, the young man was not about to give up…"I know that it was the Central Penn," he insisted!

With that comment I gave up and told him that I hoped he'd have a nice day.

Apparently my daughter, Abby, who is a surgeon, had made this trip a number of years earlier. She knew that upon our arrival at William H. Gray III 30th Street Station (doesn't that have a real ring?) without incurring any additional charges we could change to a SEPTA train and ride to either Suburban Station or to what I thought was the Market East Station (located beneath the old Reading Terminal and near the *Reading Terminal Market*) and had now been renamed the Jefferson Station after the nearby *Thomas Jefferson Hospital* paid $4 million dollars to have the station renamed in 2014. I was sure thankful that my daughter knew all of this, or who knows where I may have detrained!?!

The five of us had a great day in Philadelphia and arrived back at the William H. Gray 30th Street Station about an hour early; but thankfully train 645's Conductor spotted us approaching his train's platform and held the train about one minute for us. This permitted us to begin our journey home at 1:45 P.M. instead of waiting to board Train 609 at 2:35 P.M.

For me it was a great day; but in all honesty, I could not believe how many changes had occurred in modern day train travel since I last ridden a passenger train at least five years ago!

226

Chuck H Geletzke, Jr.

Mistaken Identities

As told by: Vyvyan Makin, Trainman, Black River & Western RR

Having grown up in a railfanning family, I suppose I've taken for granted that I've always understood more industry-specific railroad terminology than the average person. That became even more apparent in 2023 when I began volunteering as a car attendant at a local heritage railroad that runs steam and diesel excursions. Tourists invariably default to common knowledge definitions such as expecting a railroad "fireman" to be someone who puts out fires rather than someone who feeds and maintains them.

My railroad allows volunteer "Car Attendants" to wear hat badges that say "Trainman" in spite of us not being hours-of–service employees. Aside from the title on our hats, the uniform car attendants wear is the same as what the Conductor wears. Nearly every shift, several people call me "the conductor" in spite of my hat saying "Trainman" and I rarely correct them. I at least get to silently laugh it off as if I'd gotten a "field promotion" knowing that the mistaken identity is simply because in pop culture, anyone who punches a ticket gets called a Conductor. As for most of the other roles on the train crew, you'd think the general public would get them right; but there's always a time or two someone proves otherwise.

After punching tickets in my assigned coach along a slow 5-mile ride through the country, I got talking with a family of grandparents, parents, and three kids. They were inquisitive, and I was happy to share my knowledge about the history of our railroad and train cars. At the time, I'd only been a volunteer for a few months; so there was a question I didn't know the answer to, so I told them our Conductor probably knew the answer.

As luck would have it, at that moment the Conductor happened to be walking down the aisle of the coach towards us, so I snagged him to get the answer (for the family and for myself). I politely introduced him, telling the family, "This is our conductor. We can as him."

227

The matriarch of the group instantly tensed up, eyes going wide with all the color draining from her cheeks. "If he's the conductor," she asked, stifling her panic, "then who's diving the train!?!"

Deadpan, I replied, "The engineer."

The 20,000th "Smokin'Joe" drawn by Canadian National Locomotive Engineer, Joe Greyczk, was seen and celebrated on July 5, 2005 at Flat Rock, Michigan. (C. H. Geletzke, Jr. photo)

Smokin' Joe

By: C. H. Geletzke, Jr.

It was with a great deal of sadness that I learned of the passing of my friend and fellow former Canadian National Railroad Locomotive Engineer, Joseph Ernest Greyzck on January 30, 2024. In actuality, he was a "DT&I Man!"

Following graduation from high school in Carleton, Michigan, Joe joined the U. S. Navy and served in Vietnam. After completing his tour with the Navy, Joe hired out on the Detroit,

Chuck H Geletzke, Jr.

Toledo & Ironton Railroad (DT&I) in October 1969 in Engine Service.

I first met Joe on the afternoon of Halloween in 1978. I was working as Assistant Trainmaster-Agent for the Grand Trunk Western (GTW) in Kalamazoo, Michigan when the GTW announced that they were going to attempt to acquire the DT&I. Not having shot too many photos of that interesting little railroad, the late Jack N. Ozanich, who was working as a Locomotive Engineer for me at the time and a premier railfan and I decided that perhaps it was time for us to take several days and attempt to photograph the entire route of the railroad which declared, "WE HAVE THE CONNECTIONS!" So, on the morning of October 31, 1978 Jack and I headed over to Flat Rock and by that afternoon had worked our way as far south as Quincy, Ohio. Now most of you probably think that the south end of the "Dirty I" probably did not generate a huge amount of traffic!?! Well, let me tell you that what Jack and I witnessed in Quincy totally blew us away! Would you believe that upon our arrival the DT&I had a total of five trains in town…at the same time!?! I still don't believe it! It was amazing how many trains we encountered during the perfect weather of our three day journey! Anyway, while we were photographing trains of both the DT&I and the Penn Central there in town we met a DT&I engineman…I seem to recall that he was actually "firing" a work train there. He immediately introduced himself to us as Joe Greyzck and not only explained what was and was not going on; but where to go for the best photos and food! Jack and I were thrilled!

As most of you probably know, with the help of the Campbell Soup Company and several other big DT&I shippers, the GTW acquired 100% ownership and control of the DT&I on June 24, 1980. Ten months later they were also able to purchase the 50% interest that the Norfolk & Western Railroad (N&W) had in the Detroit & Toledo Shore Line giving them complete control of that railroad too.

I always loved and appreciated seeing chalk and paint stick sketches on the sides of railroad cars such as the famous "Herby" or "Bozo Texino." That said, I have never been a fan of painted graffiti applied to railroad cars or peoples' personal property. While many of these artists are exceptionally talented, I truly wish that they would confine their talent to a canvas or a spot after being granted the owner's permission.

Sometime in the early 1980's I seem to recall seeing a new sketch appearing on the sides of railroad freight cars...this time the character was "SMOKIN' JOE!" I must say that I appreciated the design and the fact that the illustrator did not ruin the entire appearance of the entire side of the car. Over a period of several years, these drawings became more profuse and I began seeing them in practically every freight train. By this time I had departed my managerial position and just like Mr. Gryzck was also working as a Locomotive Engineer. With all of the changes that subsequently took place on the "new" GTW following the acquisition of the two other railroads, I too was now going in and out of the former DT&I hump yard in Flat Rock, Michigan on a fairly regular basis. Eventually Joe Greyzck and my paths crossed and I mentioned our first meeting back in Quincy, Ohio approximately 15 years earlier. He recalled the event and the day. I also asked him about his sketches and he explained that he kept written records recording the date and the car initial and number on which they were inscribed. I was enthralled!

Apparently GTW management was also impressed by Joe Greyczk's moniker. When the railroad sold their main office at 131 W. Lafayette in Detroit, Michigan in 1987 and moved to their new "leased space" on the east side of town at Brewery Park, their interior decorator too had an appreciation for Mr. Greyczk's work! On the first occasion that I had to enter the new building, there was very little artistry or workmanship that would lead a visitor to even acknowledge that this was the headquarters of a railroad...to me, it looked more like the office of an insurance company! The one and only deviation from this was a series of perhaps ten sketches or artwork applied to one wall in the building's lobby...one of those enlarged sketches was a photo of "SMOKIN' JOE" photographed and enlarged from the side of a boxcar. I was surprised that GTW management even acknowledged it!?!

In 1993 I was appointed back into railroad management as Supervisor of Locomotive Engineers with an office in Flat Rock. My territory primarily covered Detroit, Flat Rock, Toledo, Lima, and Springfield, Ohio. The railroad had two other SLE's at that time, who interestingly were also fellow railfans and they were Jack G. Tyson covering Pontiac, Flint, and Port Huron and Lawrence R. Bolton who handled Battle Creek, Lansing, and Chicago.

A portion of each of our jobs was to either ride with and observe each engineman on trains or in the Locomotive Simulator for the federally mandated minimum of four hours annually.

Chuck H Geletzke, Jr.

Additionally, we each conducted classes on the Operating and Safety Rules in addition to train handling and an annual exam for each engineman on our respective territories.

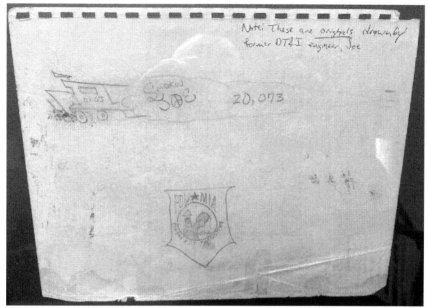

Original "Smokin'Joe" drawn by Joseph E. Greyzck on the back of C. H. Geletzke, Jr.'s Locomotive Engineers Instruction Manual in 1995.

In 1993 Joe Greyczk was working in Flat Rock (his home terminal) and ran the Locomotive Simulator when he was scheduled and I might add that he did an outstanding job! While operating over the road, I once again quizzed him about his sketches. In 1994, I rode aboard a train with Joe and again had him in one of my classes. In 1995, we had a "repeat performance." While Joe was in the class, it dawned on me that I needed an "original" of one of his drawings! Now I certainly did not have any art paper available; but I knew that I needed an alternative...I then asked Joe if he would draw a "SMOKIN' JOE" on the back of my Locomotive Engineer Instruction Manual. Naturally, he graciously responded and made the drawing for me...right there in class...several years later I found it in my archives and thought to myself, this thing definitely has "collectible value" and should be properly protected...The next day I took it to have it professionally matted and framed.

Over the years and following each of our retirements...Joe in 2004 and me in 2011, we became "Facebook Friends," and stayed in contact with one another. Last year, after moving to Pennsylvania it dawned on me that perhaps my son Travis, a Marine Corps helicopter pilot might like to have an original "Smokin' Joe" to hang on his wall. I called Joe and talked with him…and three or four days later a full sized original arrived in the mail. Once again, I had it also framed and today it hangs in Travis' home.

Yes, it goes without saying that Joe will certainly be missed and remembered by his many friends and railfans who no doubt admired his work.

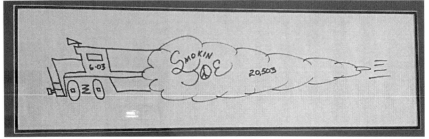

Original Joe Greyzck "Smokin' Joe" owned by: Lt/Col. Travis P. Geletzke

Chuck H Geletzke, Jr.

My grandson, Finn, and I out "railfanning," observed the arrival of a westbound Amtrak "Keystone" train at Mount Joy, Pennsylvania on June 22, 2023.

Train Whistles?

By: C. H. Geletzke, Jr.

I've mentioned before that last year my wife and I moved from Michigan to Mount Joy, Pennsylvania. In our new home we are about ½ mile north of the Amtrak (former Pennsylvania Railroad) Mainline passing through town. The other afternoon a westbound Amtrak train whistled as it was approaching the station and its next stop.

Hearing the whistle, I was really surprised when my wife said, "I really like hearing the train horn as they go through town!"

This really surprised me, you see our community does not have any grade crossings on the Mainline; so the train was only blowing to warn a track gang working ahead of its approach. Yet, I must admit it did sound especially nice.

Later in the day I thought about her statement and it dawned on me that during our previous 47 years of marriage, we never lived anywhere near a railroad track and consequently never heard any train whistles. Having been married to a professional railroader, railfan, and modeler, Leslie has never expressed any really interest or love for the railroad...other than the fact that it paid the bills! Thinking of that it really made me happy to learn that she too was finally deriving some enjoyment from the sound of a train...after all, what's not to like?

233

Chuck H Geletzke, Jr.

Author Chuck Geletzke was seen working to restore East Broad Top Railroad (EBT) Combine 14 in their Paint Shop in Rockhill Furnace, PA on May 23, 2024.

About the Author

Charles H. Geletzke, Jr. was raised in Royal Oak, Michigan and graduated from *Royal Oak Kimball High School* in 1967 and in the next month began a railroad career, which would span 45-years. Mr. Geletzke, a Marketing major, worked his way through *Central Michigan University* in Mt. Pleasant, Michigan as a roundhouse "Fire Builder" (Laborer) and Road Brakeman for the *Grand Trunk Western Railroad* and during his Senior year as a Carman Helper and Switchman for the *Delray Connecting Railroad.* He graduated with a Bachelor of Business Administration Degree in 1971. Additionally, Mr. Geletzke served in a *United States Marine Corps Reserve* Infantry Battalion and later was conscripted into the *U. S. Army's 226th Railway Shop Battalion.* In the mid 1970's Mr. Geletzke and his brother, Gerry, owned and operated a small excavating company and with their small fleet of trucks hauled perishables and steel throughout the Continental United States during the winter months. Following his college graduation he worked for the *Delray Connecting*, the *Missouri Pacific Railroad, Grand Trunk Western* (again), the *Detroit & Toledo Shore Line Railroad*, and the *Canadian National Railroad*, where he retired in 2011. During these years the author worked in both labor and managerial positions...; but mostly as a Locomotive Engineer. Chuck and his wife, Leslie, will be married 48 years this October and have three married children and seven grandchildren. Chuck and Leslie moved in 2023 to Mount Joy, Pennsylvania, and are active in their new church. Chuck is a Director of the *Grand Trunk Western Railroad Historical Society* and has become active with the *Friends of the East Broad Top Railroad.* The author's other interests include railfanning, model railroading, woodworking, college football (Chuck is still a *Navy* fan!), baseball (is a senior season ticket holder with the *Lancaster Stormers*), jazz, and writing for various railroad and historical publications. This is author Geletzke's tenth book including... ***The Detroit & Toledo Shore Line Railroad-"Expressway For Industry"*** (co-authored with the late Wilbur E. Hague); ***When Deadhead Counted As Rest and Other Railroad Stories***; ***With the Slack That Will Do, and Other Railroad Stories***; ***So, You Think You'd Like to Railroad and Other Railroad Stories***; ***Don't Flush in the Station and Other Railroad Stories***; ***Inside Railroading and Other Railroad Stories***; ***Go Ahead and Backup and Other Railroad Stories***; ***Unit Trains and Other Railroad Stories***; and ***"Soak It!!!"...and Other Railroad Stories***. Even though the last nine books contain over 650 short stories, all of which are true, I feel as though I have not as yet run out of material and providing I am able to maintain my health, I think I have

Chuck H Geletzke, Jr.

sufficient stories remaining for at least another volume or two! Once again, thank you all for your continued interest and support!

LOT SHIPMENT COLLECT (3-A 10-38)
(Printed in U.S.A.)

WHEN PARTS OF THIS SHIPMENT ARE ON SEPARATE DELIVERY SHEETS AGENT AT DESTINATION WILL ADJUST CHARGES TO PROPER AMOUNT ON THE NUMBER OF PIECES RECEIVED.

FORWARDING OFFICE

South Range, Mich. (237-0)

DELIVERY SHEET No. | DATE

DECLARED OF ENTIRE SHIPMENT | No. PIECES | WEIGHT OF ENTIRE SHIPMENT
VALUE $

RAILWAY EXPRESS AGENCY
INCORPORATED

Railway Express Agency-Copper Range Railroad Less Than Carload Shipment Collect Form

It All Starts <u>Here</u> and Other Railroad Stories

Made in the USA
Columbia, SC
26 July 2024

38844348R00130